THE VALE OF SOULMAKING

Other works by Meg Harris Williams

Inspiration in Milton and Keats

A Strange Way of Killing

The Apprehension of Beauty (with Donald Meltzer)

The Chamber of Maiden Thought (with Margot Waddell)

A Trial of Faith—Horatio's Story

For children:

Five Tales from Shakespeare

THE VALE OF SOULMAKING

The Post-Kleinian Model of the Mind and Its Poetic Origins

Meg Harris Williams

KARNAC

LONDON   NEW YORK

First published in 2005 by
H. Karnac (Books) Ltd.
6 Pembroke Buildings, London NW10 6RE

British Library Cataloguing in Publication Data

A C.I.P. for this book is available from the British Library

ISBN: 1-85575 310-3

10 9 8 7 6 5 4 3 2

Edited, designed, and produced by Communication Crafts

Printed in Great Britain

www.karnacbooks.com

To Joie Macaulay, who taught me to read poetry,
and to Donald Meltzer, who taught me to read myself

There is an active
Principle in them;
Which is not giving,
Is not receiving;
Is not the forcive
Nor the passive lust;
Which forgives tolerance
And indignation;
Is river and bed:
It is the needle
Point and thread, piercing
All receiving all;
Is identical
Imagination.

Roland J. Harris, "Prologue" to *Little Sonnets*

CONTENTS

ACKNOWLEDGEMENTS

I would like to thank my husband, Adrian Williams, who, in addition to my stepfather, has faithfully read the innumerable drafts and revisions of this book and of all my previous books and writings.

Psychoanalysis acknowledges
its poetic forebears
and joins the artistic family

Donald Meltzer

W hen in 1971 it was announced that Mrs Klein's Collected
Works were to be produced by the Hogarth Press under the
capable guidance of Roger Money-Kyrle, I was jubilant,
expecting that a sad defect in my education was to be made up as in a
Christmas gift. But it was not to be. Thirty years later, I am still struggling with classical Greek. I have learned to bear the humiliation of
being the dummy of my postgraduate class. The kindness of the
teacher, and several years' dedicated instruction by Ian Mackenzie
from mid-Wales, have been to no avail. It is a beautiful language and
beautifully taught, but I am too old and cannot learn Greek in the way
that the young gentlemen of the eighteenth century did—a humbling
experience after a lifetime of taking educability for granted.

If that were the whole story—that I was slipping into senility. . . .
But another process was going on at the same time: namely, so-called
students were taking my work seriously and blending it together with
that of Bion, Harris Williams, and a number of serious dissertations
in Italy, Spain, Sweden, and Germany, under the name of "post-

---

The title is that of a lecture given in Barcelona in 1989 jointly with Meg
Harris Williams. The following is the text of Donald Meltzer's talk, first
printed (apart from the opening two paragraphs) in Meg Harris Williams &
Margot Waddell, *The Chamber of Maiden Thought* (London: Routledge, 1991).

Kleinian". These efforts helped me to take my work seriously again. Mrs Klein's genius as a discoverer did not require that she must also be a classics scholar—which she was not, any more than I myself. The scholarship could be supplied by others—particularly Bion, Meg Harris Williams, and her late sister Morag with her work on Chaucer and American poetry. The new book, *The Vale of Soulmaking*, promises to become the text for post-Kleinian thought. It is a hard read and an exacting picture of the "poetics" of this new aesthetic dimension, going through revision after revision. And the upshot of it all is, also, to establish Mrs Klein as the first "post-Kleinian".   (September 2003)

* * *

Had psychoanalysis followed the original bent given to it by Freud at the turn of the century, it would have remained a medical sub-speciality of neurology and psychiatry, dedicated to relieving the suffering of neurotic individuals. Its method of cure, conceived in the light of nineteenth-century Germanic medical science, undertook to reach to the "cause" of the symptoms by bringing into consciousness the repressed events of earlier times, often going back into childhood. Thus it held a neurophysiological model of the disturbance analogous to an inflammation in a vestigial organ like the appendix. It is in no sense a silly model, for it has much truth in it; but it had a very restricted horizon. Once Freud had discovered the transference, in his work with Dora, this method took over the development of the science of psychoanalysis, completely placing in the shadows the massive neurophysiological preconceptions of the "Project for a Scientific Psychology" which Freud had earlier written for his friend Fliess.

The events of the transference, replacing a patient's realistic observation of the analyst by insistent preconceptions, brought into view the personality, character, way of life, values, aspirations, prejudices, hopes, and fears of the patient. While anxious that psychoanalysis should remain scientific by avoiding embracing any *Weltanschauung*, Freud nevertheless took the lead in broadening the field of observation by focusing interest on the ramifications of the libido in the form of character types, as opposed to the earlier preoccupation with the vicissitudes of the libido in symptom formation. This move was taken up in particular by Karl Abraham in "A Short Study of the Development of the Libido, viewed in the Light of Mental Disorders" (1924) and given a formal dimension as "organization" of the libido as it moved developmentally from infancy with its oral primacy towards the genitality of mature adulthood.

This broadening of the field of study eventually forced Freud to abandon the most dearly held of his neurophysiological preconceptions: the "unity of the mind". In the last decade of his life, and in particular shortly before his death in 1938, he wrote of the evidence that the mind can—and frequently does—split itself, so that the great achievements of men can stand side by side with their follies without apparent conflict. Philosophy would not brook being excluded from the study of the mind: indeed Abraham, and even more definitively Melanie Klein, gave psychoanalysis a distinctly Platonic orientation by discovering that the inner world had its own type of geographic concreteness, and that it was in the transactions of the inner world (manifest in dreams and unconscious phantasy) that the meaning of the outer world derived its origin.

It is over fifty years since Melanie Klein's seminal paper on splitting processes and projective identification established this transformation and brought "meaning" into the centre of psychoanalytic study. This naturally focused attention on emotions and on symbol formation as the means by which emotions become available for thought. In earlier days, symbols had been very little differentiated from conventional signs, with the result that thought and language were considered as conjoint, commencing in the pre-conscious where "thing-representations" were held to be transformed into "word-representations". Not only did this take no account of the severe limitations of verbal language, but it greatly reduced understanding of the impact of art and literature to interpretation of its content, its iconography. Even the stirring power of music was believed to be explicable through its programmatic imagery. The alliance with science-as-explanation—exemplified in such works as *Civilization and its Discontents* (1930a [1929]), *Moses and Monotheism* (1939a [1937–39]), *The Future of an Illusion* (1927c), and the paper on Leonardo (1910c)—alienated the artistic community from psychoanalysis. Correspondingly, this preoccupation with explanation generated an attitude of teaching rather than learning among psychoanalysts in relation to the arts, which was a barrier against their own creative response.

The coming-of-age of psychoanalysis is nowhere better illustrated than in the work of Wilfred Bion, which—for all its obscurity, flirtation with mathematical forms, and refusal to compromise with the limitations of the reader—declares the influence of the arts in promoting psychoanalytical thought and observation. Milton, Shakespeare, Keats, Coleridge, the Old Testament, the Burial Chamber at Ur, and the Bhagavadgita are not only Bion's references for exposition but also his sources of inspiration for original thought. Since the present volume is about sources such as these in English literature, it is perhaps necessary to give some precise indication of the position that psychoanalytic thought—its model of the mind—has achieved at present, as a point of reference for the essays that follow.

When Freud, in *Group Psychology and the Analysis of the Ego* (1921c) and later in *The Ego and the Id* (1923b), clarified his shift from a stratified "topographic" model to a "structural" model of the mind, consisting of id, ego and superego, he had a problem of defining the status of the superego. He thought of it as the forms of parental figures "somehow united", which had been "introjected into the ego" and subsequently separated off "by a gradient" to establish an independent function of monitoring the ego's activities. It was Abraham who recognized that, at least in manic-depressive patients, these figures of love-objects were experienced in a concrete way: that they could be destroyed, expelled, reintrojected in a destroyed form. Melanie Klein, listening to children's accounts of the internal space and its lively figures, recognized this concrete inner world and its objects. But she also saw in small children that the maternal figure and its nurturing, protective, and pedagogic functions were at least as important as the authority of the paternal figure, and also that the two figures are not, by any means, always "somehow united". This internal theatre of phantasy and drama she recognized as the scene represented in the play of children and the locus of their developmental struggles. In her hands the rather vague concept of narcissism, which in its original form had been a designation of the direction of distribution of the ego towards the body of the subject, became a firmly structural one, describing the way in which the organization of the personality fluctuated. When internal parental figures were dominant, a state of "object relations" existed; but, in contrast to this, infantile parts might unite against these figures to form their own organizations, later called "gangs" because of their rebellious and delinquent character. Even within the realm of relationships with internal parents, values could fluctuate from egocentric ones (exploiting and potentially being persecuted by parental figures) to trust, love, and concern for the welfare of the parents (the "depressive position"). Melanie Klein saw such mental states as security, optimism, joyousness, and interest in the world as emanations of a loving relation to internal parents, particularly the mother—a bond rooted in the infantile relation to the feeding breast.

Because Freud thought of the formation of the superego as a consequence of the Oedipus complex (its "heir", contingent upon the relinquishment of erotic yearnings towards the parent of the opposite sex, under the threat of castration), it was natural, given the material he was dealing with, to suppose that the superego would be more harsh than the actual parents. The nearly cannibalistic model of introjection seemed to leave no possibility that the superego might be better in its qualities than the actual parents. This invitation to pessimism was only slightly improved by Abraham pushing introjective processes into earlier phases, since he saw them as dominated by the ambivalence of oral and anal sadism. On the other hand, Melanie Klein's material from small children, while confirming the ubiquity of sadistic impulses, recognized that the first oral stage, although not free of ambivalence, was object-related, not "auto-erotic", and that the introjection of a good feeding breast did seem to take place. By recognizing the splitting of the object into good (gratifying) and bad (disappointing, deserting) parts, she could account for the establishment of an idealized breast and mother in the earliest postnatal period.

The concept of splitting-and-idealization thus mitigated the pessimism about the quality of internal objects, while still leaving the problem that their excellence was limited by the qualities of the actual parents. Freud had suggested one way of solving this: namely, by later introjection into the superego of qualities from later loved and admired figures. Melanie Klein added another avenue of improvement (one to which Freud had alluded but not developed): namely, that qualities of harshness and even cruelty in the internal parents could often be seen to be the result of infantile parts of the personality having entered into the parental figures by projective identification, thus contaminating their adult qualities with infantile attitudes and values. Withdrawal of these projections could result in improved parental function of the superego figures, including those qualities Freud had first identified as "ego-ideal" but later lost sight of—the internal sources of inspiration and aspiration.

To these two sources of hopefulness about the possible evolution of the superego—the assimilation within it of qualities of later admired and loved figures and the clarifying of it by withdrawal of projections—Melanie Klein added a third factor. In her last writings—the *Narrative of a Child Analysis* (1975), "Envy and Gratitude" (1957) and "Our Adult World and Its Roots in Infancy" (1959)—she gradually established the concept of the "combined object" (a term she had introduced in her earlier work with different, more persecutory connotations). In a sense the combined object was the same thing that Freud had located in the material of the Wolf Man (1918b [1914]), and called "the primal scene". Melanie Klein recognized its essential connection with the sexual relation of the internal parents, as a "powerful" object in its emotional evocativeness; but she also saw in it a quality not clearly visible in the external parents—namely, its mystery and creativity, its essential privacy and perhaps sacredness.

In general, it could be said that psychoanalysts followed Freud's lead in adopting a somewhat cynical attitude towards religion and its history. It is perhaps a tenable view that man has always invented gods, and naturally invented ones that suited him, being no better than himself but more powerful. But that view supposes that religions are invented by adults, rather than evolving in the minds of infants, later to be mythologized. The vision implicit in Melanie Klein's discoveries about infantile mental life is that mental life is essentially religious, and that the growth of the mind is somehow inextricably tied up with the evolution of the relationship between the self and its internal objects. Consequently, death of the mind is entailed by these objects being expelled, dethroned, invaded, corrupted, or fragmented.

What has been described so far could reasonably be claimed to be mainstream history of the psychoanalytic model of the mind, however selective. It is a history that has inevitably been deviated from, lagged behind, and converged upon, by other schools and in other geographical areas. The position by 1960 was that psychoanalysis had become a descriptive science with an artistic method of therapy and research. "Theories" were now models of the mind—that is, metaphors whose purpose was the description of phenomena; Freud's structural theory of id, ego, and superego was seen to operate as self and internal objects; the therapeutic aim had moved from the curing of symptoms to the promotion of personality development; and the pessimistic division of life- and death instincts had been replaced by a view of the struggle between narcissistic organizations and object relationships, in which Love and Envy met in combat, struggling free of egocentricity (the paranoid-schizoid position) towards object love (the depressive position). Development of the personality required reintegration of the splitting in the self and clarification of the internal objects by withdrawal of projective identification of infantile parts. It was an enriched frame of reference of clinical observation in a situation where the analyst's counter-transference was as important a function and source of understanding as the analysand's transference. Clinical results were steadily improving, but analyses were getting disquietingly longer and longer.

What follows cannot be claimed as "history" of the next thirty years in psychoanalytic thought, since it is too soon for key lines of development to have been assimilated within the movement in general. Any account of "post-Kleinian" ideas at this turbulent point in time must inevitably be a subjective one, all the more since it will be based on the personal application of Bion's ambiguously stated ideas. Yet these ideas and implications in an integrated form are germane to this book and its view of literature and history, so I will proceed with a description of the modern psychoanalytic model in terms of an account of the vale of soulmaking, which, I hope, will be seen to parallel the literary ones that follow. My own account—a subjective view of Bion's vision—has its sources of observation in the psychoanalytic situation with adult and child patients and in systematic mother–infant observation by the method developed by Esther Bick and Martha Harris, combined with recent experiences of echographic study of foetal behaviour in non-identical twins.

Long before birth, perhaps as early as fourteen weeks of gestation, the human infant can be said to manifest behaviour and to declare the fundamental qualities of its character. Not only does it relate to objects such as cord, membranes, placenta, and twin sibling interior to the womb, but also to its mother's voice and other manifestations of her state of mind and body. Mental life, as distinct from adaptational behaviour, can be seen to have begun, implying the incipience of emotional experiences, primitive symbol formation of the song-and-dance variety, and dream-thoughts. As its ambience loses the ample dimensions of the early months and becomes restrictive, the foetus develops a yearning to recover its freedom and an expectation of another world from which it receives auditory clues. When it is strong enough, it struggles to be free, and succeeds. This good experience may be blemished by exhaustion, by foetal distress; it may be curtailed by Caesarean section or, if premature, completely distorted into an expulsion. However, where the experience of birth is one of successful escape from restriction, the exterior world impinges with the shock of both panic and of ecstasy. The panic before the first breath is succeeded by the delicious expansion of the lungs; the explosion of noise becomes quickly modulated and delightfully musical; the initial chill is quickly countered; the blinding glare takes wondrous shape. But the mobile limbs have been bound down by a thousand gravitational cords, and the sense of helplessness, of being lost in limitless space, mobilizes the expectation of a saviour, and the mouth seeks it out and finds it. The infant's panicky fragmentation is pulled together by the mother's arms and her voice and smell, which are familiar; and the vast space is given a point of origin geometrically by this nipple-in-the-mouth. And when the eyes begin to see the mother's face and breast and the flesh to feel the chain of desire, her eyes are the sanctuary in which the passionate yearning towards the beauty of this new world can find the reciprocity that makes it bearable.

But the breast has its blemishes, its striae, its wrinkles when emptied; and the face is a landscape over which clouds of anxiety pass and in which storms of pain and indignation gather, sometimes obscured by mists of inattention. From the distrust engendered by these variations the baby must seek its own defence, from a rich variety easily at hand. It can internalize this good object in its full beauty but finds it takes in also its disappointing form. But that can be expelled as faeces. Once internalized, the beautiful object can afford sleep either in its arms or back inside it. Or the baby can reverse the geometry of space so that its mouth—not the mother's nipple—is the point of origin around which the variety of objects revolve as satellites, ordered by its screams. Or, most enduring of all defences, it can divide itself by variously deploying the attention of its senses so that no single object can exert the full aesthetic impact of consensuality.

When unmodulated by reciprocity, these five lines of defence against the full impact of the chains of desire—that is, introjection, expulsion, projective identification, omnipotent control of objects, and splitting processes—all weaken the passionate contact, whether they are deployed singly or in consortium; all these situations are manifest through dream-thoughts. And it is the moments of passionate contact, in which the baby is able to establish the unique transactions of cooperate projection and introjection with the unconscious reveries of the contemplating mother, that give meaning to the nourishment from the breast. The breast may then nourish the mind with symbolic representations of the baby's emotional experience and facilitate new dream-thoughts. Eventually it is the establishment of such a thinking head/breast that enables the human child to commence the process of thinking-for-itself—to create its autonomous symbols to enrich its store of received symbols and conventional signs.

This capacity for passionate contact, with its consortium of love for the beauty-of-the-world, hatred of the chains of desire felt in the flesh and on the pulses, and thirst for knowledge of the enigmatic object in its combined form as breast-and-nipple, mother-and-father, fuels the development of the soul: that interior, private core of the personality.

At the nucleus of this private core is the mysterious, sacred nuptial chamber of the internal objects, to which they must be allowed periodically to withdraw to repair and restore one another. Against acquiescence in this are deployed all the powerful forces of aversion to emotional attachment and to dependence and submission to the superiority and wisdom of these internal gods. For they are the superior, most evolved segment of the human mind, and their evolution takes place in advance of the self. Artists and poets are (as Shelley said) the "unacknowledged legislators of the world" because the internal objects are the legislators of the individual mind, and this is the artist's field of operation and the focus of his discipline; as Milton wrote, of the relation between the self and God: "who best / Bear his mild yoke, they serve him best" (Sonnet 19).

Around this core of the personality there develops, in concentric circles of diminishing intimacy, the adaptational carapace of the personality, with all its learned devices of casual and contractual relationships, simplified and impoverished in their emotionality, often stimulated by states of excitement engendered by fancy and fear of the group. Every step in development at the core must be worked through from infantile levels, in the context of emotional transference—of which the method of psychoanalysis has no monopoly. Gradually, owing to the mysterious process of aspiration towards the excellence of these evolving internal objects, the adult portion of the personality may emerge and manifest itself in the area of its passionate interests and in the desires of its intimate relationships. Its joyousness takes shape in the work of building the family of private life and contributing to the gradual evolution of the human family. Its opponents, in each individual and abroad in the world, are legion. But fortunately the forces in pursuit of truth are intelligent, and those against it are fundamentally stupid, dependent on negative imitation and perversion of the truth—or the best we can approximate to it: truthfulness of observation and thought.

Introduction

Call the world if you please "the vale of Soul-making" . . .
How are these sparks which are God to have identity given
them—so as ever to possess a bliss peculiar to each one's
individual existence? How, but by the medium of a world like
this? . . . I think it a grander system of salvation than the
Christian religion—or rather it is a system of spirit-creation—
. . . Why may they not have made this simple thing even more
simple for common apprehension by introducing Mediators
and Personages in the same manner as in the heathen
mythology abstractions are personified—Seriously I think it
probable that this System of Soul-making may have been the
parent of all the more palpable and personal schemes of
redemption.

John Keats[1]

The concreteness of psychic reality has always been dominant
and explicit in the poetic consciousness. Shakespeare gave to
airy nothing a "local habitation and a name", and Milton's Satan
announced that the mind was neither Heaven nor Hell, but "its own
place". It is not a place that can be shaped or finished by the conscious
will; it cannot—as Satan found—make heaven out of hell; rather, it is

the place where mysterious powers outside the control of the self can create meaning, in the form of symbols, and expand the horizons of knowledge through inspiration. Plato's realm of Ideas and God's ineffable effulgence have found expression through the drama of the inner world. This is the "brave new world" that overrides cynicism at the end of *The Tempest* and that lies "all before" Adam and Eve after their expulsion from Eden. Shakespeare and Milton discovered that the new world is a place not of fixities and definites, of reward and punishment, but where the idea of "the good" consists in the goal of development and the gradual, painful, but also joyful getting of wisdom. It is a place guided by ethical principles rather than by moral codes. Following this, the Romantic poets—after initially hoping to see the new world embodied in the French revolution—turned more urgently to the inner world and seized fast hold of its potential as the only real locus for mankind's regeneration and progression. Blake called this "cleansing the doors of perception" towards "a world of imagination and vision", for "all deities reside in the Human Breast". The spaces, qualities, and functions of this world are home to the type of "Mediators and Personages" Keats spoke of as presiding over the heathen "system of soulmaking"—not through didactic allegory but through sensuous metaphor. The first stage in this soul-journey Keats called the "Chamber of Maiden-Thought"—a place where the initial pleasant intoxication becomes gradually darkened by the growing awareness of sickness and misery, thereby "sharpening one's vision", until the mind achieves a state of mist and mystery:

> This Chamber of Maiden-Thought becomes gradually darken'd and at the same time on all sides of it many doors are set open—but all dark—all leading to dark passages—We see not the balance of good and evil. We are in a Mist—We are now in that state—We feel "the burden of the Mystery".[2]

From the midst of this dark cloud of unknowing, as from Dante's dark wood,[3] the soul feels its way towards the many open doors, "imperceptibly impelled by the awakening of the thinking principle within us" and guided by internal teachers and mediators. The poetry discussed in this book could be considered—in Wordsworth's words—the "master of all our seeing", not just because of its humanity, but because of its potential for guiding the creation of our own minds in their state of perpetual evolution in which, as Keats said, "the creative must create itself".

Blake said, "all deities reside in the Human Breast".[4] These are distinct from the "selfhood", and the duty of "every Christian" is to establish contact with these internal deities in order to release the mind from its claustrophobic perception and to "build Jerusalem" within himself:

> For man has closed himself up, till he sees all things thro'
> Narrow chinks of his cavern.[5]

Similarly, the Kleinian model of the mind is founded on the relation between the self and its "internal objects": mysterious godlike functions of the individual mind whose ethical awareness is more advanced than that of the everyday personality. Melanie Klein's discovery of the "combined object" pointed to the powerful impact of masculine and feminine components working in unison: initially symbolized, in its most primitive form, by the feeding-breast and guardian-nipple.[6] In relation to its objects, the self is always an "infant", limited by its achieved state of development. This is promoted by its capacity for love and trust of its object ("gratitude") and hindered by envy and egocentricity (narcissism), entailing a repeated depressive struggle towards "reparation" of the damage done to the object by infantile incursions. The Bion–Meltzer development of the Kleinian model views these internal objects not as fixed quantities but as in a continual process of qualitative evolution. Nor are they confined by the realistic capacities of the child's actual parents. The objects develop alongside the self, in response to life's opportunities. They may intuitively absorb (introject) the qualities of admired figures, in the context of circumstances that demand an expansion of their knowledge and capabilities. Bion's phrase "learning from experience" has the specific—and idiosyncratic—significance of identification with the teaching of internal objects, as distinct from the mechanical impact of external events. He directs attention to the increase in *knowledge*, in the sense of wisdom or understanding, that results when emotional awareness is contained, shaped, and thereby given meaning through trustful, non-narcissistic contact with the object. "Knowledge is as food", said Milton's Raphael.[7] For Bion and Meltzer also, knowledge is the food of the mind, which builds itself by increments through this ongoing internal dialogue. The infant-self develops according to its sensitivity and tolerance of the imminent Unknown. Keats called this tolerance "Negative Capability"—a phrase much cited by Bion: "that is when man is capable of being in uncertainties, Mysteries, doubts, without any irritable reaching after fact & reason".[8] It is a quality that underlies the acquiring of "identity" when the world is experienced as a medium for soulmaking.

In poetic literature, the mind as island, moor, or vale is a phenomenological field in which emotional experiences are continually occurring, requiring to become known to outer levels of consciousness in a symbolic form such that they can be thought about. This process of "becoming known" takes place under the aegis of the poetic Muse, or internal object in psychoanalytic terms. It is a process of "organization" as opposed to one of "tyranny", to use the Blakean distinction: a function of imaginative expressiveness, not of rationalization (Blake's "reason", which we would call "correctness"). Poets have always seen themselves as inspired by their Muse—and this is not a *metaphor only*: it is a faithful description of the internal identification with a teaching object or deity. The Muse is the symbol-making power, and the traditional invocation to the Muse indicates that this internal relationship needs to be established each time. It cannot be taken for granted—as Milton first discovered when he tried to write a sequel to his inspired "Ode on the Morning of Christ's Nativity", and the words refused to flow, but congealed into the curiously mannered and wooden "Passion". Whether or not there is a formal invocation, this relationship is usually presented as an integral part of the total poem: in shorter lyrics, it often *is* the poem. Inspiration gives structure to the imagination. A longer poem may enact in various stages and layers the quest for symbol-formation. In doing so it becomes a vehicle for the interplay and modification of the qualities of internal objects; this is its "creativity". A long poem such as an epic has room for sections that are not inspired yet may be craftsmanly and supportive. But when the symbol-making pressure makes itself felt, it is the Muse who actually finds the words and puts them in the correct order—the correct order being the order that expresses the nature of the emotional experience. "I am but the Secretary", said Blake: "the Authors are in Eternity."[9] This is poetic "truth".

The poet, with his musical skills, is equipped to hear the words that express his dream. And we, as readers, need to develop our capacity to listen to the supra-lexical or musical meaning of the poetry, its unparaphraseable expressiveness. Poetry moves on the printed line as music moves on the stave, creating meaning through its artistic form rather than its didactic intent. A line of poetry on the page, simply by virtue of having two ends, is already a potentially dramatic statement—a balance of tensions. The poetic line has the capacity to cut across grammatical syntax in a contrapuntal play; it can hold pauses and silences within the framework of metre, as in the Shakespearean half-line of blank verse which leaves a space for unspoken emotion (Hamlet's "For Hecuba! . . . What's Hecuba to him . . . ?"), or the Miltonic use of the caesura to subtly alter, even reverse, the didactic flow of the argument:

> The mind is its own place, and can make
> A heaven of Hell, a Hell of heaven;

or, "And man prefer, set God behind". Regularity makes irregularity meaningful: "Hurled headlong flaming from th'ethereal sky", or the famous repetitions "I am dying, Egypt, dying" and "My love is like a red, red rose". Or, in reverse, after a passage of clashing irregularities, Tennyson's perfectly smooth "And on a sudden, lo! the level lake", or Samson's "And I shall shortly be with them that rest". The natural rhythmicality of verse gives a sense of dimension in space and time—as Byron said, poetry's rhythm creates a "former world and a future". To these rhythmic foundations are added the non-lexical associations of visual imagery and the musical qualities of poetic diction—not just the formal devices of alliteration, assonance, etc., but the infinitely variable informal patterns of part-rhyme and sound-echo, all of which contribute to spinning the sensuous web of the symbol, capturing a non-predictable, supra-lexical meaning. Why is it that certain phrases have an untranslateable poignancy—Antony's

> Call to me
> All my sad captains, fill our bowls once more;
> Let's mock the midnight bell.

The poignancy lies in the half-rhymes (call . . . all . . . fill . . . bowl . . . bell): we can locate it, but we cannot so easily paraphrase it. And these are the meanings that accumulate through the poetic tradition, building on one another, so that we hear Antony again in Keats's

> Not a soul to tell
> Why thou art desolate. . . .
> ("soul . . . tell . . . sol")

Poetry's musical notation speaks to our internal objects even when we do not—or cannot—interpret it. This is why it is essential to immerse ourselves in the formal, symbolic qualities of the poem if we wish to make emotional contact with the mystery of its meaning—the meaning lodged by internal objects. The "deep grammar" is contained not in its didactic and discursive features, but in its underlying pattern, its poetic structure—termed by Susanne Langer "presentational form". Langer described the "cognitive value" of the *form* of the art-symbol, and how the musician needs to "think with the musical Idea" of the composer in order to allow its underlying rhythm to carry him into a "new event" in the life of his mind.[10] In a similar way, the poem can become a dream of our own and contribute to the evolving qualities of our own objects: a goal that is analogous to the psychoanalytic experience and, indeed, a primary model for it. Thus Donald Meltzer describes how the analyst needs to try to "match the poetic diction of a dream . . . with a poetry of our own", by "putting order" not into the dream itself, but into "the confusion in our own minds"; "I can tell a good story", he says, "if a patient will dream it for me".[11] For poetry's "system of salvation", as Keats calls it, is an historic "parent" of this modern "palpable and personal scheme of redemption".

The Romantic poets, whom Bion saw as "the first psychoanalysts",[12] derived their principles of creativity from their towering poetic forebears—the ancient poets, and the brave new worlds won by Shakespeare and Milton. It is no accident that both the Renaissance and the Romantic poets flourished in periods of intensely revived interest in the philosophy and drama of classical Greece, the culture that gave us the term "psychoanalysis" as well as many of the concepts that have since become technical terms—"narcissism", "oedipal", "symbol", Meltzer's "claustrum" and "aesthetic reciprocity", Bion's "catastrophic change", etc. The work of the poet we call Homer dates from the beginning of the written word; yet in that period, human culture has changed a lot, and human nature very little. The stories of Odysseus repairing his relationship with his wife with the help of Athena, and of Oedipus overcoming the blindness of ignorance with the help of his daughters, are as pertinent today as when they were first sung and danced; the more poetic an ancient work, the more modern it feels, since the more emphatically does it verify Shelley's definition of poets as the "unacknowledged legislators of the world".[13] Shakespeare, in his triumphant "tragedy of synthesis" *Antony and Cleopatra*, pursued further the implications for the poet and his feminine creativity that were suggested centuries earlier in the *Odyssey*'s concept of "homophrosyne". Milton identified with blind Oedipus even more than with blind Homer when, digesting his dreams and waiting to be "milked" in the morning, he shed his doctrinal control for the dictates of his feminine Muse, despite the emotional storm—the "hateful siege of contraries"—that this aroused in him, an intolerable mixture of love and hate. Blake recognized that this storm was not an unpleasant side-effect of creative work but the very core of its engendering. He hailed the value of the "marriage of contraries", pointing out that this emotional tension was what differentiated "vision"—the work of the Muse—from fixed schematic poetry (such as allegory), the work of the selfhood. He stressed the intensity of imaginative observation, just as later Freud was to describe how the spotlight of consciousness focused attention on internal realities and Bion was to present the interlinking emotions of Love, Hate, and Knowledge as the foundation for symbol-formation.[14] The antithesis to this confrontation with ideas or soul-knowledge is, in Blake, "single" or "negative" vision—the mind imprisoned by its own perversity—and in Bion, the "grid" of negative values—*minus* L, H, K. Bion's negative grid refers to propaganda, cynicism, stupidity; Blake located the mind's enemies didactically in terms of envy, materialism, rationalization, and sentimentality—all forms of "error" or pseudo-knowledge—instead of the traditional pride, disobedience, unbridled passion, and so on. For, as Coleridge emphasized, the mind, like a work of art, needs to be shaped by its innate poetic quality, its organic "principle of self-development", rather than by mechanical or "superinduced" requirements. This principle—the "shaping spirit of imagination"—takes the form of *ideas*, which Coleridge recognized as something not *invented* by the mind, but *perceived* by it when suitably oriented. The poetic ideas of creative thought find their pioneering expression in symbolic forms rather than in discursive philosophy: for "an idea cannot be conveyed but by a symbol".[15] Only once they have been absorbed into the culture can they be talked about through conventional means. True wisdom or soul-knowledge is not stored with the accumulations of memory but alters the very structure of the mind: it is a function of becoming, not of possessing.

The Romantics, being the first environmentalists as well as the first psychoanalysts, used the heightened vulnerability of nature in the early stages of the industrial revolution as an appropriate setting for their dramatization of the individual's interaction with the Muse as Mother Nature, a space for mental exploration newly vulnerable to the depradations of omnipotent industrial man with his tyrannical modes of slavery—the "dark satanic mills" of reductive conformity. Nobody modelled the wondrous rediscovery of nature's aesthetic potential better than Wordsworth, whose vision of the god-like child in Nature's arms, eternally encircled by mountain-breast and lake-eyes, had an authenticity that even his later fading into the "egotistical sublime" could never dispel.[16] It is the first "thought", in the post-Kleinian definition, the original and universal symbol. In other ways, however,

Wordsworth avoided confronting the implications of his own meta-phor—the deep grammar of the poet's ambiguous and complex rela-tionship with his feminine Muse: the doubts, jealousies, fragmentation, fears of unreciprocated desire. Instead of achieving trustfulness, he relaxed into complacency, relinquishing the invitation to emotional tumult, and took early retirement from creativity when he became established as a "genius". In elevating poetry together with childhood into an idealized condition, he made no allowance for childhood's struggle and anxiety over the internal enemies of negativity and phil-istinism—the withdrawal from aesthetic conflict in the face of uncer-tainty over the unknown qualities of the Muse, so well charted by Milton. The poetic experience, like the childhood experience, lost its grip on reality and became a false heaven rather than a vale of soul-making. It became vulnerable to the wolf that, like Milton's Satan, "leapt with ease into the fold".[17] The wolf in the fold was recognized by Byron, and to some extent capitalized upon: the image of the Byronic hero that dominated the literary culture of that period descended di-rectly from Satan, heroic in its tormented self-worship. Byron was too intelligent to be much of an idealizer; but his ambivalence towards poetry prevented him also from tackling the implications of the fiend within. He regarded poetry as a fury-like pursuing female that would overcome him in the end, like Coleridge's "Nightmare Life-in-Death"; yet meanwhile, impelled by resentment against his neglectful mother, he would seek his revenge on other women.

It was Keats who took up the poetic burden that Wordsworth had set down. The adjective "Shakespearean" which is often applied to Keats indicates his revivifying of the Romantic status quo by a return to Shakespeare's complex, "negatively capable" mentality. "Who am I to be a Poet, seeing how great a thing it is?" he asked in the early days of his infatuation with poetic language. Yeats said, "Myself must I remake"; but Keats recognized intuitively from the beginning that he could not make himself a poet—only the Muse could do that. As the short period of time available to him unfolded and the pressure of the concept of impending death alchemically fused his perceptions, it be-came crystal clear to him that the poet's quest to make his soul was essentially a story of the poet's romance with his Muse, with all its turbulent implications. He accepted that the Muse of poetry would not bring Rousseauist freedom (as the older Romantics had hoped) but, rather, a form of dependence that might appear as servitude. He was not a "Godwin perfectibility man" but a "negative capability" one.[18] His identity was to be moulded, under the pressure of "circumstances", not by his own will, but by the knowledge attained by and contained in his internal objects. Like Byron (whom he hated), he regarded his "demon Poesy" as an ambiguous female figure who might either support or overwhelm his own vulnerable infant-poet self; but, in contrast to Byron, his tenacious grip on his complex concept of "the beautiful" enabled him to work through the consequences. Milton, who shared the poetic goal of Beauty, was equally with Shakespeare a component of Keats's internal poetic object. Assimilating Milton's experience of mourning in *Lycidas*, Keats plunged into the aesthetic conflict and followed his Muse of the "Belle Dame" through the "vales of heaven and hell" to rebirth in the "Ode to Psyche" and relinquishment in the "Ode to a Nightingale". "Psyche", with its rediscovery of a "neglected goddess", may be taken—as its title indicates—as the work that establishes the possibility of psychoanalysis from the poetic perspective. The crucial period of working-through, at the end of which Keats dazzlingly metamorphosed into a great poet, occurred during the winter of 1818–19 after the death of his beloved youngest brother Tom, and we may follow its evolution "as if we were God's spies"[19] in the classic journal-letter to his brother and sister-in-law in America, written really for posterity, to model and record for those "hungry generations" one man's experience of soulmaking.

"La Belle Dame Sans Merci" is the poem that marks the threshold of Keats's "leap of faith"; being the work that proves his own identity as a poet, newly "fledged". It could have been written by "John Keats and no other"—as Keats defined his poetic ambition, when he was feeling overwhelmed by the "shadow of the great poets" before him, fearing that he would only ever be an imitator. At the same time, it is steeped in medievalism, and there is no better way to approach its subject of an adolescent falling-in-love with an ambiguous fairy Muse than through the medieval masterpiece *Sir Gawain and the Green Knight*, whose author is known to us only as "the Gawain poet" in recognition of this poem's importance to the English literary tradition, despite the problems of modern accessibility that derive from the difficulty of the original language.

NOTES

1. John Keats, journal letter of February–May 1819 to the George Keatses, in: *Selected Letters of John Keats*, ed. R. Gittings (Oxford: Oxford University Press, 1975), pp. 249–51.

2. Keats, letter to Reynolds, 3 May 1818, in Gittings, *Letters*, p. 95.

3. Dante begins the *Inferno* with the words: "In the middle of the journey of our life I came to myself within a dark wood where the straight way was lost", transl. John D. Sinclair (Oxford: Oxford University Press, 1971).

4. William Blake, *The Marriage of Heaven and Hell*, plate 11, in: *Complete Writings*, ed. G. Keynes (Oxford: Oxford University Press, 1972), p. 153.

5. Ibid., plate 14, in Keynes, *Writings*, p. 154.

6. The combined object—essentially, the creativity represented by the internal parents in sexual intercourse—is that which "insists on development"; Meltzer, *The Kleinian Development* (Strath Tay: Clunie Press, 1978), Part 2, p. 103.

7. *Paradise Lost*, VII.126.

8. Keats's famous criterion of "negative capability" was formulated when he was aged 22 in a letter to George and Tom Keats of 21, 27 December 1817, in Gittings, *Letters*, p. 43.

9. Blake, letter to T. Butts, 6 July 1803, in Keynes, *Writings*, p. 825.

10. Susanne Langer, *Philosophy in a New Key* (Cambridge, MA: Harvard University Press, 1942), and *Feeling and Form* (London: Routledge and Kegan Paul, 1953).

11. Donald Meltzer, *Dream Life* (Strath Tay: Clunie Press, 1984); and a lecture given at the London Centre for Psychotherapy in 2001, one of a series on "Spirituality", in: N. Field et al. (Eds.), *Ten Lectures on Psychotherapy and Spirituality* (London: Karnac, 2005).

12. Wilfred R. Bion, *A Memoir of the Future*, single-volume edition (London: Karnac, 1991), p. 385.

13. Shelley, concluding words in his *Defence of Poetry*.

14. Freud, letter to L. Andreas-Salome, cited in Bion, *Attention and Interpretation*, (London: Tavistock, 1971), p. 57.

15. Coleridge, *Biographia Literaria* (1817), ed. N. Leask (London: Dent, 1997), p. 91.

16. Keats's description; letter to Bailey, 27 October 1818, in Gittings, *Letters*, p. 157.

17. "As when a prowling wolf . . . Leaps o'er the fence with ease into the fold"; Milton, *Paradise Lost*, IV.183–87.

18. Keats criticized his friend Charles Dilke for being a "Godwin perfectibility man"—a reference to William Godwin's *Political Justice*; letter to the George Keatses, 14–31 October 1818, in Gittings, *Letters*, p. 164.

19. To borrow Lear's phrase, later echoed by Keats in a letter to Reynolds, 11–13 July 1818, in Gittings, *Letters*, p. 122.

CHAPTER ONE

The stroke of the axe

The process of condensation operates on the myth of the emotional experience in the same manner as a set of chessmen stand in symbolic relation to Gawain and the Green Knight, Morte d'Arthur etc. In the mythic stage of recording an emotional experience, as in many discursive dreams, the meaning is still open to many interpretations. But as the condensation proceeds, and finally results in a highly condensed symbol, say the Queen in chess, the meaning is now "contained", no longer open to multiple interpretation. It must now be "read" or understood, grasped. Thus a symbol may be said to be "close to the bone" of mental pain, for it pinpoints the zone of conflict.

Donald Meltzer[1]

Milton said it was not necessary to have spurs on the feet and a sword laid on the shoulders to become a knight in the service of truth; and he exchanged his long-cherished intention to write an Arthurian epic for the subject of *Paradise Lost*.[2] Once upon a time, however, the sword and spurs were obligatory equipment in any romance about soulmaking. Chivalric quests and rambling dream-poems are the standard genres of medieval literature.

The fourteenth-century poem *Sir Gawain and the Green Knight* is exceptional in the tautness and sophistication of its telling. Written in dense and vigorous alliterative verse,[3] it crystallizes the stylized elements of medieval fiction into a richly woven tapestry of emotional tensions. Yet it is essentially a fairy-tale, with the same enduring qualities of archetypal significance. It tells of Gawain's interaction with the mysterious forces represented by the Green Knight and his Lady, the spiritual governors of the Castle of his inner world. In the Lady with her ambiguous love we can see the original Belle Dame Sans Merci of the aesthetic conflict; in the Green Knight with his dual nature, both human and transferential, we can see the beginnings of the psychoanalyst and his "countertransference dream".[4]

As in all tales of a knight winning his spurs, the glorious paraphernalia of a knight and his horse, a king and his castle, form a vital celebratory aspect of the romance. Yet *Gawain* represents a turning-point: the heroism of his task lies not in action but in inaction, as when he is imprisoned by the Lady in his own bed or is, by the terms of his "covenant" with the Green Knight, bound to suffer a blow to the neck without blenching. His quest is not for success in arms but to discover the meaning of "courtesy", a term imbued with religious significance of a neo-Platonic kind, relating the earthly self to its source of ideas. The literal monsters and marvels of his journey—dragons, wolves, satyrs, giants—are mentioned only in cursory fashion; they have become vestigial. It is the internal emotionality that interests the poet—the drama of the Castle and the Green Chapel, where the narrative becomes essentially a dream-poem. The story begins on Christmas Day at Camelot, with a sketch of the adolescent community playing their festive "kissing games" under the benign rule of King Arthur, who is described as "somewhat childgered" (boyish), continually stirred by his "young blood and wild brain".[5] The company, according to his custom, are awaiting a "marvel" before sitting down to dinner—some sort of appetising hors d'oeuvre. Into this entertainment-absorbed society the Green Knight thunders on his green horse, penetrating their youthful complacency with his beheading challenge, saying he wants a "Christmas game" of a more serious type. He offers his axe to anyone who dares to behead him and then to agree to suffer a reciprocal blow in a year's time at his home, the Green Chapel. The Knight is an "elvish (unearthly) man", of giant stature and more than human powers. His green colouring, splashed by red (as in his beard, his "red eyes", or his blood) is suggestive of pagan gods and forces of nature; at the same time these are Christianized, as in the holly bough that he carries instead of a sword. He is the mysterious and awesome force that will initiate a "catastrophic change" in the prevailing mentality of Camelot, drawing it forth—either to ruin, or to greater maturity and self-knowledge.[6]

It falls to Gawain, the most thoughtful of the knights, to take up the challenge and explore further the nature of this serious type of love, on behalf of the Camelot-mind. "Now think well, Sir Gawain", says the poet, "not to shrink from the danger of this adventure" (l. 487). As the year of mental preparation draws to its close, Gawain is equipped with his knightly apparel and his horse Gringolet. He sets forth bearing on his shield Solomon's pentangle and the image of the Virgin Mary, signs of his received wisdom—the internal combined object as perceived up to now, in its wisdom and purity. Initially Gawain's journey is geographically a realistic one, northwards along the Welsh coast then across into the "wilderness of the Wirral". It is midwinter, and the birds "pipe with cold". The poet stresses Gawain's loneliness. Forsaking the comfortable environment of Camelot and its group assumptions, he prepares for his mental ordeal by partaking of the privations of wild nature—sleeping in his armour amidst naked rocks under the sleet and icicles. It comes to Christmas Eve, and so far no sign of the whereabouts of the Green Chapel has materialized. Gawain prays to Mary for a "harbour"—not for his body but for his soul—and immediately "becomes aware" of a Castle "shimmering and shining through the white (hoar-frosted) oaks" of a dense forest (l. 772). It is the Virgin Mary's way of introducing him to the ambiguous fairy world, the other side of femininity. The delicate clusters of white pinnacles prefigure the Lady with her jewelled hair-net, while the strength of the Castle walls and the burning "fierce fires" of its hall intimate its association with the Green Knight, as do many other hints as to the identity of the Lord of the Castle—his "bright beard", his face "fierce as the fire", and in particular his forthright manner, being "free of his speech" and direct, just within the bounds of courtesy, in his dealings with Gawain (l. 847). For the Chapel is the Castle's wild back-yard, lying only "two miles away", the pagan source of primitive energies lying behind its civilized Christianity. And Gawain's sojourn in the civilized microsociety of the Castle during the Christmas period, with its warm reception of the wanderer and its strict observance of the rituals of religion and courtesy, represents his preparation for the ordeal at the Chapel where he will discover the meaning behind his trial of courtesy.

The Lord who plays host to the testing of Gawain's soul is simultaneously the incumbent of the Chapel, where he plays the part of a devil-in-disguise. He demands that Gawain demonstrate his reputation for courtesy and "love-talking", spurring him on with a jovial irony—his own form of courtesy: "While I live, I shall be better / Because Gawain has been my guest at God's own feast" (ll. 1035–36). The Lady of the Castle is from the beginning an ambiguous figure—in fact there are two of her, a beautiful young version and an old hag (just as in there are in the other famous legend about Gawain and the Lady Ragnell). The lady is led by the left hand by the "ancient one", and they are described in tandem throughout a long stanza, interweaving details of the one with contrasting details of the other, like a tableau of Youth and Age:

> For if the young one was fresh, withered was the other;
> Rich red arrayed the first one everywhere,
> Rough wrinkled cheeks rolled over the other;
> That one wore a kerchief with many clear pearls,
> Her breast and bright throat bare displayed,
> That other had a gorger covering her neck,
> Her black chin choked in chalky veils . . . [ll. 951–57]

Later we are told that the ancient lady is Gawain's aunt Morgan le Fay, enchantress of many guises and seducer of Merlin, inimical to the Round Table yet with healing powers that are ultimately (in legend) directed to the healing of Arthur's mortal wound. She and the Lady "take Gawain between them" for courteous conversation, and he addresses himself to them equally. He is caught "between two dyngne [dignified] dames, the older and the younger" (l. 1316).

The chastity-test of Gawain's courtesy, with its three mornings in the bedroom with the Lady and its three kisses, is the prologue to the three strokes of the axe that he will receive from the Knight at the Green Chapel. Taken together, not separately, they will close the symbol of his ambiguous emotional experience, "pinpointing the zone of conflict". The savage and exhilarating activity of the Lord amidst the bustle of huntsmen, dogs, and horses is juxtaposed to Gawain's enforced passivity as he is penned in bed conversing with the Lady:

> Thus the lord plays by the side of the lime-woods,
> And the good Gawain lies in his gay bed. [ll. 1178–79]

The narrative has an envelope structure: on each day the indoor hunt is enfolded by the description of the outdoor hunt in two parts, and they have equal imaginative impact. The hunt of the first day is expressly

for female deer: "At the first cry of the quest the wild creatures
quaked" (l. 1150), while Gawain, simultaneously, is woken "slyly"
(warily) by the "little noise" of the lady creeping lightly into his chamber. "You are a sleeper unsly", laughs the Lady, as he retreats beneath
the bedclothes. She points out that she has "taken him tightly" and will
"bind him in his bed". He produces the courtly formula that he wishes
only to be at her service and asks to be "released from his prison", but
she tucks in the bedclothes on the other side and states categorically:
"you shall not rise from your bed". Now that they are there alone with
the door locked, she hopes he will live up to his reputation; he is
"welcome to her body", and she desires with "fine force" that he will
take action—so she, in courtly terms, can be his "servant". Gawain
protests that she must be thinking of someone else—he is unworthy,
there must be some other service he can supply. No, she insists, he is
"all that she desires", and must have been brought by the Lord in
Heaven "to her hand" (l. 1257). She implies she is unhappy in her
marriage, and were she able to choose her own husband, he would be
the one. Gawain counters this by saying she has already fared better;
he takes care to answer "each case" (point) in her arguments. The one
that always dismays him is her oft-repeated tease that he "cannot be
Gawain"; he wonders, has he failed in courtesy? He is trapped on both
sides of the bedclothes by the danger of discourtesy towards the
Lady—either by refusing her or by accepting her temptation. It would
be similarly discourteous to lock the door; in any case, though the
chamber is lockable, dreams are not.

The interweaving of the bedroom scenes with those of the hunt
demonstrates the sexuality of the combined picture—not in the fixed
sense of allegory, but in the fluid sense of emotional atmosphere. The
deer who are the quarry of the first day's hunt raise a resonance with
Gawain, who is being hunted, and also with the Lady, who is "that
dere one"; the tribute of the deer-flesh to Gawain is a reminder of the
Lady's body that she had offered. The butchering, like the hunting, is
lengthily described, with due propriety and appreciation, in celebratory mode, suggesting the sensual act that was not performed in the
bedroom. The prime impression is of the goodness of the meat and the
skilfulness of the huntsmen in processing it. Producing his own prize,
the Lord jovially probes Gawain, implicitly, about the results of his
day's hunting-in-bed, as he

Shows him the fair flesh shorn on the ribs.
How like you this play? Have I won the prize? [ll. 1378–79]

The goodness of the meat is equivalent to the quality of the Lady's kisses, attested to by the Lord, when Gawain transfers them to him at the end of the day, according to the terms of their "contract". He transfers not just the fact but the spirit—delivering warmly the "comeliest" kisses he can muster. On the second day the quarry is a boar, remarkable for its size, fierceness, and courage—the "sellokest [most wonderful] swine" that had long since, owing to its age, singled itself out from the herd (l. 1439). The boar's tough mantle is proof against all the huntsmen's arrowheads, and in the end it comes to a duel between the Lord and the beast: the boar sets himself at bay against a bank beyond a swift-flowing stream, intelligently "aware of the weapon in the man's hand". The boar springs out,

> So that the man and the boar were both in a heap
> In the whitest of the water; the worst had that other,
> For the man marked him well as they met,
> And set his sharp point straight in the slot,
> Up to the hilt so his heart sundered . . . [ll. 1590–94]

Man and boar are of a similar physical type—splendid huge mature specimens—and already the boar has terrified and wounded both men and hounds. The hunt therefore testifies to the Lord's own courage and accurate application of strength—he "marks well" and, even in the turbulence of the collision over the foaming water, drives the point of his sword through the boar's only vulnerable spot. His precision is significant for the delicacy of the wound he later delivers to Gawain even with the four-foot blade of his axe; it is analogous to the irony of his verbal taunts, couched within their veil of courtesy.

The Lord's identification with the boar is emphasized when, in the procession home, "the boar's head was born before the lord himself" (l. 1616), reminding us of the Green Knight carrying off his own head. The Lady, meanwhile, has entered Gawain's bedroom to tempt him with the idea that he, too, might prove the strength of his desire by acting boarishly. He fires up at her suggestion that he could easily take her by force—"constraine with strength"—if she were discourteous enough to resist. "In his country", he insists, "goodwill" is a prerequisite for the "gift" of courtship (ll. 1495–1500). Then the Lady wonders whether, despite his fame as a ladies' knight, he is really "ignorant" of the "game" of love that she has come to learn from him, emphasizing again that she is "single" and her "lord is from home". Gawain parries this by acknowledging his insufficiency; she certainly "wields more skill in that art" than he does, and he is in no position to teach her "text and tales of arms". This is modified by his assuring her that he finds it a most "joyous game" and it gives him "delight" that she should "play with her knight though so poor a man". By the end of Day Two they have come to a draw: "There was no evil on either side, neither did they know anything but happiness" (l. 1552). For the time being, the poison has been drawn from the game of courtly love. That evening, however, Gawain feels deeply disturbed by the Lady's advances, made more openly in public, so that "the man was all astonished and upset within himself" (l. 1660). The Lord, for his part, gives the increasing impression that he is being left out of something and that Gawain has been having the best of the bargain. There is perhaps a tinge of genuine suspicion, not just ironic good manners, in the Lord's quip that Gawain will be richer than any of them if his "trade" in kisses continues so well (l. 1645). The metaphor of "traded goods" has become an inadequate description for what we have witnessed of the love-play between Gawain and the Lady.

The tension reaches its peak on the third day, with its expectations of "third time throw best" (l. 1680). The hunt this day is for a fox, which has the more significance in that fox-hunts are rarely described in mediaeval literature—a fox is not worth hunting. By the end the Lord has only a "foul fox-skin" and a brush that bears a strong resemblance to his own ruddy beard to exchange for Gawain's Lady's kiss. "Let the Devil have it!" exclaims the Lord as he hands over his worthless prize to Gawain. By contrast, in terms of nature, this is by far the most beautiful day, vividly observed by the poet:

> Wonderfully fair was the land, for the frost clung;
> Fiery red from a drifting rack rose the sun
> And clear floated the clouds from the welkin. [ll. 1694–96]

The fair day, and the foul fox-skin, remind us of the twin aspects of womanhood in the Lady and Morgan the enchantress. There is now a turbulence in the minds of all the protagonists. We suspect it is not only Gawain but also the Lord who is being required to grasp some essential aesthetic point, regarding the ambiguity of their own feelings. Is the Lady merely acting mechanically as temptress (the official version of the story), or is she stirred by genuine feeling? To what extent is she perhaps sending a message to her Lord by means of Gawain's kisses? There are elements of both Gawain and the Lady in the fox's slyness: Gawain, after all, had only pretended to be asleep when the

Lady slid into his chamber. Unlike the deer with their speed and the boar with its ferocity, the more human "Reynard" has nothing but his wits to rely on and leads the huntsmen a merry dance of double-dealings and backtrackings:

> And he led them by lagman [strung out in a line], the lord and his men,
> In this manner among the mountains till mid-afternoon. [ll. 1729–30]

Reynard's fate is sealed, however, not by skill with sword or bow, as previously, but by the operation of the medieval hunting-machine, with groups stationed round the hill so that there is literally no escape. The Lord can take no pride in his catch because it merely the product of society's assumptions, not of any skill or strength, and this is mirrored by the uselessness of the flesh. It is the first case of "the unspeakable in pursuit of the inedible".[7]

Gawain, in contrast to the Lord, seems to feel for the first time that morning a hint of desire for the Lady, "with joy welling up in his heart", rather than the usual terms of chivalric defence. The poet's plea to Mary to take care of her knight, because "great peril stood between them", echoes Gawain's own prayer to Mary before entering the castle, mirroring his dependence on the Muse to provide a happy outcome as the "dint" of the axe approaches. And we know the meaning, the feeling, of peril, from following the wild creatures of the hunt. The peril derives from the greater empathy between Gawain and the Lady, transcending the forms of courtesy. For the first time the Lady asks him a true question (as distinct from a rhetorical, teasing one)—asking whether he has another lover whom he likes better. When Gawain answers no, and nor is he ready for one, she accepts that she has been "truly answered, though it pains" her. Is this a moment of sincerity, or her ultimate betrayal, putting him off his guard so she can trap him with the present of the girdle, literally enwrapping him in it, just as she imprisoned him in the bedclothes, while the "hunt" is now closing in upon him, as the time of "chekke" [checkmate] looms? As often in literature, the girdle is an emblem of her femininity, and Gawain—identified with the animals of the wild—accepts it for its life-saving properties:

> "Now do you forsake this silk", said the lady then,
> Because it is simple in itself? And so it may seem.
> Lo! so it is little, and so less it is worth;
> But whoever knows the costes [nature, quality] that is knit within it,
> He would appraise it perhaps at a greater price; ... [ll. 1846–49]

Later it is described as a love-token, "drurye". Yet it is not literally her body, as in the temptation of the first day; it is more like a vehicle for her knowledge, which she is passing on to Gawain. Only once the girdle is tied round him does she beseech Gawain not to tell her husband, "for her sake". For it belongs (as its green and gold colours indicate) to the Lord—in society's terms, the possessor of her sexuality—and she presents it as a thing "of little worth", recalling the trading terms employed by the Lord. Yet we wonder, does the Lord himself know the worth of the girdle, so "simple in itself"? Does he suffer from a confusion of values, resulting from his own submission to the heavy machinery of society's basic assumptions? The fox, deprived of its inner wits, turns out nothing but a stinky hide—the ugly or sinister aspect of Morgan le Fay. Does the Lady, when entered mechanically or with violence, turn out not worth the catching?

The fact remains that even at the end of the poem we never know, nor does Gawain ever know, the Lady's innermost heart. The Lord thinks he knows—but by the time he explains to Gawain how he has masterminded the entire plot, using his wife as the instrument of temptation, we have become sceptical of his omniscience. He knows only the mechanics of the relationship between Gawain and the Lady, but the poet, in retelling this well-known tale, has—to his own anxiety—evoked its complex and unparaphraseable emotional nuance. Indeed, the Lord himself is merely an agent for Morgan le Fay, though he never fully digests the implications of this. The question will always remain to what extent the Lady's love may have been genuine and served as Gawain's protection, even at the cost of a minor nick in the neck. On the most basic level, the girdle improves his morale, which turns out itself to be crucial in his verbal exchanges with the Knight at the Green Chapel; for despite the Knight's assertion of predetermination, the poetic impression remains that it is the final stage of their relationship that really clinches Gawain's survival.

On the day of the tryst, the weather has changed. It is no longer "wonderfully fair", as on the day the Lady seemed to indicate her protectiveness, but inclement and threatening. Gawain, waking early, "lowers his lids" against the sounds of sleet and "werbelande [wuthering] wind" and the shivering of the wild animals. Outside, mist drizzles on the moor, and each mountain wears a hat, a huge "mantle of mist", with the drear suitability of sinister giant-like forms surrounding the Green Chapel. Nature reflects the mysterious grandeur of the Green Knight, Nature's child, in a foretaste of Romanticism. This is to be the day on which the masculine component of the internal object reveals its nature as guardian and possessor of the feminine. First a Guide is selected by the Lord to put Gawain on the "right path". Speaking in the same forthright manner as the Lord and the Knight, the Guide advises Gawain to run away. Somewhat nettled ["gruching"], Gawain refuses to do so, and the Guide sneers at this failure of common sense, implying that he has been brainwashed by the knightly code of honour, which is merely foolish vanity: "Now farewell, on God's side, Gawain the noble!" His taunts serve to strengthen Gawain's resolve—and though we are never told, we suspect that this was their intention, and that the Knight has himself been playing devil's-advocate.

The Green Chapel turns out to be an ancient mound, grown into the landscape: "hollow within, nothing but an old cave" (again, reflecting the fox-skin). To Gawain it appears to be the caricature of a Christian chapel—an "ugly oratory" fit for the devil himself to say matins in:

> This is a chapel of mischance, chekke [checkmate] betide it! [ll. 2193–95]

Such caves were used in legend by enchanters like Morgan for the preparation of their arts. Such containers for knowledge are ambiguous, with power for good or ill, like the ancient Greek *Eumenides*. Gawain sees it as "ugly" (a word used several times in this poem, the first recorded in English), indicating the aesthetics of ambiguity. It is the place of "checkmate" regarding his own emotional turmoil—the place where he will survive or lose his head (his reason). Instead of a love- or sleep-potion being prepared, Gawain hears the fierce din of an axe-head being whetted on the other side of the mound:

> What! It whirred and whetted, as water at a mill;
> What! It rushed and rang, rueful to hear. [ll. 2203–4]

—the poet making the most of alliterative potential. "Let God work!" says Gawain to himself, again suggesting that the contraries of God and the Devil are "whetting" together. The whetting recalls the other movements of preparation—the Knight stroking his beard, Gawain stroking the axe at Camelot, the Lady tucking in the bedclothes. They meet with reciprocal formality, as in a duel. The Green Knight echoes his words of sinister courtly welcome from when he was Lord of the Castle—saying he will give Gawain "everything that he ever promised" (ll. 1970, 2218). Gawain echoes his own formula of courtesy when he was the Lord's guest—"I give you myself for your own, if you like".

When he kneels to receive the blow, Gawain's posture reflects the tableau of the bedroom, with the Lady "leaning luflily" [graciously] over him to deliver the kiss. However he has commended himself to "God's will", and all the while his mind is alert to the potential of each moment, practising his ideal of courtesy with a strenuous passivity. He intends to stick to his word but not to submit to his destruction: hence the tension of the exchanges with the Knight. The Knight aborts the first blow because Gawain flinches as the axe descends: taunting him, as did the Lady, with "Thou art not Gawain . . . fleeing for fear before you feel harm!" (l. 2270). This proves, he says, that he must be the better man. Gawain, uncrushed, retorts that his own trial is a real one, not a magical fairy-tale—he cannot replace his head once it has fallen to the ground. The Knight whets the sparks of Gawain's spirit just as he whetted the blade of his axe. The effect is to spice Gawain's restrained chivalry with some of his own fire-and-brimstone character. He challenges the Knight to "be brisk" and "bring me to the point":

> For I shall stand thy stroke, and start no more
> Till thine axe has hit me: here is my truth.
> Have at thee then! quoth the other, and heaves it aloft,
> Looking as furious as though he were mad. [ll. 2286–89]

This time, Gawain stands as still as a stone, or as a tree entwined by a hundred roots in rocky ground (introjecting the Green Knight's force-of-nature aspect). In response, the "green man" yet again aborts the blow, and teases him playfully ["murily"]:

> So, now you have your heart whole, it behoves me to hit you.
> Hold on now to the high knighthood that Arthur gave you,
> And keep your neck at this cut, if you can. [ll. 2296–99]

This time, since he had not flinched, Gawain fires up with anger—again taking emotional colouring and strength from the Knight. He makes a pointed accusation that has the effect of finally stinging the Knight into action:

> Why! Thrash on, you fierce man, you threaten too long;
> I think your heart is awed by your own self. [l. 2300]

When Gawain makes this verbal cut, after which he realizes that "no marvel" can save him now, the Knight finally, with surgical precision, delivers his "nick to the neck". The blood that shoots out over the white snow—"the blood blenk on the snow" (l. 2315)—recalls how the

Knight's blood "blinked on the green" at the outset of the story when his own head was chopped off: it has found its reciprocation.

Gawain's identification with the Knight's "fierceness" results not in literally putting his head back on, but in a feeling of rebirth:

> Never since he was a baby born of his mother
> Was he ever in this world a creature half so blithe. [ll. 2320–21]

It is as though it were his birth-blood on the snow; he has survived the "check" of the catastrophe. The verbal counterpart, however, is more complex, as the Knight reveals his identity and the involvement of the Lady. When the Knight says Gawain has now performed "penance at the point of my edge", we understand that the "edge" is not merely the concrete blade of the axe but the total impact of the emotional knowledge as it now appears, as in a flash of insight. Through the Knight's cut, Gawain experiences the dual significance of the Lady's gift as protector and wounder. She is the power behind the stroke of the axe— "Morgan the goddess" (l. 2452). Meltzer has the phrase "the blow of awe and wonder",[8] referring to the aesthetic impact of the mother on the newborn baby; an analogous blow is sustained by Gawain. His "penance" leaves him, the Knight says, as pure "as if he had never sinned since he was first born" (l. 2394).

As soon as Gawain has received his "check" and confessed his own guilt and fearfulness, the character of the Knight changes. He abandons his ferocious mannerisms and stands resting on his axe, as peaceably as a farmer leaning on his spade. Shedding his transferential or confessorial mantle as devilish priest-of-Nature, he becomes the human Sir Bertilak de Hautdesert. In fact, he takes on a benign paternal role and tries to persuade Gawain to return to the castle and be part of the family. When Gawain (in reaction to the "blow") tries to hand back the girdle, calling it "foul" and "false thing" (like the fox-skin), he does not allow it. He encourages Gawain to accept responsibility for his feelings: the foulness lies in himself not in the girdle. "And in his heart he liked him" (l. 2335). This is a revealing moment, the first indication the poet has ever given of the Knight's having feelings. It contrasts, in its spontaneous and unpredicted quality, with his complacent assertion that he knows everything about the relation between Gawain and his wife:

> Now I know well your kisses and also your costes [quality]
> And the wooing of my wife: I wrought it myself. [ll. 2360–61]

It is true that the Knight "knew", through a species of countertransference, the quality of the "kisses" (imaged in Gawain kissing him directly). Yet his directorial role is responsible for only the bare bones of the action, not the intimate meaning. The "costes" of the interaction between Gawain and the Lady are as intricately woven as the "costes" of the girdle. Somehow the Knight has encouraged Gawain to "know" more about femininity than he knows himself—for he is still stuck in the old mentality, assured—by virtue of his masculinity—of Morgan's favour and protection. This differs from Gawain's reliance on Mary and God as internal objects who will respond to his faith and somehow save his life. Like Prospero in the hunt for Caliban, the Knight practises converting vengeance into virtue with a godlike omnipotence, but without the painful consciousness of the loss of Ariel—the femininity that must be free if it is not to be sly and foxlike. He can "laugh as though he were mad" and stop it at will, just as he can put his head back on, but can he lose his head in the sense of falling in love? The Green Knight, successful in his analytic role as tester and developer of Gawain's soul, has perhaps fared less successfully in developing his own soul, when he returns to his ordinary human state. Unlike Gawain, he remains blind to his own vulnerability. Nonetheless, the growth of his unpredicted "liking" for Gawain indicates the change of heart that may, for all we know, have been instrumental in saving Gawain's neck: the Knight respects his "care for his life" just as he sympathizes with his susceptibility to his "winsome wife". What message from the Lady does he really see in the "costes" of the girdle? Indeed, is the Lady as much an avatar of Mary as of Morgan?[9] Had Gawain arrived at the Chapel *without* the girdle, we wonder, might the axe have slipped? The Knight's ironic words at the castle may have acquired more truth in them than he anticipated when he said that he "would be better for having had Gawain as his guest". The inscrutability of the poem's deep grammar testifies to the unknown workings of the poet's own Muse (he also appeals to Mary), infusing with ambiguity the unconscious communications that the Knight's words are inadequate to explain.

Gawain, meanwhile, acknowledges the justice of the Green Knight's blow of knowledge, as paternal object guarding access to the ambiguous castle-chapel with its poetic contents. The stroke of the axe reveals, but does not explain away, the mystery of the Lady and her relation to the Virgin Mary—who first introduced to him the white pinnacles of the erotic castle—on the one hand, and to Morgan le Fay on the other. He will always wear the scar on his neck, the sign of his blood coursing: it is the mark of his destiny, as in Greek tragedy, imprinted on his personality. But he will also always wear its complementary colour, the green girdle bound up with the "costes" of love and its life-saving properties, in the spiritual rather than the literal sense. Whenever pride pricks him, he says, for his prowess in arms, "a look at this love-lace shall humble my heart" (l. 2438). The two knightly functions—the two types of "arms"—complement one another. He is no longer Mary's pure knight—purity will belong to the later and more boring Galahad, the only knight to achieve the quest of the Holy Grail. His internal idea of Mary and her expectations of him has changed. His new object integrates Mary's truth and Morgan's ambiguity—with a tinge of the Green Knight's own fiery colouring, yet without the complacency of Sir Bertilak as a man. The combined-object love-knot is "locked under his left arm" in the place where he wears his shield, layered on top of the signs of the Pentangle and the Virgin,

> In token that he was taken by a stain of guilt,
> Thus he came to the court, a knight safe and sound. [ll. 2487–89]

Despite—or, rather, because of—his scar, the poet can now pronounce him "a knight safe and sound". His internalization of his dream-experience is his new protection. So when he returns to Arthur's court, fortified by a new readiness to fall in love—not merely to sit enthroned by Guinevere's side and make courteous speeches—he finds that all the other young people wish to emulate him: they all decide to wear a green girdle, in token of the new game that must be played in deadly earnest.

NOTES

1. D. Meltzer & M. Harris Williams, *The Apprehension of Beauty* (Strath Tay: Clunie Press, 1988), p. 229.
2. Milton, *An Apology for Smectymnuus*, in: *Poetical Works*, ed. D. Bush (Oxford: Oxford University Press, 1942), p. xxx.
3. *Sir Gawain* was contemporaneous with Chaucer, but written in the north-Midlands dialect that was superseded by the smoother southern English used by Chaucer in his championship of native English as the language of poetry (rather than French, as at court, or Latin, as in church). This southern English eventually became established as modern English.
4. Meltzer's term; see Chapter 8, this volume.
5. Quotations, followed by line-numbers, are based on *Sir Gawain and the Green Knight*, ed. J. R. R. Tolkien and E. V. Gordon; second edition by Norman Davis (Oxford: Oxford University Press, 1967). I have modernized the spellings but kept the original words where possible, even though

their meanings may have slightly changed in some cases. This suggests the flavour of the original and pinpoints some of the word-resonances. "Luflily", for example, translates best as "graciously", but in so doing loses the sound of "love"; "costes" translates as "quality" but then loses the ambiguity of the trading metaphor; "chekke" translates as "doom" or "destiny" but loses the analogy with the game of chess. However to read the poem as a whole, it is best to turn to the modern verse translation by Bernard Stone (Harmondsworth, Middlesex: Penguin, 1964).

6. For an analysis of Bion's concept of catastrophic change, see Meltzer, *The Kleinian Development* (Strath Tay: Clunie Press, 1978), Book 3, Ch. XIV.

7. Oscar Wilde's definition of fox-hunting.

8. Meltzer & Harris Williams, *Apprehension of Beauty*, p. 57.

9. Since Gawain goes light-heartedly to confession immediately afterwards and is "securely absolved", it is clear that for the poet his acceptance of the girdle, and hiding it from the Lord, is not in religious terms a sin.

CHAPTER TWO

The evolution of Psyche

The tragic element in the aesthetic experience resides, not in the transience, but in the enigmatic quality of the object: "Joy, whose hand is ever at his lips / Bidding adieu." Is it a truthful object that is always reminding the lover of the transience, or a tantalizing one, like La Belle Dame? The aesthetic conflict is different from the romantic agony in this respect: that its central experience of pain resides in uncertainty, tending towards distrust, verging on suspicion. The lover is naked as Othello to the whisperings of Iago but is rescued by the quest for knowledge, the K-link, the desire to know rather than possess the object of desire. The K-link points to the value of the desire as itself the stimulus to knowledge, not merely as a yearning for gratification and control over the object. *Desire makes it possible, even essential, to give the object its freedom.*

Donald Meltzer[1]

The genesis of the Romantic poets' view of the aesthetic object— the Muse with her storehouse of poetic images—lay in Satan's description of Eve in *Paradise Lost:*

> She fair, divinely fair, fit love for gods,
> Not terrible, though terror be in love

> And beauty, not approached by stronger hate,
> Hate stronger . . .[2]

Satan discovered, through tentative unfolding steps—ungrammatical in prose but eloquent in poetry—how the aesthetic object is defined by the contraries of love and hate, beauty and terror, inherent in the relation between the object and the poet-adventurer. These comprise the "hateful siege of contraries" that were to become Blake's philosophy of the "marriage of contraries" in *The Marriage of Heaven and Hell* and the concept of "fearful symmetry" in The Tyger:

> Tyger Tyger, burning bright,
> In the forests of the night;
> What immortal hand or eye,
> Could frame thy fearful symmetry?
>
> In what distant deeps or skies,
> Burnt the fire of thine eyes?
> On what wings dare he aspire?
> What the hand, dare seize the fire?
>
> And what shoulder, & what art,
> Could twist the sinews of thy heart?
> And when thy heart began to beat,
> What dread hand, and what dread feet?
>
> What the hammer, what the chain,
> In what furnace was thy brain?
> What the anvil? What dread grasp,
> Dare its deadly terrors clasp?

The poet, like Prometheus, wonders whether he "dare seize the fire" of the core of poetic energy housed in the eyes of the tiger. The building of the poem follows, in imagination, the building of the tiger, feature by feature, by the power of Los, the god of creativity-as-construction. Los with his hammer rhythmically beats the tiger into shape, line by line, and at the same time sets its heart beating—his "dread grasp" matching the power that is being unleashed. In this way the nature of the aesthetic object is evoked as something known by means of the tension between contrary emotions, resulting in the cry of recognition:

> Did he who made the Lamb make thee?

It is a rhetorical question, answering itself. The Tyger–Muse cannot be "framed" by the poet—he cannot simply seize the fire from heaven. Rather, the poet adjusts his vision to correspond to the frame of this awesome conjunction of objects. Now he understands creativity-as-inspiration. It turns out that the hammer of Los has in fact been work-ing on his inward perception, forging and purging until he is correctly aligned in beauty and awe of the object.

This reflection of the eternal fount of inward fire in the distant depths of the skies of the unconscious is the Romantic alternative to the infernal fires of the industrial furnaces. The soul, to "create itself", must have an inherent vitality beyond the control of society or the selfhood. In Wordsworth it appeared as the "visionary gleam", which, like a shaft of sunlight animating a natural form, would suddenly irradiate his perception, bestowing meaning on nature and turning it into the stuff that dreams are made of. This irradiation is not so much pleasurable or even enlightening, as awesome. One such "spot of time" in *The Prelude* describes rowing in a boat as a boy and being frightened by a cliff:

> She was an elfin Pinnace; lustily
> I dipp'd my oars into the silent Lake,
> And, as I rose upon the stroke, my Boat
> Went heaving through the water, like a Swan;
> When from behind the craggy Steep, till then
> The bound of the horizon, a huge Cliff,
> As if with voluntary power instinct,
> Uprear'd its head. I struck, and struck again,
> And, growing still in stature, the huge Cliff
> Rose up between me and the stars, and still,
> With measur'd motion, like a living thing,
> Strode after me.[3]

The boy in his "elfin pinnace" feels himself a magically protected explorer upon the lake of his mind, ringed by mountains that seem to contain rather than threaten. The pattern of rise and fall that ripples the surface of the "silent lake" is initiated by himself: "I dipp'd my oars . . . I rose upon the stroke". Suddenly the nature of the horizon, which securely bounds his world, changes: the "craggy Steep" releases the figure of the huge cliff, whose genie-like powers dwarf those of the elfin rower. Now his panicky striking is aggressive, as if against the cliff itself: "I struck, and struck again". This action, or feeling, seems to animate the cliff further, till "growing in stature" in response to the boy's fear, it pursues and seems to swallow in its shadow the figure of the boy in the boat. The pursuing cliff becomes the source of a "dark-ness" in his mind, which takes the fairy-tale shape of

> huge and mighty Forms that do not live
> Like living men mov'd slowly through the mind
> By day and were the trouble of my dreams. [ll. 424–26[

In this way Wordsworth effortlessly relates the origins of religious and poetic (and psychoanalytic) experience. As Susanne Langer points out:

> Aesthetic attraction, mysterious fear, are probably the first mani-festations of that mental function which in man becomes a peculiar "tendency to see reality symbolically", and which issues in the *power of conception*, and the life-long habit of speech.[4]

Wordsworth's giant cliff, like the Green Knight whetting the axe in his Chapel, is a masculine aspect of the feminine goddess-mountain whose arms encircle the scene of the poet's life experiences in a way both secure and frightening. The oar-strokes of his tiny kicking limbs trouble the water of his dreams as the huge and mighty forms of his inner gods—"not like living men"—move slowly through his con-sciousness in response, and evoke what (in Book 2) he calls "the ghostly language of the ancient earth", the source from which he "drank the visionary power".[5]

When Wordsworth felt the visionary power receding, instead of delving deeper into the waters of the unconscious, he attributed its retreat to the inevitable process of growing up:

> Shades of the prison-house begin to close
> Upon the growing Boy,[6]

He accepted the "prison" of society's basic assumptions. Coleridge, however, having a greater spirit of inquiry, took—like Byron—a meta-physical interest in the more tortuous aspects of the relation between the infant-self and its objects. In contrast to Wordworth's conclusion that he must be one of Nature's "favoured Beings",[7] Coleridge empa-thized with the fear of being thrown out, abandoned in his guilt to spiritual drought. "Remorse", he said, was "the most difficult & at the same time the most interesting Problem of Psychology".[8] In *The An-cient Mariner* the poet-voyager takes the form of a Wedding Guest who is prevented from entering the church by the compelling story of the Mariner, who "holds him with his glittering eye". Through this he discovers what it is to be cut off from the sources of spiritual nourish-ment:

> All in a hot and copper sky,
> The bloody Sun, at noon,
> Right up above the mast did stand,
> No bigger than the Moon.

Day after day, day after day,
We stuck, nor breath nor motion;
As idle as a painted ship
Upon a painted ocean.

Water, water, everywhere,
And all the boards did shrink;
Water, water, everywhere,
Nor any drop to drink. [ll. 111–22]

This starvation of visionary drink, leading to a drained mind and a type of sterile artificial poetry—"a painted ship on a painted ocean"— is the result of the Mariner's omnipotent shooting of the albatross with his "cross-bow", his temper. The sun fixes the ship to the ocean by standing at the masthead where the albatross used to perch. The great bird, like "a Christian soul", had overseen the mariners' simple child-like pieties, coming daily for food, play and "vespers nine". It had perched on the top of the mast, level with the huge icebergs in the midst of their fearful cracking, roaring and growling. The feminine Muse of the poetic nursery phase guided the Mariner among the awe-some aspects of these giant powers (like Wordsworth's Cliff) and steered the ship through the Storm, bending before the masculine blast:

And now the STORM-BLAST came, and he
Was tyrannous and strong:
He struck with his o'ertaking wings,
And chased us south along. [ll. 41–44]

Yet the albatross with its huge wing-spread is itself born of the Storm-blast with its "o'ertaking wings", just as the Storm himself was intro-duced by means of the rhythmic pacing of the bride, who sweeps before her the "merry minstrelsy" in a movement that then immedi-ately transmutes into the wind sweeping the shipful of men towards the icebergs of the southern ocean. Thus the bride, the albatross, the Storm, are part of the same object-network. Then after the Mariner has shot the albatross, these male–female components take the retributive form of the "bloody Sun" and the "Nightmare Life-in-Death", who "veers and tacks" like a missile towards the grounded ship:

Her lips were red, her looks were free,
Her locks were yellow as gold:
Her skin was white as leprosy,

> The Night-mare LIFE-IN-DEATH was she,
> Who thicks man's blood with cold.
> The naked hulk alongside came,
> And the twain were casting dice ... [ll. 190–96]

The bride who was "red as a rose" becomes the fearful spectre of sexual torment, "free" in the sense of loose, painted in false colours to disguise the inner "leprosy". The sexual act, and the poetic one, become a deadly gamble, dicing for the spiritual death of one party: much worse, the Mariner discovers, than the physical death of his fellows. In this context the poet loses his faculty of expression, his heart becoming "dry as dust", producing nothing but a "wicked whisper". Only after the scene is transfigured by the light of the moon, imaging the return of overseeing femininity, does the Mariner's appreciation of beauty return, in the form of the water-snakes that he had at first found so hideous:

> Within the shadow of the ship
> I watched their rich attire:
> Blue, glossy green, and velvet black,
> They coiled and swam; and every track
> Was a flash of golden fire.
>
> O happy living things! no tongue
> Their beauty might declare:
> A spring of love gushed from my heart,
> And I blessed them unaware: [ll. 277–87]

The play of light traces the restored line of identification between the poet and his Muse, the moon, who transforms the dry burning shadow into a vital inner world of flashing lights and fountains (Coleridge's characteristic imagery for "reason", his term for inspiration). When the ugly is seen to become beautiful and the vision of poetry and beauty is restored, the "naked hulk" aspect of the feminine principle is exorcized—represented by the corpse of the Albatross falling "like lead into the sea", while its spirit rises with the Moon:

> The moving Moon went up the sky,
> And nowhere did abide ... [ll. 263–64]

The ugliness that had been in the mind of the beholder is lifted when the doors of perception are cleansed. It happens "unaware", without conscious volition. The inspiring force of the moving Moon, with its long lullaby vowels, restores movement to the Mariner's mind, repairing the damage caused by the arrow shot from the cross-bow of his ignorant omnipotent self.

In this way the Romantics were discovering, or rediscovering, the essential features of the infantile basis for the romance between the poet and his Muse. The principle of going back to Mother Nature was associated with the idea of a "natural" language of poetry—rather as Shakespeare had supposedly "warbled his native woodnotes wild". Only Wordsworth believed in this literally; but in his work, the languages of external and internal nature did indeed appear a seamless whole, in a way that other poets would find inimitable. Keats, however, had an experimental and critical interest in the varied qualities of poetic language as well as a deep-rooted faith in their organization by the Muse. The relation between "native English music" and its complication by such things as Miltonic or Latinate idioms is a constant preoccupation in his letters. In this context, we may take the ultimate *Lyrical Ballad* to be Keats's "La Belle Dame Sans Merci".[9] It is the logical culmination of the earlier Romantics' immersion in traditional ballad forms and of their Rousseauist mission to portray the original, primitive, or essential nature of poetic composition.

Before "La Belle Dame", however, Keats wrote *The Eve of St Agnes*, another very different approach to the familiar theme of the poet-as-knight errant in search of the prize of love.[10] The medievalism of the two poems has different linguistic roots—one in Spenser's neo-mediaeval faeryland, the other in the sparse Romantic ideal of a native or natural music, free in its simplicity. *St Agnes* was written at Chichester in January 1819 and marries a Spenserian verse form with Gothic romance and historical medievalism as seen in the cathedral monuments. The theme is the popular superstition that on St Agnes' Eve (20 January) maidens may see a vision of their true love—their virginity like St Agnes' "lambs unshorn". The luxuriant evocativeness and careful craftsmanship comprise a new level of technical achievement in Keats's work: an intense focus on how to get the utmost from the language used, by means of association, condensation of phrase, and complementary contrasts—warmth and cold, noise and hush, light and shade, distant past and vivid present. We see Porphyro "buttressed from moonlight", Madeline "Half-hidden, like a mermaid in seaweed". The sensuous links thread delicately through the poem like a medieval tapestry: thus the hare who "limped trembling through the frozen grass", as an image of constrained warmth and vitality, leads directly to Madeline "trembling in her soft and chilly nest", feeling

As though a tongueless nightingale should swell
Her throat in vain, and die, heart-stifled, in her dell. [ll. 206–7]

The Keatsian use of the alexandrine—the long last line—creates a parabolic swelling-and-fading effect.

The sexual awakening of Madeline, "asleep in lap of legends old", is founded—as is often pointed out—on *Romeo and Juliet*, but even more fundamentally on the pubertal fairy-tale of the Sleeping Beauty. She is a rose who "shuts to be a bud again"; erotic fantasies enfold her like petals, "Hoodwinked with fairy fancy". Porphyro fills the air with the scents and colours of a feast; he discovers her "lute tumultuous" (a beautifully compact phrase) and plays on it that ancient song of Provence, "la belle dame sans merci". His music corresponds to Madeline's swelling nightingale desire, stifled by the baronial restrictions of her family castle (her dutiful chastity). Their sculpted monuments "ache in icy hoods and mails", "imprisoned in black purgatorial rails". Like the prince in the Sleeping Beauty, Porphyro pierces this thorn-thicket and creeps inside her bedroom, then her bed, then her "dream":

> Into her dream he melted, as the rose
> Blendeth its odour with the violet,
> Solution sweet—meantime the frost-wind blows
> Like Love's alarum pattering the sharp sleet
> Against the window panes; St. Agnes' moon hath set. [ll. 321–24]

Keats immediately alleviates the saccharine coyness of the moment of climax with the tapping of the storm-wind on the window panes. It is a technical sleight of hand, resulting in the popular distinction between indulgent dream and harsh reality that has so often been taken to characterize Keats's thinking. Madeline awakens to "moan forth witless words", declaring herself "a dove forlorn and lost". It is a good opportunity for Porphyro—unlike Hamlet, who missed the chance with Ophelia in her madness—to carry her over the moors to the haven of marriage and respectability. There is a touch of impatience in the poet's wish to be rid of the lovers by means of a slightly stagey distancing in sense and time:

> And they are gone—aye, ages long ago
> These lovers fled away into the storm. [ll. 371–72]

For the erotic centre of the poem is lacking in spirituality—it is *merely* sensual. The "storm" which might have accompanied the ensuing "wedding" as in the *Mariner* is hinted at, then immediately dispelled into the "ages long ago" of fairyland.

Keats had a row with his publisher, John Taylor, over the consummation stanza: Taylor was worried it would make the poem unsuitable for ladies, and Keats, forced to revise the original version, retorted that he did not wish to write for ladies. The subject of the poem had in fact been suggested by Mrs Isabella Jones, a widow who was having an affair with Taylor at the time and with whom Keats also had some sort of unsatisfactory erotic liaison. She insisted he keep this secret from Taylor, to Keats's annoyance; and, indeed, he felt she treated him as a boy, giving him presents of grouse and fancy food instead of her body. The quality of this association pervades the poem. Even from the time of writing, Keats judged *St Agnes* indifferently, considering it too sentimental or "smokeable". He printed it in his 1820 volume, having a dispassionate eye for its genuine merits, its "colouring"; yet it was never part of the mainstream of his poetic ambition (unlike *Hyperion*, which he was writing during the same period). His dissatisfaction was not technical but spiritual and emotional. The split of femininity into young and beautiful and old and ugly exists here as in *Sir Gawain and the Green Knight;* but there is no aesthetic tension between them, no merging of identity. This requires a sense of mystery, of fluid boundaries and unknown quantities. Madeline's chaperone is Old Angela, "with meagre face deform" and "aged eyes aghast / From fright of dim espial", but she is no Morgana, any more than naïve Madeline is a Lady; and Porphyro is no Gawain. Rather, Angela is a straightforward bawd like Juliet's nurse, begging Porphyro to wed Madeline if he must take her virginity. She bears within her ague-stricken brain the excitement of eroticism in the context of secrecy and parental (authoritarian) prohibition; and Porphyro's partnership with her—which is both contemptuous and expedient—reflects this feature of his own attitude to the conquest of Madeline. He intrudes into Madeline's dream by a trick of projective identification. It is associated with some characteristically Keatsian remarks about women (always making specific exceptions) to the effect that he would rather give them "a sugar plum than my time", etc.[11] Elements of the pornographic and the silly accrue unresolvedly to the Angela–Madeline Muse, however evocative the swelling nightingale and the tumultuous lute. The sugar-plum maiden finds her partner in a knight-errant who, once stripped of the glamour of *St Agnes'* medieval trappings, bears a certain resemblance to the "naughty boy" whom Keats had pictured for his young sister Fanny some months earlier, in a typically humorous and modest self-portrait:

> There was a naughty boy,
>   And a naughty boy was he,
> For nothing would he do
>   But scribble poetry—[12]

This was the little boy who "followed his nose to the north", as he had done in childhood play, in search of fishes, fountains, ghosts, and witches to make a collection for his forthcoming volumes of poetry.

Keats finished *St Agnes*, a poem much loved and much anthologized, at the beginning of February 1819. It meant nothing to him—in terms of the subterranean spiritual struggle he was undergoing at the time, following Tom's death two months previously and during the initial stages of his relationship with Fanny Brawne. He had complained in October of feeling "all the vices of a poet—irritability, love of effect and admiration."[13] This referred mainly to the Miltonic cadences of *Hyperion*, which he was writing at the time; but the writing of *St Agnes*, which has its own brand of poetic self-consciousness, did nothing to dispel this feeling of being prey to "vices". Indeed his letters of that winter and early spring tell of his having written "nothing—nothing—nothing", "for to tell the truth I have not been in great cue for writing lately—I must wait for the spring to rouse me up a little".[14] By "writing" he meant writing poetry of the type that would help to forward his ambition to "be a Poet—seeing how great a thing it is."[15] However, there was a sense in which, instead of poetry itself, his long journal-letters to George and Georgiana Keats in America were fulfilling that function—in the sense of mental preparation, as distinct from technical preparation. Keats was acutely sensible of his new loneliness, now that the intimate trio of brothers had been dispersed. When George had hurriedly emigrated with his new wife in June, Keats had steeled himself for the forthcoming tragedy, saying that, because of his remaining sister, he "may not follow [his brothers], either to America or to the Grave—life must be undergone."[16] Tom died on 1 December, aged 19. Keats used the pain of these physical absences to establish an analytic mode of internal communication, in which he felt himself to be mediating between their souls:

> I have scarce a doubt of immortality of some nature or other—neither had Tom . . . sometimes I fancy an immense separation, and sometimes, as at present, a direct communication of spirit with you. That will be one of the grandeurs of immortality—there will be no space and consequently the only commerce between spirits will be by their intelligence of each other—when they will completely understand each other—while we in this world merely comprehend each other in different degrees—[17]

The long journal-letters take the place of a prose "tale", which he had promised George he must write in order to satisfy his mind's "inability to remain at rest".[18] The tale never materializes; but the February–May letter, in particular, becomes his own version of a "Prelude, or Growth of an Individual Mind".[19] It is the prelude to the "Ode to Psyche"—the poem that materializes from Keats's expressed wish for his letters to somehow enable George and Georgiana to give birth to "the first American poet", infusing a spirit of "sublimity" into the new country's pragmatism.[20] His mental activity would support, and transform, George's material colonization of "the Wilds of America";[21] for "Psyche" is for John Keats—to borrow the words of John Donne—"my America, my new-found land."[22]

The great leap forward occurs on 21 April, when Keats spontaneously drafts "La Belle Dame Sans Merci" in the middle of his letter. Meanwhile, however, the soul-seeds have been quietly germinating, despite his feeling that his Muse may have deserted him entirely. He wrote on the 13th of March: "I know not why Poetry and I have been so distant lately—I must make some advances soon or she will cut me entirely". The implication is that the poetry-god may have abandoned him on account of his poetic "vices", just as two years earlier he had said there was "no greater sin" than that of being a "Self-deluder . . . flattering [oneself] into the idea of being a great Poet".[23] Now, he distinguishes between the type of poet who "cuts a figure" but yet is "not figurative" in himself (he selects his *bête noire* Byron to exemplify this) and the Shakespearean type, whose (poetic) life is allegorical or mysterious. For "a man's life of any worth is a continual allegory—and very few eyes can see the Mystery of his life."[24] He thought of Shakespeare as being the "Presider" over his poetic attempts; and the implication here is that his own life may be figurative—not in the grandiose sense of being like a great poet but, rather, as having a mystery as yet unknown even to himself. So although as late as 15 April he sincerely believes he is on the verge of giving up poetry altogether,[25] his life's allegory is writing itself subterraneously. This serious confrontation with the idea of "giving up" derives less from his depression than from his learning a new helplessness and dependence on the Muse, splitting this off from the "vices and irritability" of the self-made poet.

Keats was learning, in fact, a Socratean ignorance—he was reading about Socrates at the time—and coming gradually to the realization that this improved his spirits and his mental health. He had suggested some months earlier the way that "a little more knowledge . . . makes us more ignorant".[26] Following this, he had completed his Scottish tour at the top of Ben Nevis, in a "mist" of ignorance—"not only on this height, / But in the world of thought and mental might."[27] On 19

March he transcribes a sonnet that is similarly bare of any attempt at what he terms "poetical luxury" (sensuous beauty). It begins "Why did I laugh tonight?" and in it Keats declares: "Heart, thou and I are here sad and alone". The sonnet is a meditation on the concept of a figurative "death" that is in fact "life's high meed"—a catastrophic change. Lest George should mistake this for suicidal gloom, he tries to explain that it is really part of his life's allegory unfolding, part of his search for knowledge:

> Do you not think I strive—to know myself? ... I am ever afraid that your anxiety for me will lead you to fear for the violence of my temperament continually smothered down: for that reason I did not intend to have sent you the following sonnet—but look over the last two pages and ask yourselves whether I have not that in me which will well bear the buffets of the world. It will be the best comment on my sonnet; it will show you that it was written with no Agony but that of ignorance; with no thirst of any thing but knowledge when pushed to the point . . .[28]

This formulation of his condition of ignorance, alone with his heart, led Keats to triumphantly conclude: "Sane I went to bed and sane I arose." That day he had received a black eye in a game of cricket—a "buffet" that he used to indicate to George his mental resilience. It prompted the following meditation, preparatory to the "vale of Soul-making" passage of a few weeks later:

> Circumstances are like Clouds continually gathering and bursting—While we are laughing the seed of some trouble is put into the wide arable land of events—while we are laughing it sprouts it grows and suddenly bears a poison fruit which we must pluck—[29]

Even life's poison fruits have potential for a developmental role—in contrast to the anodyne of *St Agnes'* argosian spices. As the burden of poetic sins or "vices" fell from his shoulders, Keats came to appreciate the darkness of his ignorance, saying he was "striving at particles of light in the midst of a great darkness" and interpreting this in religious terms of his own as implying the existence of a higher kind of knowledge (that of "superior beings", inner gods):

> Yet may I not in this be free from sin? May there not be superior beings amused with any graceful, though instinctive attitude my mind may fall into, as I am entertained with the alertness of a Stoat or the anxiety of a Deer?[30]

He identifies with the animals of the wild—stoat, deer, field mouse—in pursuing this "instinctive course", which, as in *Gawain*, have an association with femininity. This receptive and non-dogmatic mentality has a type of "grace", a lighter touch than the strivings for greatness and the anxiety of never achieving a position in "the Mouth of Fame". Instead of poetic fame, Keats was now absolutely clear that his duty towards his family and, in a wider sense, towards humanity was to get to "know himself" and to instinctually pursue the path that he glimpsed towards soulmaking, just as in the "chamber of Maiden Thought" letter he had imagined how the dark passages are set open: "We are in a Mist . . . We feel 'the burden of the Mystery'."[31]

The dark passage along which he set out was that of mourning and identification with Tom. He did not have to choose it: it chose itself, for he had always felt Tom's "identity pressing on him" during the period of his illness. Tom represented a spark of his family identity that had not had the chance to fully become a soul, as in the description of the innocent children in the "vale of Soul-making" passage. Keats felt particularly protective towards him and bound as if to a gentler, more feminine aspect of himself. One of the factors he believed had contributed to Tom's emotional distress in his final illness was an epistolary romance with one fake "Amena"—really their acquaintance Charles Wells. At the time of writing the "Belle Dame" Keats had been looking over this tawdry correspondence and was disgusted by the deception, concluding Wells to be "a rat".[32] Tom's naivety in believing the love of "Amena" to be genuine—despite what Keats could immediately tell was "a man's hand imitating a woman's"—came to symbolize the spirit of the infant-poet whose lack of knowledge made him prey to the delusions of a false Muse. The year before, Keats had described to Reynolds how the poet's susceptibility to "sensations" needed to be "fledged" by knowledge:

> The difference of high Sensations with and without knowledge appears to me this—in the latter case we are falling continually ten thousand fathoms deep and being blown up again without wings and with all the horror of a bare shouldered Creature—in the former case, our shoulders are fledge, and we go through the same air and space without fear.[33]

For the sake of Tom, who was in a sense floating in purgatory, Keats felt he had to rectify this lack of knowledge, this vulnerability to seduction, this inability to distinguish between true and false art, and to become a "fledged" poet and lover. He decided to "leave [Wells] to his misery except when we can throw in a little more" and to devote his energies to the positive and reparative activity. "I will clamber through the Clouds and exist", as he had written to Haydon in the spring.[34]

It is no accident that his meditation on the "rat" Muse is juxtaposed to his dream of being in Dante's purgatory, which follows immediately in the letter:

> The dream was one of the most delightful enjoyments I ever had in my life—I floated about the whirling atmosphere as it is described with a beautiful figure to whose lips mine were joined as it seem'd for an age—and in the midst of all this cold and darkness I was warm—even flowery tree tops sprung up and we rested on them sometimes with the lightness of a cloud till the wind blew us away again—[35]

He is in the region of Paolo and Francesca, the self-absorbed lovers, wafting about the tree-tops in a way that echoes Apuleius' account of the myth of Psyche, itself a source for the Ode that Keats is soon to write. Meanwhile he writes the dream into a sonnet, beginning "As Hermes once took to his feathers light":

> Pale were the sweet lips I saw
> Pale were the lips I kiss'd and fair the form
> I floated with about that melancholy storm—

In the sonnet, he tells how the very process of writing poetry inoculates him against the infernal "dragon world" of spying, criticism, and gossip—recalling the "sleeping dragons" of the establishment who guard the castle in *St Agnes* while the lovers flee away into the storm.

Yet there is a difference between this windblown dreamer and the "fledged" poet who is Keats's ideal—the poet who exists "partly on sensation, partly on thought", who can "buffet the storm" instead of being blown about by his emotions. The Paolo–poet is like Tom, in his desperation to have some kind of love affair before dying, or like Porphyro in his reliance on the phantoms and legends of voluptuousness. He is associated with the insubstantiality of Hermes' "feathers light", not with the "eagle-winged" poet to whom Keats aspired. This type of poet is vulnerable not only to the inner temptations of "cutting a figure", but also to external attack by the enemies of promise such as those marketed by the powerful and fashionable reviews of the time, *Blackwood's* and the *Quarterly Review*. Keats had defiantly dismissed the mean-spirited stupidity of the review of his *Endymion* and was certainly not "snuffed out by a critique" in the manner of the posthumous myth.[36] But this minor "buffet" helped him to focus on the point of vulnerability and played its part in his mental digestion at this time, as is shown by his appreciative transcribing of long passages from Hazlitt's brilliant piece of invective against Gifford, editor of the *Quarterly*. "You are the government critic", wrote Hazlitt: "a character nicely differing from that of a government spy—the invisible link, that connects literature with the Police".[37] Spying, voyeurism, "smokeability", the thought-police of the political-literary establishment—in short, the Claustrum—were the factors that smothered the soul in purgatory. And they all came under the heading of "lack of knowledge". Keats was well aware that "few think for themselves" and that this was what gave the reviews their power. A year later, when Keats reworks *Hyperion* into *The Fall of Hyperion* in the form of a dream-poem, this purgatorial wafting on the outskirts of knowledge will become the basis of his distinction between true "poet" and false "dreamer". The dreamer, a type of "self-deluder", is closely associated with the poetic "sins" or "vices" that Keats sees as suffocating the confused infant-soul, hindering communication with its Muse, as happened with the depressed emotional paralysis of *Hyperion*, which Keats had recently abandoned. The "mist" never transforms into the "Mystery". Likewise, the spark of Godlike "intelligence" represented by Tom—in the terms of the "vale of Soul-making" passage—had not yet made contact with its Beatrice-like "Mediator" to dispel the claustrophobic clouds of purgatory and irradiate his soul with knowledge. What was required was not even the advent of a new "circumstance" in his life, but an adjustment of vision, as with Blake and the Tiger.

Keats had met Fanny Brawne a short while before Tom's death, and throughout this period his thoughts about poetry are increasingly bound up with his feelings towards her. Keats was 23 years old; Fanny was 18. He gets to know her by means of the occasional "chat and tiff", calls her a "minx" whose behaviour can "fly out in all directions", and, crucially, finds her "strange"—she does not fit into his preconceived notions of womanhood as sentimental, blue-stocking, or sisterly.[38] And by the time Keats next takes up his journal-letter (six days after transcribing his Dante dream), this new strangeness has transferred itself, along with Tom's spiritual needs, to his poetic Muse:

> And sure in language strange she said
>   I love thee true.

The quality of strangeness, which implies acceptance of ignorance, is complementary to the desire for knowledge that has been infusing Keats's journal with a crescendoing urgency. "La Belle Dame" is the succinct poetic expression of the emotional tensions on this tantalizing threshold of knowledge. The poem appears in mid-letter, when he returns to it on the evening of Wednesday 21 April, after having noted his appreciation of the panorama of the North Pole, which was then on show in London:

> I have been very much pleased with the Panorama of the ships at the north Pole—with the icebergs, the Mountains, the Bears the Walrus—the seals the Penguins—and a large whale floating back above water—it is impossible to describe the place—Wednesday Evening—
>
> La belle dame sans merci—
>
> O what can ail thee knight at arms
>   Alone and palely loitering?
> The sedge has withered from the Lake
>   And no birds sing!
>
> O what can ail thee knight at arms
>   So haggard and so woe begone?
> The squirrel's granary is full
>   And the harvest's done.
>
> I see a lily on thy brow
>   With anguish moist and fever dew,
> And on thy cheeks a fading rose
> Fast withereth too—

Tom–Paolo has become the "palely loitering knight at arms" (or in arms, in the infantile sense), paralysed on the purgatorial threshold of experience, the lake of love. The blush of emotion has taken the sinister form of a hectic tubercular flush on the cheeks. The "paleness" is a quality reiterated by Keats throughout these weeks. (Fanny Brawne's complexion, also, was pale.) It contrasts with the self-satisfied hoarding of the squirrels in their granary of worldly and emotional securities. The knight has partaken instead of unearthly fairy food, as he relates to the listener:

> I met a Lady in the Meads
>   Full beautiful, a faery's child
> Her hair was long, her foot was light
>   And her eyes were wild—

I made a Garland for her head,
    And bracelets too, and fragrant Zone,
She looked at me as she did love,
    And made sweet moan.

I set her on my pacing steed
    And nothing else saw all day long
For sidelong would she bend and sing
    A faery's song.

She found me roots of relish sweet
    And honey wild and manna dew
And sure in language strange she said
    I love thee true.

She took me to her elfin grot
    And there she wept and sigh'd full sore
And there I shut her wild wild eyes
    With kisses four.

And there she lulled me asleep
    And there I dream'd—Ah woe betide!
The latest dream I ever dreamt
    On the cold hill side.

I saw pale kings and Princes too
    Pale warriors, death-pale were they all
They cried, La belle dame sans merci
    Thee hath in thrall.

Essentially the knight's story shows how his original belief that he was the active partner in the relationship—setting the lady on his pacing steed—is gradually eroded by the growing awareness that it is she who sets the rhythm and marks out the mental territory. This time it is not a Porphyro–knight who produces the banquet, love's sustenance, but the fairy Lady who finds "roots of relish sweet / And honey wild and manna dew", and she who takes him to her "elfin grot". This process of gradual reversal, corresponding to his dawning knowledge, is characteristic of the ballad genre, whose rhythmic inevitability traditionally suggests fatalism; it is also analogous to the classical *peripateia*, the march of fate. Moreover, a ballad has no time for accidents, no space for wandering by the wayside or elaborate fine phrases; it follows, with inherent logic, a paratactic sequence predetermined by the first stanza, then unfolding step by step towards revelation. The "steps" are delineated with deadly precision by the effective use of repetition, the denouement being: "And no birds sing." Keats terms this, afterwards, his Muse's "headlong impetuosity". Similarly in Coleridge's ballad the bride paced into the marriage hall only to leave the Wedding Guest paralysed by the door, wondering what he was doing there. So in choosing the ballad form, Keats allows the subject to pace towards its own conclusion. It is the first time he has allowed this to happen in his own work, though he knew very well that "the creative must create itself".[39]

For in the "Belle Dame" he is not the instigator nor even the protagonist of the poetic experience: he is identified primarily with the questioner to whom the knight relates his story and thus becomes an analytic observer of the emotional conflicts that are close to his heart, but at one remove: like the psychoanalyst, he has a dream of the knight–patient's dream. The knight–patient is a combination of himself and Tom, both belonging to the group of adolescent "pale kings and princes" who find the prospect of falling in love threatening, liable—if unreciprocated—to lead to spiritual starvation:

> I saw their starv'd lips in the gloam
>   With horrid warning gaped wide
> And I awoke and found me here
>   On the cold hill's side.

> And that is why I sojourn here
>   Alone and palely loitering;
> Though the sedge is wither'd from the Lake
>   And no birds sing.

In St Agnes it was Madeline who was held in the grip of "pale enchantment", the web of superstition rather than of poetry, with Porphyro hovering round the coverlet of her dreams like the "legioned fairies", trying to peer inside:

> Never on such a night have lovers met
> Since Merlin paid his Demon all the monstrous debt. [ll. 170–71]

In reversing the perspective in "La Belle Dame", so that it is not voyeuristic but communicative, Keats both protects himself against the sinister potential of this Morgana-demon (the Merlin-poet's seductress) and investigates more deeply the ambiguous feelings aroused by the fairy's ambiguity, her "wildness".

Keats's knight originally met his Lady "in the Wilds" before altering it to "Meads" in the process of composition, so that he can use the word to focus more specifically on the Lady herself—in particular her "wild" eyes, which later in the poem expand frighteningly to "wild wild" eyes, in a context which clarifies the knight's self-delusion:

And there I shut her wild wild eyes
  With kisses four.

In the repeated wildness he sees the reflection of himself falling with "the horror of a bare-shouldered creature", the unfledged poet. The colonial notion of being able to control the "wild" comes from the realms of dragon eyes, satanic mills, and purgatorial repression—from society's basic assumptions and, specifically, poetic omnipotence. In the fairy's wildness lies her strangeness, her innate freedom, her organic link with the unknown. And in her double wildness—the four kisses—lies her sinister potential, with its Blakean quality of "fearful symmetry". At the end of the poem, in fact, Keats jokes about the "four kisses"—recognizing with hindsight that four is the right number for maximum effect.[40] The "wild wild" is also an echo of Burns's ballad "My love is like a red, red rose" with its similar play on the pleasing, and frightening, attributes of redness—the rose and its thorn. Keats had been much preoccupied with Burns and the "misery" of his life during his Scottish tour that summer, which became as "horribly clear" to him "as if we were God's spies". Burns seemed to him another poet in purgatory, associated this time not with literal death, but with a type of poetic madness. Keats wrote some strange lines after visiting this "bard's low cradle-place about the silent north", ending with a prayer

That man may never lose his mind on mountains bleak and bare;
That he may stray league after league some great birthplace to find,
And keep his vision clear from speck, his inward sight unblind.[41]

The concept of "unblindness", with its double negative and its Miltonic inversion, loaded with significance, refers back to Milton's "things invisible to mortal sight". In this area of mental "mist" and ambiguity lies the challenge of the Belle Dame's eyes. Are they a window to the world of love and poetry, or a trap leading to insanity, isolation, delusion?

Keats follows his knight, therefore, to this erotic threshold or fledging-point, equivalent to winning his spurs; it is the same emotional territory as that entered by Gawain in his encounter with the Lady and the animals of "the wild". When the knight makes a garland for the fairy's head, her response is to look "as she did love", leaving it ambiguous whether she really loved or appeared to love. Can the knight really understand the "language strange" in which she says "I love thee true"? Some days later, after writing the "Ode to Psyche", he explains that he has been experimenting with the sonnet form, to loosen the "pouncing rhymes" that, he feels, restrict the Muse's expression: so "if we may not let the Muse be free, / She will be bound with garlands of her own."[42] Keats now recognizes that the headiness of his vision—"And nothing else saw all day long"—must be accepted as subjective, not as an indication of controlling the Muse; that delusion could now be left to critics and dragons. He has learned to accept the Muse's ambiguity, confronting simultaneously the loved and hated aspects of the Muse in the true sense of aesthetic conflict. Now he can see that the rat–Muse is a fake, an irrelevance; the source of real pain lies not in female impersonation, but in the feminine Muse herself; it was she who demanded the "monstrous debt" of perpetual enchantment from Merlin. At last it becomes clear that she who deals delight and death is the same person: the mermaid Madeline and the spectral Angela as Gawain first encountered them, hand in hand.

In this way Keats exorcises the "Nightmare Life-in-Death" aspect of the Muse. Indeed, the brief account of the North Pole exhibition, with its whales and icebergs, suggests a preparatory association with Coleridge and his albatross of the southern ocean—the monstrous white breast with its skeletal transformation. Keats had in fact recently met Coleridge on Hampstead Heath and had listened for an hour to his talk of poetry, nightmares, "the second consciousness", monsters and mermaids—all material for the "wilds" of the poem's scenery.[43] Another piece of prose-work had also provided relevant preparation for the poem; this was Keats's review of his friend Reynolds's satire on Wordsworth's much-publicized forthcoming work "Peter Bell". The review, like "La Belle Dame" itself, was spontaneously composed in the letter a little earlier on the same day. In it, the falseness that accrues to even the true poet (Wordsworth) when he becomes complacent is exposed by means of the satirist himself entering into the poet's clothes (his exoskeleton), borrowing his manner and diction. Reynolds's cathartic piece of dressing-up was the perfect complement to the "cruel deception" of Wells who disguised his destructive intent through the superficial appearance of femininity. Keats was clearly delighted with it and wrote in his review:

> This false florimel has hurried from the press and obtruded herself into public notice while for ought we know the real one may be still wandering about the woods and mountains. Let us hope she may soon appear and make good her right to the magic girdle . . .[44]

The false Florimel and the false Duessa are the Spenserian forms of the untrue knight errant and his Muse—they mimic the attributes of the real protagonists. Reynolds's satire was published before Wordsworth's poem had a chance to come down from the woods and mountains not of vision but of vanity (the claustrum of the head-breast in Meltzer's terms). The question Keats poses is, when the poem does arrive, will it be a real one, deserving of the "magic girdle", the medieval iconography for the poetic garland? Rather than condemning Wordsworth in advance for having in a sense defrauded himself, he points to the poem itself as the only thing that can settle the argument. If the poem is worthy of the girdle, it will already be wearing it, regardless of critics, public, dragon eyes, and false florimels. And after writing his own poem, Keats's elation expresses his own belief that at last he has been the vehicle for a true florimel—not hurried by the press but driven by the "impetuosity" of his Muse:

> Why four kisses—you will say—why four because I wish to restrain the headlong impetuosity of my Muse—she would have fain said "score" without hurting the rhyme—but we must temper the Imagination as the Critics say with Judgment. I was obliged to choose an even number that both eyes might have fair play: and to speak truly I think two a piece quite sufficient . . .[45]

As Ferdinand asked of Ariel's song, "where is that music—in the air, or the earth?" The poem materializes on the page as though Keats had caught it "on the wing"—as he described Milton's poetic faculty—while it was passing by, its rhythmic patterning the result not of his own "pacing steed" but of the Muse's spirit. Keats knew very well that "the creative must create itself"; now, as when he first "looked into Chapman's Homer", it is as though a "new planet [has swum] into his ken".[46]

Thus the new poetic power attained by Keats derives from a new passivity or acceptance of helplessness. It was adumbrated in his impressionistic philosophy long before—as in, the image of the thrush who passively awaits the warmth—but in a sense he had not devoted his energies to achieving this "negative capability" until the death of Tom, with premonitions of his own death, made it imperative for him to engage committedly in soulmaking. In prose initially, he wrote himself into the frame of mind in which "La Belle Dame sans Merci" could arrive and, in a sense, write itself down. The ballad ends with the customary emphasis of returning to the first verse with a difference. But it is not the claustrophobic circularity of the Mariner, forever bound to repeat his tale to whoever may seize his eye. The "Belle Dame" ends with a sense of mystery and an implicit question, *what will happen next?* The option was no longer available to Keats to follow the dumb "squirrels" who inhabited the woodland verges of the Belle Dame's lake into their seasonal hibernation. He was poised to explore another realm of knowledge, on behalf of the "pale warriors" starving like fledgling birds on the "cold hill side" of their deserted nest. The illusion of floating about like Dante's "pale lovers" with lips eternally joined together could no longer sustain these unfledged souls—whom in the "Ode to a Nightingale" Keats calls the "hungry generations". The idea of the infant–poet being symbiotically fused with the Muse– nipple was indeed warm and delightful—but not true. Other modes of spiritual nourishment must be discovered, making allowance for greater seasonal variation than the Wordsworthian "visionary gleam". Keats recollected his thoughts on the buffets of the world and circum- stances like clouds, and he came up with his famous parable of the world as a "vale of Soul-making", as an alternative to the superstitious and pessimistic "vale of tears". It was in this context that he discovered the "neglected goddess" who had been inhabiting the deeper reaches of his mind, not invented but Platonically pre-existing—the "personi- fied abstraction" Psyche.

The "Ode to Psyche" was, Keats said, the first time he had taken "even moderate pains" with his writing, which had previously been rushed and careless. This poem has been written "leisurely":

> I think it reads the more richly for it and will I hope encourage me
> to write more things in even a more peaceable and healthy spirit.[47]

He adds that though Psyche was not formally instituted as a goddess before the time of Apuleius the Platonist, he himself is "more orthodox than to let a heathen Goddess be so neglected". The Ode was written at some point during the ten days following "La Belle Dame", when Keats also experimented with ways of expanding and loosening the sonnet form, softening its "pouncing rhymes". When his own ode form comes into being, it is irregularly based on extended, interlinked sonnets but discards the aggressiveness of the final couplet.[48] Instead, he pivots the sections on short lines drawn from the ballad form. Thus echoes of the ballad's onward movement reinforce the ode's unfolding pageantry. The poem has direction and moves, but without the ballad's predeter- mined inevitability. Instead, it has a variable pace founded on a differ- ent structural core, which allows for discovery, question, loss, and affirmation—a psychological structure that has roots—as we shall see later—in the mourning processes of Milton's *Lycidas*. Keats "loads every rift with ore" (as he had once advised Shelley to do), and there is room for meaning to gather and expand. This more capacious and fluid form is capable of responding to the type of mental search that the poet needs to conduct within it. It transcends the trickiness of the sonnet, the shapelessness of the "floating" dream, and the fatefulness of the ballad. It can accommodate the Spenserian richness of *St Agnes* but does not have its indulgent artfulness and verbal ingenuity—its poetic "vices". Yet unlike "La Belle Dame", the diction is allowed to vary between Keats's characteristic sensuous word-clusters ("cool-rooted flowers, fragrant-eyed") and emphatic simplicity ("Holy the air, the water and the fire"). Above all, the focus is both outward and inward-looking—preserving the space or caesura between the goddess Psyche and the individual poet's own soul:

> Surely I dreamt to-day, or did I see
> The winged Psyche with awakened eyes?

Her story and his co-exist, his soul and the Soul awakened simultaneously within the dream.

Instead of the defensive windows of ambiguity and illusion that are drawn between the protagonists in "La Belle Dame", we have a reflective drama between soul and Soul-goddess, a gradual drinking in of meaning. The beginning is tentative, apologising for singing Psyche her own secrets and making the cause of the poem into the subject:

> O Goddess! Hear these tuneless numbers, wrung
> By sweet enforcement and remembrance dear . . .

The poet "wanders in the forest thoughtlessly"—that is, without intent, such that the vision of the bower of Cupid and Psyche is a discovery, representing the recent awakening of Psyche from neglect. He recognizes Psyche by means of Love:

> The winged boy I knew;
> But who was thou, O happy, happy dove?
> His Psyche true!

As the abstractions are embodied, he realizes for the first time that they are part of the same system. This corresponds with Keats's description (in the "Soul-making" entry in his letter) of how "Mediators" such as those of heathen mythology greatly simplify the "system" of soul-making by making a bridge between the infant consciousness and the growing personality to which "identity" is beginning to accrue. In October, shortly before his own birthday on the 31st, he had written a premonitory lullaby for the expected arrival of George and Georgiana's first child, saying that he "had a mind to make a prophecy and they say prophecies work out their own fulfilment":

> See, see the lyre, the lyre
> In a flame of fire
> Upon the cradle's top
> Flaring, flaring, flaring.
> Past the eyesight's bearing—
> Awake it from its sleep
> And see if it can keep
> Its eyes upon the blaze.
> Amaze, amaze![49]

Keats here anticipates the "amazed" feeling of his forthcoming discovery of Psyche, when he himself becomes the newly-born "bard of the western wild", the first poet of this new-found-land.

We see how the forest bower of Cupid and Psyche has moved on from both the Titans' "nest of woe" and the restless floating among the treetops of the Paolo and Francesca dream. It has discovered its own cradle of creativity. The dreamer does not long for an escapist eternity of oblivion; in the dream he is awake and asks questions (like the ballad). In "La Belle Dame", the fairy had said, or had seemed to say in "language strange", "I love thee true". The rhyme and rhythm are echoed here in "His Psyche true". It is a different type of subjectivity, without the dangerous ambiguity of the fairy dream, since the poet is not swept up in the same close identification. He never believes the goddess is in love with *him*, nor does his salvation depend on being in control of the vision. Instead, the "love" shines on him mediately. The figure of Cupid replaces the poet as lover, and, unlike the dream, "their lips touched not"; the moment is of arrested time, before and after a continually renewed lovemaking, "ready still past kisses to outnumber". Thus there is no voyeuristic quality; the moment responds to the dreamer and, as he enumerates its features, gives him the opportunity for leisurely recognition, at his own pace:

> O latest born and loveliest far
>   Of all Olympus' faded hierarchy!
> Fairer than Phoebe's sapphire-regioned star,
>   Or Vesper, amorous glow-worm of the sky;
> Fairer than these, though temple thou hast none,
>   Nor altar heaped with flowers:

Nor virgin-choir to make delicious moan
    Upon the midnight hours . . .

At the beginning, the poet felt his "tuneless numbers" were inadequate
to approach the goddess. Now as he enumerates the attributes of
worship that this new "neglected" goddess would appear to lack, he
finds that, paradoxically, they do in fact seem to accrue to her, but in a
way generated by her own internal qualities rather than by religious
custom, as in those days of "happy pieties"—the days of the old Olym-
pian gods. The voice, the lute, the pipe come to be emanations of
Psyche herself, like her own "lucent fans, / Fluttering among the faint
Olympians". At the same time, the ode becomes infused with music.
And now the poet can make the confident and emphatic statement:

I see, and sing, by my own eyes inspired.

This line is the hinge of the poem—when the poet commits himself to
the reality of his vision and the worship of the new goddess. His
previous gods of poetry fall back into the shadows as Keats repeats the
lines, almost word for word, with an aura of ritual transfer and confir-
mation—their music is now *his*:

So let me be thy choir and make a moan
    Upon the midnight hours—
Thy voice, thy lute, thy pipe, thy incense sweet
    From swinged censer teeming;
Thy shrine, thy grove, thy oracle, thy heat
    Of pale-mouthed prophet dreaming.

Inspired by internal qualities of the Muse, the poet now sees that his
job is to echo and reflect them, using the sensuous materials of his art:
"let me be thy choir . . . thy voice, thy lute, thy pipe . . ." With repetition
comes commitment and the establishment of a teaching relationship. It
is the moment equivalent to Blake's

And when thy heart began to beat
What dread hand? And what dread feet?

The inner life of the goddess is transferred through the "fluttering" of
her fans to the breath of the poet as prophet, in the form of "heat"—the
"heat . . . of prophet dreaming"—later to "let the warm love in". The
warm air-current is picked up from the "delightful" dream of Paolo
and Francesca; it contrasts with the "dying" or "ebbing" chance gusts
of wind that Keats had described in his abandoned epic *Hyperion*, its

life-breath paralysed by depression at the time of Tom's approaching death:

> Tall oaks, branch-charmed by the earnest stars,
> Dream, and so dream all night without a stir,
> Save from one gradual solitary gust
> Which comes upon the silence, and dies off,
> As if the ebbing air had but one wave . . . [I.74–78]

Here the tall oaks, embodying Titanesque woes, too great for man to bear, had stirred no music in the heavens—their branches a static tracery, like the cold "purgatorial rails" of *St Agnes*, whose "carved angels ever eager-eyed" resemble these "earnest stars" with their artful illusion of caring.

The "pale-mouthed prophet" is a reformation of the ghostly or death-pale infant poet who has appeared in Keats's writings throughout these months: a complex fusion of the dead Tom, whose voice was stopped by a cruel Muse, and of the poet struggling to find a voice. Keats had contrasted Tom's gentle nature with his own "violence", his determination to buffet the world. Now his identification with Tom emerges, transformed, into the "pale-mouthed prophet dreaming", the baby at the breast after feeding, mouth slightly open like Cupid and Psyche but not like the gaping lips of the Belle Dame's victims and not pressed adhesively like Paolo and Francesca in an illusory eternity. Now the baby is fed by its dreams.

This establishment of the baby-and-Muse relationship is the firm psychological basis on which Keats founds the glorious affirmation of the final stanza of the ode:

> Yes, I will be thy priest, and build a fane
>   In some untrodden region of my mind,
> Where branched thoughts, new grown with pleasant pain,
>   Instead of pines shall murmur in the wind:
> Far, far around shall those dark-clustered trees
>   Fledge the wild-ridged mountains steep by steep;
> And there by zephyrs, streams, and birds, and bees,
>   The moss-lain Dryads shall be lulled to sleep;
> And in the midst of this wide quietness
>   A rosy sanctuary will I dress
> With the wreathed trellis of a working brain,
>   With buds, and bells, and stars without a name,
> With all the gardener Fancy e'er could feign,
>   Who breeding flowers will never breed the same:

And there shall be for thee all soft delight
   That shadowy thought can win,
A bright torch, and a casement ope at night,
   To let the warm Love in!

No longer wandering thoughtlessly, the poet has discovered his vocation: to build the shrine in the forest of his mind in which soulmaking
can take place. This new knight is not a rider, a drifter, or a colonizer;
he has discovered that he is in fact a builder and gardener. He gardens
his own brain, in preparation for her poetic visitations. As priest to
Psyche, he must prepare the ground for his own "salvation", without
capture or ownership, for poetry must "work out its own salvation in a
man". Steep by steep, step by step from "far, far around", the mental
landscape unfolds, "fledging" the brain by following its terraced con-
tours. The Belle Dame no longer sways "sidelong" or "headlong" in
response to the poet's pacing steed. The relentless march of her message is replaced by this unfolding process, and her spirit finds a resting-place in the landscape. The persecutory quality of her "wild wild
eyes" modulates to an aura of mystery and inaccessibility as her features set themselves in this structure "dark" "wild" and "steep", awesome in its scale as Wordsworth's Cliff.

The previous summer, Keats had written to Tom of "the counte-
nance or intellectual tone" of the first mountains he saw on his walking
tour (in the Lake District) and how by the magnitude of contrast this
"set his imagination at rest": "I never forgot my stature so completely."[50] They were not treeless mountains but "fledged with ash",
just as here the mental landscape evoked by Keats suggests a hair-
covered ridge of bone above a recess. As Ruskin said, empathizing
with Keats's particular dislike of treeless landscapes, this "marvellous
Ode to Psyche" demonstrates "the influence of trees upon the human
soul". The traditional idea of a poet having wings undergoes a sea-
change as a result of the intense meaningfulness Keats gives to the
word "fledge", which he uses both to describe the growth of poetic
powers and the way that trees grow out of the clefts in a mountainside.
Keats has, in fact, made the fledging of the distant mountains by
branched thoughts a metaphor for soulmaking itself, the growth of
knowledge. Later that year he expresses a wish to "diffuse the colouring of St Agnes Eve throughout a Poem in which Character and Sentiment would be the figures to such drapery".[51] He means a large-scale
poem, Shakespearean drama, or Miltonic epic. But in fact his words
describe precisely what he has already done, on a small intimate scale,

in the "Ode to Psyche". The music and colouring of poetical "luxury" sits on the shoulders of structural knowledge, as the poem attentively traces the features of the goddess–mountain. He has evoked not merely the rocks beneath the foliage, but the muscle and the heart-beat—"what art / Could twist the sinews of thy heart?" The affective condition for this is one of "pleasant pain"; at the same time, impercep-tibly, the branches of thought multiply. In this "rosy sanctuary" the hostility melts from "red, red" and "dread, dread". *Hyperion*'s treetops come to life, dissolving the static quality of the fixed stars in their unregarding heaven: they become points of sound and colour—birds, bees, buds, bells. The descending movement revises the floating from treetop to treetop of the Paolo and Francesca dream, and the myth in which Psyche was carried to earth by gentle winds. It comes to rest in the garden, with its "wreathed trellis" mirroring the convoluted brain-folds. The garden is the intimate, personal area of cultivation, the genital area, intense with bee-sounds (zephyrs-streams-birds-bees-moss-Dryads-sleep-midst-quietness), like Yeats's "bee-loud glade" and recalling Keats's own earlier concept of the active and passive elements in creativity expressed by the co-operation of the busy bee and the flower "budding patiently under the eye of Apollo".[52] Now Apollo has been superseded by Psyche as the god of poetry.

In this way the feminine principle, so long "neglected" or held in suspicion by the Romantic poets, is revealed through Keats's priest-like process of negative capability, to constitute the core of the poetic Muse. It is achieved by a poetic "imagining into" the qualities of the opposite sex, as distinct from the Porphyrean self-insinuation beneath the colours of his own verse.[53] Keats does not need to ask, "Did he who made the Lamb make thee?" Blake's, and Shelley's, image of the Promethean poet daring to seize the fire from the gods in their "distant deeps or skies" has been transformed into Keats's idiosyncratic vision of Psyche's flame: for the final image of the open window is a joyous reversal of the myth in which Cupid was burnt by Psyche's candle-flame when he visited through the window at night. This window with its welcoming light is a means of communication, not a barrier of separation, ever receptive to the visits of "shadowy thought". It be-comes a characteristic image in Keats, indicative of the threshold of a new experience, a Bionic catastrophic change. Keats banishes the Belle Dame's warning of being abandoned "On the cold hill's side", together with Coleridge's Nightmare Life-in-Death, when he echoes their bal-lad-rhythm in his triumphant, short last line: "To let the warm Love in". The year before, he had written, in anticipation: "It is impossible to know how far knowledge will console us for the death of a friend".[54] He has not been consoled, but he has gained in knowledge. His shoulders are fledged; he has understood how to work on his own soul. In Milton's words,

Tomorrow to fresh woods and pastures new.

NOTES

1. D. Meltzer & M. Harris Williams, *The Apprehension of Beauty* (Strath Tay: Clunie Press, 1988), p. 27.
2. Milton, *Paradise Lost*, IX.489–92.
3. Wordsworth, *The Prelude*, I.401–12.
4. Susanne Langer, *Philosophy in a New Key* (Cambridge, MA: Harvard University Press, 1942), p. 110.
5. *The Prelude*, II.328.
6. Wordsworth, "Ode: Intimations of Immortality from Recollections of Early Childhood".
7. *The Prelude*, I, 364.
8. Coleridge, *Notebooks*, ed. K. Coburn (London: Routledge & Kegan Paul, 1957), Vol. 3, No. 4047.
9. The *Lyrical Ballads* of Wordsworth and Coleridge were published in 1798; Blake's *Songs of Innocence and Experience* in 1789–94.
10. A longstanding theme in Keats—as in his earliest verse romance "Calidore".
11. Letter to the George Keatses, 14–31 October 1818, in: *Selected Letters*, ed. R. Gittings (Oxford: Oxford University Press, 1975), p. 170.
12. "A Song about Myself", written July 1818, in: *Complete Poems*, ed. J. Barnard (Harmondsworth, Middlesex: Penguin, 1973); following quotations are from this edition.
13. Keats, letter to Haydon, 22 December 1818, in Gittings, *Letters*, p. 173.
14. Keats, February–May journal-letter to the George Keatses, in Gittings, *Letters*, p. 214.
15. Keats, letter to Leigh Hunt, 10 May 1817, in Gittings, *Letters*, p. 10.
16. Letter to Bailey, 10 June 1818, in Gittings, *Letters*, p. 99.
17. December 1818–January 1819 journal-letter to the George Keatses, in Gittings, *Letters*, pp. 175–76.
18. Letter to the George Keatses, 14–31 October 1818, in Gittings, *Letters*, p. 168.
19. The full title of Wordsworth's *Prelude*.
20. See letter to the George Keatses, 14–31 October 1818, in Gittings, *Letters*, pp. 164–65.

21. Keats, letter to the George Keatses, 16 December–4 January 1819, in Gittings, *Letters*, p. 185.

22. John Donne, "To His Mistress Going to Bed". Keats later became very bitter about America—a land "unowned of any weedy-haired gods"—after George proved more unlucky and more gullible than anticipated in his business affairs there.

23. Letter to Haydon, 10, 11 May 1817, in Gittings, *Letters*, pp. 12–13.

24. February–May journal-letter to the George Keatses, in Gittings, *Letters*, p. 218.

25. Ibid., p 233.

26. Letter to Bailey, 21, 15 May 1818, in Gittings, *Letters*, p. 98.

27. Sonnet of 2 August 1818, "Read Me a Lesson, Muse".

28. In Gittings, *Letters*, p. 230.

29. Ibid., p. 228.

30. Ibid., p. 230.

31. Keats, letter to Reynolds, 3 May 1818, in Gittings, *Letters*, p. 95.

32. February–May journal-letter to the George Keatses, in Gittings, *Letters*, p. 239.

33. Letter to Reynolds, 3 May 1818, in Gittings, *Letters*, p. 92.

34. Letter to Haydon, 8 April 1818, in Gittings, *Letters*, p. 83.

35. February–May journal-letter to the George Keatses, in Gittings, *Letters*, p. 239.

36. Byron's satirical view (in reaction to Shelley's idealized myth of Keats in *Adonais*) was: "'Tis strange the mind, that very fiery particle / Should let itself be snuffed out by an article."

37. February–May journal-letter to the George Keatses, in Gittings, *Letters*, p. 222.

38. December–January journal-letter to the George Keatses, in Gittings, *Letters*, p. 178.

39. Letter to J. A. Hessey, one of his publishers, regarding the "slipshod Endymion", the reviews, and his own self-criticism: 8 October 1818, in Gittings, *Letters*, p. 156.

40. It has been suggested that two of them recall pennies on the lids of death.

41. "Lines Written in the Highlands after a Visit to Burns's Country", July 1818.

42. "If by dull rhymes our English must be chained", copied at the end of this journal-letter.

43. Keats recounts his walk with Coleridge in the February–May letter, in Gittings, *Letters*, p. 237.

44. Ibid., in Gittings, *Letters*, p. 242.

45. Ibid., in Gittings, *Letters*, pp. 243–44. Keats makes corrections in the process of writing the draft (not reproduced above).

46. Keats's sonnet "On First Looking into Chapman's Homer".

47. February–May letter, in Gittings, *Letters*, p. 253.

48. Of the two sonnet forms (Petrarchan and Shakespearean), the Shakespearean consists of three quatrains and a concluding rhymed couplet.

49. Keats, lines beginning "'Tis the witching time of night", in Gittings, *Letters*, pp. 165–66.

50. Letter to Tom Keats, 25–27 June 1818, in Gittings, *Letters*, p. 103.

51. Letter to Taylor, 17 November 1819, in Gittings, *Letters*, p. 340.

52. Letter to Reynolds, 19 February 1818, in Gittings, *Letters*, p. 67.

53. Keats's "negative capability" letter is that of 21, 27 December 1817 to his brothers, in Gittings, *Letters*, p. 43. His description of Milton's "imagining-into" capacity is made in his notes on *Paradise Lost:* see Barnard, *Poems*, p. 518.

54. Letter to Reynolds, 3 May 1818, in Gittings, *Letters*, p. 92.

CHAPTER THREE

Milton as Muse

What is to be sought is an activity that is both the restoration
of god (the Mother) and the evolution of god (the formless,
infinite, ineffable, non-existent), which can be found only in
the state where there is NO memory, desire, understanding.

Wilfred Bion[1]

When Keats was on his Scottish walking tour the summer
before Tom's death, gathering materials for poetry, in particular for his projected Miltonic epic *Hyperion,* he wrote to
his friend Bailey that the first thing he intended to do when he got back
was to "read that about Milton and Ceres and Proserpine".[2] The passage he refers to is marked in his copy of Milton's *Paradise Lost,* with
the following note:

There are two specimens of a very extraordinary beauty in the
Paradise Lost; they are of a nature as far as I have read,
unexampled elsewhere—they are entirely distinct from the brief
pathos of Dante—and they are not to be found even in Shakespeare. These are according to the great prerogative of poetry
better described in themselves than by a volume. The one is in the
following—"which cost Ceres all that pain"—the other is that ending "Nor could the Muse defend her son"—they appear exclu-

59

sively Miltonic without the shadow of another mind ancient or modern.[3]

Both the Orpheus and the Proserpina myth are stories about the limited powers of the mother-child relationship on which the flowering of nature depends. In one the poet is separated from his Muse-mother and becomes vulnerable to the gangsterism of "the rout that made the hideous roar", a poetry-killing noise; in the other the poetic spirit—the beautiful idea—is seized by the powers of darkness and withheld from the Muse to whom it belongs, though on a less damning, "seasonal" basis. They are well-known myths, part of received culture, yet Keats sees them as being *about Milton and nobody else*—Milton has retold them such that they form an organic part of his personal poetic history, "without the shadow of another mind". Such stories only achieve their full impact when they have a role in the soulmaking of an individual mind. When a myth is incorporated as an "idea", it can then—in Bion's terms—become "generative".[4] In fact, Milton mentions the myths fairly briefly at certain key points, but Keats has recognized that their significance is diffused throughout the wider story and seems to have guessed how Milton himself once expressed his vocation in terms of searching for "the idea of the beautiful through all the shapes and forms of things . . . with the same diligence as Ceres seeking her lost daughter Proserpina".[5] The link is the Platonism, echoed by Keats many times; looking back on his life, he described himself as having "lov'd the principle of beauty in all things".

For both poets the relationship with the Muse came to have a mother–child analogy; though at points, initially, they each held a more narcissistic ideal of the Apollonian poet who held the key to godlike, universal knowledge. Their experiential view was that the Muse, though the source of poetic richness, is by no means omnipotent, for the flow of inspiration—the "principle of beauty"—depends on the nature of the poet's communications. For Keats, Milton-as-Ceres formed a significant component of his own internal Muse, together with that of his "Presider" Shakespeare, though their influence appears in a different way owing to their different character as poets. Coleridge described them as "twin peaks of the poetic mountain", with Shakespeare having the "protean genius" of entering into a wide variety of different identities and Milton the subjective or egotistical genius of drawing other types inside himself. Yet Milton, as much as Shakespeare, practised a projective-introjective method of getting to know his subject—what Adrian Stokes describes as "envelopment and incorporation".[6] Indeed, it was Milton whose "imagining-into" the head of the serpent Keats so much admired. For Keats's interest in Milton had two (interrelated) facets, one being the expressive power of his language, the other being the *nature of his inspiration*—that is, the nature of his relation with his Muse. If we follow Milton's developmental struggle, looking simultaneously through the window of Keats's struggle during the evolution of Psyche, we can see structural parallels that tell us a great deal about the process of establishing contact with the Muse. The influence of Shakespeare, in Keats, is everywhere—naturalized, invisible. But to read Keats with one's Miltonic "bleep" switched on enables one to detect every significant nodal step forward in his development; it shows up every crux, every conflict, every fledging-point. Shakespeare dissolves; Milton stands out. Similarly, to read Milton, led by the hand of Keats, gives us a privileged insight not only into the development of two poets, but into the process of object-evolution that is so fundamental to the psychoanalytic method and the foundation of the post-Kleinian aesthetic view of its operation.

Keats was always dubious about Milton's "philosophy", his achieved knowledge, though, like all the Romantics, he shared his republican views and thought that the nobility of Milton's phrase "for fear of change perplexes Monarchs" should have had power in itself "to pull that feeble animal Charles from his bloody throne."[7] Like Blake, who took Milton's God to be a function of Milton's selfhood, Keats was suspicious of Milton's dogma and theology when in his political or preaching mode and considered this to be split from his poetical self, whose medium was the sensuous luxuriance of language. "With some exceptions", he said, Milton's best poetry was when he forgot about the "ardours" of Song and devoted himself to its "pleasures"; but these "exceptions" were the greatest passages of *Paradise* Lost, and they occurred when he went beyond both pain and pleasure and "committed himself to the Extreme" in his daring flights of imagination:

> Had he not broken through the clouds which envelope so deliciously the Elysian field of verse, and committed himself to the Extreme, we should never have seen Satan as described—
>
>   "But his face
> Deep scars of thunder had entrench'd", &c.
>
> There is a greatness which the Paradise Lost possesses over every other Poem—*the Magnitude of Contrast*, and that is softened by the contrast being ungrotesque to a degree.[8]

The delicious clouds of Elysium, as well as the torments of hell, can have a claustrophobic quality, as the knight discovered in "La Belle Dame". Whereas the "extreme" moments of breakthrough into great poetry, occur when they are brought together in aesthetic confrontation, as in Satan whose archangelic beauty is scarred with thunder.

It is interesting that Keats singles out "magnitude of contrast" as a notable feature of the greatness of *Paradise Lost* and stresses that it is in no way "grotesque", as might be expected—or indeed, as Pope made it, in his satire *The Rape of the Lock*. The dizzy changes of scale in the epic, as when the little devils swarm into Pandemonium like bees, evoke the contrast between an infant-view and parental or godlike view. The fallen angels never have sufficient height or breadth of vision to see themselves and to diagnose their infantile logic. Yet these scale-switches are not grotesque because they are meaningful, poignant. They could be said to have their genesis in an intimate picture that Milton gave of his poetic ambitions at the beginning of his career, in which he refers to himself as a two-year-old child learning to speak:

> Hail native language, that by sinews weak
> Didst move my first endeavouring tongue to speak
> And mad'st imperfect words with childish trips
> Half unpronounced, slide through my infant lips,
> Driving dumb silence from the portal door,
> Where he had mutely sat two years before . . .[9]

These lines are part of a "Vacation Exercise"—a public address given while he was at university. In them he "leaps over the statutes" (as he puts it), since only Latin, not English, was permitted on such occasions, to hail the "native language" that he believed to be the proper emotional and educative source for poetry. He deliberately, even provocatively, created a confrontation between oratorical conformism and the inspired poetry that he hoped to write later under the aegis of the Muse (Native Language), just as his two-year-old self had learned his mother-tongue. Milton was a great linguist and was first recognized as a poet in Italy, as a result of his poetry written in Italian. Yet years later, even in the midst of the complex and involved clauses of *Paradise Lost*, he would still in emotional terms have "infant lips" in relation to the Muse of his own language. And, as in a religious ceremony, he chose this public occasion to declare his private intent and thus, in a sense, bind himself to it.

Shortly after this university episode, in 1629, Milton spontaneously wrote his "Ode on the Morning of Christ's Nativity", telling the story of how the poetic spirit is born or implanted in the mind's "new-enlightened world", and marking the beginning of his life as a poet:

> It was the winter wild
> While the Heav'n-born-child
> All meanly wrapped in the rude manger lies . . [ll. 30–32]

The simple historic past (once-upon-a-time) is brought into the present: the word-order of "heaven-born-child" (suggesting a slow snowfall of single flakes, and prefiguring the arrival of Peace . . . stanzas later) conveys the transmutation of heavenly into earthly being. The abstract and mystical idea instantaneously becomes embedded in earth in a humble and concrete situation: "wrapped in the rude manger" with its rough sounds, gives a sensuous actuality to the place of birth and the child's existence, fallen from intangible heaven; and Milton has invented a new verse form that, through its masque-like interweaving of long and short lines, continually echoes this movement of the arrival of spirit in sense. He uses the Spenserian alexandrine (a six-stress line), like Keats, for sensuous emphasis—a curling back and wrapping effect. Thus Peace, prefiguring the later descent of Psyche through the tree-tops, comes "softly sliding / Down through the turning sphere", then

> She strikes a universal peace through sea and land.

The crucial feature of the poem, however, is not its inventiveness but its inspiration. The introductory stanzas, which invoke the Muse, stress the immediacy and sensuous actuality of the vision that he sees and the place where he is—the state in which he finds himself. Whatever happens, happens "Now". These stanzas are not, as is generally explained, merely conventional. It is clear that the poet feels himself forced to address the Muse: not politely or reverentially, but as the words come into his mouth, urgent, eager, and colloquial:

> Say heavenly Muse, shall not thy sacred vein
> Afford a present to the infant God?
> Hast thou no verse, no hymn, or solemn strain,
> To welcome him to this his new abode,
> Now while the heaven by the sun's team untrod,
> Hath took no print of the approaching light,
> And all the spangled host keep watch in squadrons bright?

In the mysterious moment before dawn, the boundary between night and day, sense-experience seems fluid and magical; abstraction and metaphor fuse into one another, as "light insufferable" becomes the sky peopled by stars (the angelic army); and the poet's own state of wonder demands that the "approaching light" be printed not only on the face of heaven, but in the words of poetry:

> See how from far upon the eastern road
> The star-led wizards haste with odours sweet,
> O run, prevent them with thy humble ode,
> And lay it lowly at his blessed feet . . . .

The "humble ode" is his equivalent of the journey towards knowledge made by the star-led wizards. It is the Muse's reciprocation towards himself: the aesthetic impact on him echoing the incarnation of the deity. Milton writes to a friend at the time, in a tone of excitement and astonishment, that the verses were "brought to me by the first light of the dawn".[10] The infant-poet's first contact with the age of gold, with the bright realities of the Platonic sunlight, is one in which the Muse–mother not only glorifies and irradiates but also protects the mind. It is what Meltzer calls the "dazzle of the sunrise":

> There could well be countless babies who do not have ordinary devoted beautiful mothers who see them as ordinary beautiful babies, and who are not greeted by the dazzle of the sunrise. Yet I cannot claim with conviction that I have ever seen one in my consulting room.[11]

The most poignant and musical passages of the poem concern the way the banished pagan gods flame into life at the very moment of their dying and provide an exquisite setting for the infant idea at this catastrophic point of change:

> The oracles are dumb,
> No voice or hideous hum
>   Runs through the arched roof in words deceiving.
> Apollo from his shrine
> Can no more divine,
>   With hollow shriek the steep of Delphos leaving.
> No nightly trance or breathed spell
> Inspires the pale-eyed priest from the prophetic cell.
>
> The lonely mountains o'er,
> And the resounding shore,
>   A voice of weeping heard, and loud lament;
> From haunted spring and dale
> Edged with poplar pale,
>   The parting Genius is with sighing sent;

With flow'r-inwoven tresses torn
The nymphs in twilight shade of tangled thickets mourn.

In consecrated earth,
And on the holy hearth,
    The Lars and Lemures moan with midnight plaint . . . [stanzas xix–
xxi]

Reading this after reading Keats, one might almost think they were the same poet. The influence of Milton's banishing of the pagan gods on the "Ode to Psyche" with "Olympus' faded hierarchy" is well recognized. Both poets are describing a new idea that supersedes the old religious world. Keats's ode, and his others of that spring, interweave images and echoes from Milton's: his "virgin-choir to make delicious moan / Upon the midnight hours" comes from the nymphs who "in tangled thickets mourn" and the "moan with midnight plaint" ("mourn" also leads to "dawn of aurorean"); the "haunted forest boughs" come from the "haunted spring and dale"; the "wreathed trellis" from the "flower-inwoven tresses torn"; the "dark-clustered trees" which "fledge the wild-ridged mountains" from the "lonely mountain o'er" and "edged with poplar pale"; "steep by steep" from "the steep of Delphos leaving"; "no shrine, no grove, no oracle, no heat / Of pale-mouthed prophet dreaming" comes from the dumb oracles with "no voice" and the "breathed spell", which "inspires the pale-eyed priest in his prophetic cell", which, in turn, becomes the cell-like structure of Keats's "working brain" with its interlaced branches deriving from Milton's "arched roof", the shelter for shades and shadowy thought.

At the end of the poem, the prevailing descending-and-wrapping movement of the poem is checked by "the dreaded infant's hand" stretching out like the sun's ray to organize the landscape into one mighty symbol, binding the pagan elements in harmony:

Our Babe, to show his Godhead true,
Can in his swaddling bands control the damned crew.
So when the sun in bed,
Curtained with cloudy red,
    Pillows his chin upon an orient wave,
The flocking shadows pale
Troop to th'infernal jail;
    Each fettered ghost slips to his several grave,
And the yellow-skirted fays
Fly after the night-steeds, leaving their moon-loved maze. [stanzas xxv–
xxvi]

Here Milton sets the new "sun" (son) in its shadowy pagan context like a jewel in a brooch, cradling the Christian in the pagan. It is a marvellous description of the shoal-like horizontal clouds of a sunset melting rapidly into the sea. Like Keats's "shadowy thought", which "breeds flowers", these "flocking shadows pale" finally win a position, an incarnation, centred round a source of rosy light ("cloudy red", Keats's "rosy sanctuary"). Like Psyche's "lucent fans" the layers of light breathe heat and life. The "fays", the "night-steeds", and the "moon-loved maze" of Milton's poem become, through sound-association, Keats's "zephyrs, streams, and birds and bees", the vital elements. Finally, we see how the "pale-eyed priest in the prophetic cell" has opened like a flower, metamorphosing into the infant Christ, from whence he becomes the "pale-mouthed prophet" who is Psyche's baby and priest.

Milton's infant, like Keats's, appears to be initially starving—"pale-eyed", fearful that the "hideous hum" from the high-arched roof of its mother's mouth is not music but "words deceiving" like those of the Belle Dame or like *Hyperion*'s "fit roofing to a nest of woe".[12] Its hopes are fed and fears allayed, ending with rosy cheeks "pillowed" on the "orient wave" of its mother's breast. Suddenly the baby appears powerful, shown by its clenched hand. This hand reaches out to collect the ambiguous fays and fairies from the pagan world and transforms them into "bright-harnessed angels" ranged round in "order serviceable". In Keats this process becomes the building of the sanctuary, the garden. "Serviceable" is a key facet of the concept of reciprocation. We remember the "prophecy" he made for his brother's unborn child in America ("amaze, amaze . . . past the eyesight's bearing"). That lullaby referred back to the "dazzle of the sunrise" of the "Nativity Ode", both in language and in its idea of a new poet who had "something working in him" in the nature of a "Prophecy being accomplished". Here we see the origins of the Milton who could not rest in pure luxuriousness of song but who felt he must strive to discover the meaning embodied within it. Keats, "following in the steps of the Author", came to the same conclusion after writing *St Agnes*. His poem had "colouring" of a type similar to that in the "Nativity Ode" but lacked its "structure"—the mental form that would qualify it to be a contribution to soul-making.

We see how Keats's thinking process is modelled on Milton's—not on his doctrine but on his deep meaning, contained in the music and structure of his verse. It is the preacher–Milton who calls the superseded gods a "damned crew". Keats, in the equivalent mental position in the "Ode to Psyche", has no notion of "damning" the Olympians; their vestigial elements merely fade away, while their live spirit continues, fanned back into life. The Keatsian doctrine is not one of good versus evil, but of a "grand march of intellect" in which successive generations base their thinking on the utmost implications of the previous one. He takes a more historical, less political view of mental achievement. But in both poets, the old worship, purged of its ugly superstitions, becomes the setting for the new vision, the cradle of the new idea. Indeed Keats, in his letters, is well aware that the more civilized orientation of his own era is not the result of greater "powers of intellect" but of its privileged basis in the struggles of previous generations of poets.

I now wish to return to the struggle itself—to see what Milton learned, and what he could therefore teach subsequent poets, about the negative aspects of "learning from experience" (in the Bionic sense). A few months after writing the "Nativity Ode", Milton attempted to write a companion poem on the theme of "The Passion", beginning by referring to his previous achievement and continuing in language that becomes increasingly strained and mannered as he tries to inject "passion" into it by the force of his own artistic will. He nominates "Night" to be his Muse, since she is "best patroness of grief", and asks that she "work my flattered fancy to belief / That heaven and earth are coloured with my woe". But after a few stanzas he complains that despite his technical control—his "ordered characters" and "well instructed tears"—his verse does not seem "as lively as before". Psychologically, what is fascinating is the way Milton seems to abandon his intended subject—Christ on the cross—and, as the poem continues, to focus instead on his own reaction to the subject, as if trying to analyse the reasons why the poem refuses to come to life. In a little note appended to the published poem to explain why it is unfinished, Milton says he found the subject "above his years". But his verdict within the poem itself is somewhat different: he suggests it fails not because it is about suffering and death, but because of its narcissistic clamour, straining for control without the overseeing power of the Muse, resulting not in "notes of saddest woe" but in a self-stimulated "infection of sorrows loud":

> And I (for grief is easily beguiled)
>   Might think the infection of my sorrows loud
> Had got a race of mourners on some pregnant cloud.

The poem thus demonstrates Milton's sharp self-observational capacities, always keeping the "Nativity Ode"—the real thing—at the back of his mind. He made "The Passion" into a lesson for himself: that inspiration could not be commanded by the self—it really was an attribute of the Muse. In a sonnet "O Nightingale", written at about this time, he exchanges the Night–muse for the Nightingale. Here he contrasts the true bird of poetry with the false cuckoo, the "rude bird of hate", concluding that he wishes to be a follower of the "Muse, or Love", whichever is the Nightingale's mate: for "Both them I serve, and of their train am I".

Keats was interested in "The Passion". His famous phrase the "viewless wing of poesy" in the "Ode to a Nightingale" is taken from "The Passion"; while the "Ode on Melancholy", the last of the group of spring odes, expressing the aftermath of inspiration, is steeped in echoes from it—Milton's "fitly fall in ordered characters" becomes "the melancholy fit shall fall", and so on. He uses it to close a period of creativity, to say farewell to inspiration. But he makes a more important use of it, during the period leading up to the Odes, in terms of learning to ride poetic failure and depression—the period when the Muse did not seem to speak at all and he was on the verge of giving up writing poetry altogether. This was also the time when he was having his most intense love–hate struggle with Milton, focused on his epic *Hyperion,* which he kept starting and stopping throughout that autumn and winter. In contrast to *St. Agnes' Eve,* which he dashed off quickly and easily, *Hyperion* was the almost obsessive vehicle for his serious poetic ambitions. It tells how the ancient giant race of Titans is superseded by the "more beautiful" Olympians—in particular, how Hyperion the old sun-god is replaced by Apollo, god of healing and of poetry. The principle of evolution, which underlies the "Ode to Psyche", had its first formulation here in the mouth of Oceanus, who is an impersonation of Milton, the intellectual debater of the high moral ground. Oceanus, the Titanic god of the sea, arises with "locks not oozy" and begins to address the assembly of fallen Titans. He is one of those "weedy-haired gods" that, Keats complains later, seem to be absent from America.[13] Indeed, Oceanus is dripping with Miltonic references, and Keats uses a strange echo of the "Vacation Exercise" and its picture of the origins of speech, to describe the sea-god's manner:

In murmurs which his first-endeavouring tongue
Caught infant-like from the far-foamed sands: [II.171–71]

But Oceanus takes a purely intellectual stance, displaying no emotional sympathy for his stricken fellow-Titans. He tells them they must "receive the truth" and "let it be [their] balm":

> So on our heels a fresh perfection treads,
> A power more strong in beauty, born of us
> And fated to excel us, as we pass
> In glory that old darkness . . . [II.212–14]

Oceanus's recommendation of "the truth" is a type of catechism, a ritual instruction, not an idea that is brought to life through a symbol. Keats puts his own doctrine of the beauty-truth equivalent in Milton's mouth, as if to borrow his philosophical weight, his certainty. Inevitably, this cannot sustain the poem, which shortly collapses; Keats abandons the poem, in fact, in the middle of a line, sentence unfinished. Apollo is left in the process of anguishing and convulsing into birth, while the Muse, Mnemosyne, holds her arms over him "as one who prophesied". The episode is a kind of strained caricature of Keats's hopes for his own birth as a new kind of poet under the aegis of previous great poets such as Milton and Shakespeare. In fact Milton-as-Muse does not sustain the narcissistic vision of the beautiful Apollo, despite Keats's effective reproduction of a Miltonic style in the first two books. This is not the Milton with whom Keats, as a poetic son, needs to communicate. He needs a different type of identification in order to incorporate the Miltonic strength within his own object-structure: not impersonation, but inspiration. Even as Apollo insists that "Knowledge enormous makes a God of me", we—and Keats himself—are impressed by the poem's failure to become a vehicle for soul-knowledge, in contrast to his letters of the same period with their quiet and unpretentious progress towards the concept "agony of ignorance". Keats learns, by this negative means, that he needs to forsake his idol Apollo and open the window in his mind that will reveal the "neglected goddess" Psyche.

During those winter months Keats was gradually coming to the realization that what was wrong with *Hyperion* was something similar to what was wrong with "The Passion". Its false assumption of knowledge of the nature of mental pain merely masked the underlying ignorance. Genuine ignorance, with its need for communication with the Muse, could not find a voice because it was smothered by a false veneer—the purgatorial clouds of stilted stylistics. Later, he judged *Hyperion* to have "too many Miltonic inversions" in it—such as, "locks not oozy", "indulged tongue presumptuous".[14] Milton's "well instructed tears" are equivalent to the groans of Apollo or the lecturing of Oceanus. Milton has his metaphysical conceits; Keats has his Miltonic inversions and cadences. However, the obtrusive stylistic devices are merely a symptom, not the disease itself. The core of the problem is a wrong type of identification: it is the poet in projective identification who speaks, not the Muse. The Miltonic Muse of *Hyperion* becomes like the rocky landscape of the poem—a type of exoskeleton composed of linguistic constructions and themes, consciously and cleverly imitated. It is hard but at the same time brittle, without inner strength. Keats described it, with somewhat harsh self-criticism, as "the false beauty proceeding from art" rather than "the true voice of feeling".[15] What Keats needed was not imitation of, but inspiration by, Milton—not to copy the technique, but to follow the inner pathway. He needed to "clamber through the clouds to exist", in the same way as Milton "broke through the clouds" and "committed himself to the Extreme".

Nonetheless, *Hyperion* contains the seeds of potential communication with its Milton-object: that is, with the inspired Milton, not the egocentric Milton. Milton clearly felt that "The Passion" had failed owing to hubris, a sort of poetic arrogance; *Hyperion* fails, however, because of the frozen weight of depression that inspiration cannot pierce. The object-failure is that of Ceres rather than of Orpheus. Each faint move towards communication is endstopped, smothered in mid-air—the poet, like the fallen Saturn, king of the Titans, unable to find the reciprocation he seeks:

> Forest on forest hung about his head
> Like cloud on cloud. No stir of air was there,
> Not so much life as on a summer's day
> Robs not one light seed from the feathered grass,
> But where the dead leaf fell, there did it rest.
> A stream went voiceless by, still deadened more
> By reason of his fallen divinity
> Spreading a shade; the Naiad 'mid her reeds
> Pressed her cold finger closer to her lips. [I.6–14]

The fallen Titans inhabit a "nest of woe" where "crags and rocks / Forehead to forehead held their monstrous horns", reminding us of Christ's "sad sepulchral rock" in "The Passion". The resonance of sound, the ability to speak out, is dramatically absent in Saturn. He is smothered in a stillness in which "unbelief has not a space to breathe". Nonetheless this passage, from the opening of the unfinished epic, conveys the "pain of suffocation" that Keats admired in Milton's description of the serpent;[16] it has an empathy that goes beyond mere artfulness of style and approaches a deeper, if somewhat adhesive, identification with the model poet-as-Muse. It is the best writing in the poem. Materials are gathered here from their source in the "Nativity Ode", as if in readiness for their later revised use in "Psyche". The Nativity's "nymphs in tangled thickets" become the Naiad in the reeds and later Psyche in her bower; the nymphs' "twilight shade" becomes the shade of Saturn's "fallen divinity"—which lies quiescent, as if in hibernation, until it can be used for Psyche's "shadowy thought". The "nightly trance or breathed spell" of Milton's pagan gods passes through *Hyperion*'s "tranced" and "branch-charmed" trees before it reaches Psyche's partly-open lips, a reformation of the Naiad with her finger to her lips. Like Lear, Saturn is a baby–king who feels he has lost his powers, cruelly weaned from mother earth; indeed, he is sneered at by another of the Titans for his "baby words". He feels suffocated by the "monstrous truth" that weighs upon him, "smothered up" by his fall from grace. His "hand" lies "nerveless, listless, dead", unlike the "dreaded infant's hand" in the "Nativity Ode"; but it is resurrected in "Psyche" as the gardener discovers a new function for it. For ultimately, this rocky cradle of woe—a ledge in Dante's infernal terrace—will be transformed into Psyche's wild-ridged mountains.

This transformation is a function of a changed identification, and the means of change are suggested by Milton himself in *Lycidas*, the greatest of English elegies. It was written in 1637 after the death of his mother, though ostensibly about a university acquaintance drowned at sea whose body was never recovered. Here Milton confronts what he had failed to do in "The Passion"—namely, the idea of death in poetry: a catastrophic change that could not be sustained without the aid of the Muse. A few years previously, he had savagely condemned the pursuit of poetry as a profession, calling it an "unprofitable sin of curiosity" that interferes with normal worldly ambition: it is a type of hell in itself, "whereby a man cuts himself off from all action and becomes the most helpless, pusillanimous, and unweapon'd creature in the world".[17] It is interesting that the object of his hate is in effect his own creativity—the sense of helplessness that derived from allowing his talent to be used by the Muse for the service of humanity. This is the Milton admired by Keats when he saw him as "suffering in obscurity for the sake of his country"; he was empathizing not merely with Milton's failed republican ideals, but with his internal courage and the struggle that is conveyed through his poetry.[18]

Milton placed this expression of hatred of poetry in a "letter to a Friend" in the midst of drafts of his early poems. In effect it was a letter to himself, to give a first formulation to the violence of emotion that— at the end of that same manuscript of poems—eventually found a place in his poetry. In *Lycidas*, for the first time, Milton brings together these clashing emotions of love and hate, demanding that the Muse prove her spiritual resilience and forge in him a reciprocal capacity for internalization. When Keats begins the "Ode to Psyche" with the lines

O Goddess! Hear these tuneless numbers, wrung
    By sweet enforcement and remembrance dear,

he is calling deliberately on the qualities that Milton invoked in his Muse when he began his elegy with a harsh and irregular sonnet, broken by the force of the emotion it contains:

Yet once more, O ye laurels, and once more,
Ye myrtles brown, with ivy never sere,
I come to pluck your berries harsh and crude,
And with forced fingers rude
Shatter your leaves before the mellowing year.
Bitter constraint, and sad occasion dear,
Compels me to disturb your season due . . . [ll. 1–7]

Keats apologizes for singing Psyche's "secrets"; Milton asks, "Who would not sing for Lycidas?" In muted form, the entire impact of *Lycidas* is compressed into those two lines of "Psyche", with its idea of "sweet enforcement". Keats knows from Milton that the Muse will hear the poet's appeal even—or especially—if it is dull or dissonant; and that his own avowed "violence of temperament" is no disqualification. Milton's "forced fingers rude" tear apart the laurel wreath of poetry; Keats's "tuneless numbers" do not do justice to its music. Yet they are "wrung" from him by inner urgency, just as Milton is "compelled" to disturb the propriety of the season. With "remembrance dear" he recalls that "sad occasion dear". This inner need and appeal is what the Muse will respond to; it is the Muse who must eventually give shape to the poem, since it is evident that the poet alone cannot.

In "Psyche" the goddess appears to have been neglected; she cannot be found until known through Love. In the case of Lycidas, the "remorseless deep" has closed over his body, and it too cannot be found. The image of the drifting, unanchored body—the poetic principle in life—is that of Proserpina and Orpheus, and of Tom Keats. The progressive surges of the poem, like the sea itself where Lycidas was drowned, delineate the search for this unpurged, unreclaimed body, wafting and "weltering" on the wave. The drifting, in *Lycidas*, contrasts with an early time when the dead brother-figure and the elegist had seemed inseparably joined, "nursed upon the self-same hill". Then there was a death, a parting, narrated to the accompaniment of a nostalgic vowel-music, a faint echo of the departure "with sighing" of the pagan gods in the "Nativity Ode":

> Now thou art gone, and never must return!
> Thee, Shepherd, thee the woods and desert caves,
> With wild thyme and the gadding vine o'ergrown,
> And all their echoes mourn. [ll. 37–41]

The beauty of such music has lost its power. It is faded and tentative, like the opening of the "Ode to Psyche". Instead, Milton delves behind the nostalgia to tackle his bitterness and anger. During the course of the poem, all the poet's hatred of poetry is laid bare—the sense of degradation and humiliation that accompanies the "homely slighted shepherd's trade"; the "thankless Muse"; the false prelates and poets of the "blind mouths" and "lean and flashy songs". And at the core of the poem's violence lies the fear that, when it comes to the breaking point, the Muse will be insufficient and unable to withstand the poet's own rage and despair:

> What could the Muse herself that Orpheus bore,
> The Muse herself for her enchanting son
> Whom universal nature did lament,
> When by the rout that made the hideous roar,
> His gory visage down the stream was sent,
> Down the swift Hebrus to the Lesbian shore. [ll. 58–63]

This is the "savage clamour" that reappears in *Paradise Lost*, again with the reminder of the Muse's insufficiency: "nor could the Muse defend / Her son".[19] The poetry-killing forces are the weakness, fame, and hypocrisy that substitute their "hideous roar" and "flashy song" for the true voice of feeling. They are similar to the forces that , in Keats's dream-phantasy, killed his brother Tom—the delusory enchantment of the rat–muse. This is why, in *Paradise Lost*, where Milton feels he is charting very dangerous territory, he is careful to invoke the "heavenly Muse" whom at one point he calls Urania; but, lest the name should be mistaken, he guards himself with: "The meaning, not the name I call".[20] He recognizes that if this internal object is in some way deficient in quality or strength, he may fall back on the delusory support of narcissism or become prey to the gangsterism of internal basic assumption groups ["the rout"].

The climax of rage at this point in *Lycidas* derives from a sense of helplessness. However, this contact with vulnerability is in fact the turning-point of the poem. It releases the river of weeping and awakens "enamel'd eyes" within the landscape, covering the banks with newly-opened flowers:

> Ye valleys low where the mild whispers use
> Of shades and wanton winds and gushing brooks,
> On whose fresh lap the swart star sparely looks,
> Throw hither all your quaint enamel'd eyes,
> That on the green turf sucks the honied show'rs,
> And purple all the ground with vernal flow'rs.
> Bring the rathe primrose that forsaken dies,
> The tufted crowtoe, and pale jessamine,
> The white pink, and the pansy freaked with jet,
> The glowing violet . . . [ll. 136–45]

Previous imagery had been of "parching" winds, the salty desert of the sea, the "shrunken streams" of the rivers, the "desert caves" of the empty land. Now the river of life returns and "purples all the ground"—as if blood were enlivening the pale flesh. As the river starts to flow, the "eyes" of the flowers open. The "green turf sucks the honied show'rs". Keats draws on this passage in his description of Psyche's bower with its "cool-rooted flowers, fragrant-eyed"; here is the "eye-dawn of aurorean love", and he sees it with "awakened eyes", which seem to breathe life into the goddess in reciprocation. The idea that, in imagination, the drifting body has been found and given ritual funeral tribute enables mourning—the process of bringing to life in the mind—to begin.

But there is a further phase to this mourning process. The literal recovery of the body is separated off into the realms of "false surmise" (since it did not, in fact, happen). This makes it clearer that what is now to be described is purely spiritual, an abstraction. The triumphant finale of *Lycidas* images the recovery not of the poet–body but of the Muse–mother—not as an alternative, but as a further stage of recognition. The earthly remains of the previously known container of knowledge are superseded by a dream of their spiritual source: in Bion's terms, it is the foundation for not just the "restoration of god (the Mother)" but also "the evolution of god". The elegist now imagines the body of Lycidas to be in a place that is unknown and therefore forever mysterious, in the full turbulence of its storm-tossed experience:

Ay me! whilst thou the shores and sounding seas
Wash far away, where'er thy bones are hurled,
Whether beyond the stormy Hebrides,
Where thou perhaps under the whelming tide
Visit'st the bottom of the monstrous world;
Or whether thou, to our moist vows denied,
Sleep'st by the fable of Bellerus old,
Where the great Vision of the guarded mount
Looks towards Namancos and Bayona's hold;
Look homeward, Angel, now, and melt with ruth;
And, O ye dolphins, waft the hapless youth. [ll. 154–64]

The place where Lycidas now "sleeps" is in essence unknowable; it is as much a sanctuary as Psyche's bower. It is a place where unknown future experience is generated, a crucible of creativity. "In what furnace was thy brain?" In the "sounding-hurling-whelming" part, Lycidas plumbs the "monstrous" depths of emotional turbulence. Then suddenly there is a transformation. The active verbs change: he "sleeps by a fable". What happens here is a change in abstraction, a gathering into symbol formation. The next verb, repeated, is "Looks" or "look". In the climactic, famously moving line

Look homeward, Angel, now, and melt with ruth

we hear the poet's appeal to the Muse to "tell the truth". The transition point, when symbol closure takes place, is the word "now". It is the point at which the Angel, who has been facing in the other direction, turns and *looks at* the poet, homeward where he is, fused with his idea of Lycidas. The dolphins raise his body above the waves, in parallel to the "dear might of him who walked the waves" (Christ). The baby–poet who has been fed, raised in its mother's arms, confirms the experience through the link with its mother's eyes, like the "day-star" that rises from the sea and

Flames in the forehead of the morning sky.

Here again we recognize the infant of the "Nativity Ode" whose arm reaches out like the sun's ray, firmly committed in its desires, while the Muse, the Archangel, embodies the bisexual qualities of both "might" and "ruth", strength and tenderness, which enable the poet to cross the seas of life unharmed. These qualities, together, *tell the truth.*

Keats, like Milton, did not want to be a protagonist, but a priest: to discover not a way of doing but a way of seeing. Interestingly, even before he plunged into *Hyperion* that autumn, he had established at the back of his mind the image of a Lycidas-muse that had presented itself to him in the form of an unpremeditated phantasy when he was visiting Fingal's Cave at Staffa, with its distinctive columnar rock-formations. These looked, he said, like a bundle of matchsticks thrown together by giants (like the Titans). He imagined himself, as in a dream, approaching the *genius loci* of this place to ask for poetic directions and seeing a figure shrouded in white sleeping on the rocks at the threshold of the cave while the waves surge around him. He approaches and touches the figure, whom he now terms "a spirit", and it awakens and declares itself to be Milton's Lycidas:

> I am Lycidas, said he,
> Famed in funeral minstrelsy!
> This was architected thus
> By the great Oceanus!
> Here his mighty waters play
> Hollow organs all the day . . .
>
> . . . . . .
>
> I have been the pontiff-priest
> Where the waters never rest,
> Where a fledgy sea-bird quire
> Soars for ever; holy fire
> I have hid from mortal man . . .[21]

The lines are semi-serious and turn into a light satire on how fashionable verse, like the tourist "fashion boats" that row out to peer at this natural "cathedral of the sea", shuts itself off for ever from the "holy fire" that is the lifeblood of inspired poetry—the fire of Blake's tiger-eyes. Lycidas is the "priest" or guardian of the poetic cavern—the mouth or head of the Muse, "fledged" by its seabird choir. His white shrouded body among the rocks recalls the Christ of Milton's "Passion" as well as the apotheosis of Lycidas' drowned body. One thing that is clear from this quizzical little sketch is that for Keats, the Titanic god Oceanus who "architected" Fingal's Cave is equivalent to the Milton who architected the epic *Paradise Lost*. Now his progeny, or priest, Lycidas, lies at the threshold of poetic creation. The Oceanus of *Hyperion*, when he was drafted a few months later, was the cruel and austere philosopher of the "beauty is truth" doctrine, oblivious to the sufferings of his fellow-Titans. This puritanical superego seemed to punish the new poet, not so much for hubris (for believing he could write a great poem, that he could save the soul of his brother Tom) but for supposing that the minute scale of his individual human desires should have any bearing on the overall march of humanity as seen from a gods' eye view. This seemed to crush the life out of poetic ambition: in the face of death, poetry seemed pointless. A year previously, Keats had wondered how he could ever become a poet, "seeing how great a thing it is". Then the experience of writing *Hyperion* had made him ask, what are love and death in the lives of the Keats brothers, to a poet of such "oceanic" mentality as Milton? In other words, who cares?

Yet even while he appears crushed by this stern and elevated Milton, the more ambiguous Milton-of-the-rocks hovers in the background. The Milton lightly sketched in the lines on Fingal's Cave suggests that there is a choice of poetic models that may be followed. Keats never finished these lines; they stop in mid-sentence, as does *Hyperion*, their questions not yet answerable, and he dismisses them, saying "I am sorry I am so indolent as to write such stuff as this".[22] But the questions play a crucial part in the prelude to the spring Odes. Is Milton's "rocky portal" here the gateway to a "cathedral" or a sepulchre, as in "The Passion"? Does its "pontiff priest" keep in, or keep out? Is "holy fire" really hid from modern man owing to his prying and intrusive ways? Is Lycidas the type of guardian who locks up the poetic treasure, rather than the inspiring voice that rescues the seaborne poet from shipwreck? Is it only the sea-birds of the natural world that "fledge" the heavenly choir, rather than modern poets who may become fledged and learn to "fly through air and space without fear"? Is Keats himself just another of those tourists in pleasure-boats? Milton's emphatic statement, after meeting the eyes of the archangel and then turning towards the unembodied *idea* of Lycidas, had been:

> Henceforth thou art the Genius of the shore,
> In thy large recompense, and shalt be good
> To all that wander in that perilous flood. [ll. 163–65]

In what sense, now, could Keats benefit from the "goodness" of this power that offers itself as a "Mediator" between Milton's Muse and subsequent generations of poets—all those who "wander in the perilous flood"? Keats's answer is given most beautifully, perhaps, in the second-to-last stanza of the "Ode to a Nightingale":

> Thou wast not born for death, immortal bird!
>   No hungry generations tread thee down;
> The voice I hear this passing night was heard
>   In ancient days by emperor and clown:
> Perhaps the self-same song that found a path

> Through the sad heart of Ruth, when, sick for home,
>   She stood in tears amid the alien corn;
>   The same that oft-times hath
>   Charmed magic casements, opening on the foam
>   Of perilous seas in fairy lands forlorn.

The voice of the Nightingale is no catechismic truth, like that of Oceanus; it is real emotional truth, the only food for the hungry generations amid the alien corn of their world of circumstances, where "youth grows pale and spectre-thin, and dies". Just as the music of *Lycidas* leads to "fresh woods and pastures new", an ambiguous landscape both shadowy and fertile, so the Nightingale opens the window to fairy seas, while at the same time its song is "buried deep / In the next valley-glades". It becomes "generative". The door to the next emotional experience opens even at the moment of resolution of the present conflict. There are many dark passages, all open.

In this way we can see Keats allowing his internal objects to "create themselves", in gradual stages, by means of a varying, struggling identification with Milton and with Milton's own process of object-evolution. In so far as Milton was viewed by the Romantics as internally split in his identifications, he afforded a model that could help to distinguish between narcissistic imitation and the trust in "goodness" that would ultimately dissolve the Muse's apparent cruelty and reveal her soulmaking capacities. So in the winter months after beginning *Hyperion*, when Keats was himself adrift in "fairy lands forlorn" and certainly no tourist in the realms of pain, he clarified for himself the helpful, and unhelpful, aspects of Milton as a poetic model:

> Why did I laugh tonight? No voice will tell;
>   No God, no Demon of severe response,
> Deigns to reply from Heaven or from Hell.
>   Then to my human heart I turn at once—
> Heart, thou and I are here sad and alone.

He finds he has shaken off the "demon of severe response", the Oceanus–Milton. Heaven and hell have passed away in the sense of moral judgements, guilt, and retribution. They bare his "heart", "sad and alone"—a type of purgation. His aloneness prepares him not to *be like* Milton, but *to see as Milton saw*, when he committed himself to the Extreme. Keats can now follow the identification with the Genius of the Shore whose mediation can turn "tuneless numbers" and "savage clamour" into orphic song. By this means Milton's Muse can be incorporated as a function of his own internal object. But this time she will speak not in a Miltonic manner, but in a voice "without the shadow of another mind, ancient or modern". Only when poetic influence comes in the form of inspiration, transmitted via the model–poet from its source in his objects, as distinct from that poet's own character, does it have the potential to transcend that character, placing the abstract qualities of his objects in a context of object-evolution that can become part of the next generation's learning-from-experience. The Song is buried deep in the valley-glades; next time it will be of the same essential pattern, but a different song.

After the Odes, when his illness begins its relentless deterioration, Keats has another period of bitterness against Milton, and indeed against Fanny Brawne, who both become for a short time associated with the deceiving Muse (as in his poem *Lamia*). But after he has worked through this, he chooses a quotation from *Lycidas* to epitomize his empathy with Milton's experience of being-a-poet. In one of his last letters he writes to Fanny Brawne that

> I have lov'd the principle of beauty in all things, and if I had had time I would have made myself remember'd . . . now you divide with this (may *I* say it?) "last infirmity of noble minds" all my reflection.[23]

The "principle of beauty" is Milton's "idea of the beautiful". Fame is in *Lycidas* the "last infirmity of noble mind"—interestingly, Keats says "minds", which makes it more intimate. "Yet may I not in this be free from sin?" he had asked a year earlier, in the context of appreciating the value of his own ignorance. Finally, in the following haunting lines from *The Fall of Hyperion* (his revision of the original epic in the form of a medieval dream-poem like *The Romance of the Rose*), he formulates the distinction between the true poet-dreamer and the false or omnipotent "fanatic", a distinction that he had learned and explored through his relationship with Milton-as-Muse:

> For Poesy alone can tell her dreams,
> With the fine spell of words alone can save
> Imagination from the sable charm
> And dumb enchantment. Who alive can say,
> "Thou art no poet; may'st not tell thy dreams?"
> Since every man whose soul is not a clod
> Hath visions, and would speak, if he had loved
> And been well nurtured in his mother tongue.

Whether the dream now purposed to rehearse
Be poet's or fanatic's will be known
When this warm scribe my hand is in the grave. [ll. 8–18]

He knows there is something of the "fanatic" within even a "noble mind"; no poet, in so far as he is a mere mortal, can be "free from sin"—the sins of his selfhood. Correspondingly, there is something of the poet within every man "whose soul is not a clod", whether or not he can find the words for his "visions". The true poet voices the dreams of everyman, on his behalf. It is not for him to judge, nor for his contemporaries, but for posterity: "Who am I to be a Poet, seeing how great a thing it is?"

NOTES

1. Wilfred Bion, *Attention and Interpretation* (London: Tavistock, 1970), p. 129.
2. Keats, letter to Bailey, 18, 22 July 1818, in: *Selected Letters*, ed. R. Gittings (Oxford: Oxford University Press, 1970), 1987, p. 135.
3. Keats, Notes on *Paradise Lost*, reprinted in: *Complete Poems*, ed. J. Barnard (Harmondsworth, Middlesex: Penguin, 1973), 1988, p. 525. The passage occurs in *Paradise Lost*, IV.268–72.
4. Bion, *A Memoir of the Future* (London: Karnac, 1991), p. 572.
5. Milton, letter in Latin to Charles Diodati, written at about the time of writing *Lycidas*; in: *Complete Prose Works of John Milton*, ed. Don M. Wolfe (New Haven, CT: Yale University Press, 1953), Vol. I, p. 324.
6. Adrian Stokes, *The Invitation in Art* (London: Tavistock, 1965); for my discussion see "Holding the Dream", in: Meltzer & Harris Williams, *The Apprehension of Beauty* (Strath Tay: Clunie Press, 1988).
7. Keats, note on *Paradise Lost*, in Barnard, *Poems*, p. 520.
8. Ibid., p. 517.
9. "At a Vacation Exercise in the College", ll. 1–6. Milton's poems are quoted from *Poetical Works*, ed. D. Bush (Oxford: Oxford University Press, 1966).
10. Milton, "Elegia Sexta", translation of verse letter to Charles Diodati; in Bush, *Poetical Works*, p. 76.
11. Meltzer & Harris Williams, *The Apprehension of Beauty*, p. 29.
12. *Hyperion*, II.14, in: Barnard, *Complete Poems*.
13. Keats's phrase "unowned of any weedy-haired gods" refers to his impression of America's lack of soul or "sublimity"; Ode "To Fanny", October 1819; letter to the George Keatses, 14–31 October 1818, in Gittings, *Letters*, p. 165.
14. Inspired examples of Milton's own inversion are the phrases "human face divine" and "bush with frizzled hair implicit"; *Paradise Lost*, III.44, VII.323.

15. Letter to Reynolds, 21 September 1819, in Gittings, *Letters*, p. 292.

16. Keats, notes on *Paradise Lost*, in Barnard, *Poems*, p. 526.

17. Milton, manuscript "Letter to a Friend", in the *Trinity College Manuscript* held at Cambridge containing drafts of his early poems; facsimile edition, ed. W. A. Wright (Menston: Scolar Press, 1972), pp. 6–7.

18. Keats, letter to the George Keatses, 14–31 October 1818, in Gittings, *Letters*, p. 164.

19. Paradise Lost, VII.32–38.

20. Ibid., VII.5.

21. Keats, lines beginning "Not Aladdin magian".

22. Keats, letter to Tom Keats, 23, 26 July 1818, in Gittings, *Letters*, p. 144.

23. Keats, letter to Fanny Brawne, February 1820, in Gittings, *Letters*, p. 361.

CHAPTER FOUR

The fall and rise of Eve

A Poet can seldom have justice done to his imagination . . . it can scarcely be conceived how Milton's Blindness might here aid the magnitude of his conceptions as a bat in a large gothic vault.

John Keats[1]

Daylight is safer; although one must remember that so great a protagonist of Heavenly Light was not saved from blindness, the domain of the infinite and the horrors of the formless, any more than the Forms of Plato saved him and his public-thing from the poets.

Wilfred Bion[2]

The Keatsian ideal of becoming a "fledged" poet who can "fly through air and space without fear" is founded on the poetic flights of Milton in *Paradise Lost*. "Through utter and through middle darkness borne", or floundering between "waters dark and deep" and the incomprehensible "void and formless infinite", the poet is as much an explorer within the extraordinary landscapes of his own poem as is Satan, winding his "oblique way" in pure air, or "Treading the crude consistence, half on foot, / Half flying". This sense of a difficult adjustment to the texture of his own poem, and to the new areas of experience that each section explores, is expressed by Milton vividly and sensuously in the four invocations of the Muse, which occur at the beginning of Books I, III, VII, and IX. In these Milton portrays with a unique clarity the relationship between the infant–poet struggling to develop and his dependence on the maternal Muse, who both makes known the mental dangers of poetry and guides the poet through them. This could be said to be the primary subject of his poetry, continually revised and re-experienced in the light of the world of circumstances. The Muse both dipped him in and saved him from the "horrors of the formless", just as Satan was rescued from the "bottomless abyss" by his still smouldering spark of godliness and led to discover the shape of his inward agony in God's new creature, man—which is why Blake considered Satan to be Milton's hero, saying, in his famous cruel joke, that Milton was "a true Poet and of the Devil's party without knowing it."[3]

Milton began to write *Paradise Lost* when he had been blind for six years. The Commonwealth was collapsing, together with his dreams of a just society on earth; his second wife had recently died in childbirth following a brief period of marital happiness.[4] The restoration of the monarchy in 1660 meant not only the end of his career and the loss of most of his money, but also that his life was in danger for a period, until influential friends got him an unofficial pardon, which seems to have been granted sneeringly on the grounds that God had already punished him by means of blindness, so life would be a greater inconvenience to him than death. He was left dependent in his daily life on his friends, illiterate servants, visiting students, and three young daughters. (He did not marry again until 1663, two years before finishing the epic.) The Genius of the Shore, with its predominantly masculine quality, appeared to have deserted him; but instead, in *Paradise Lost*, he pursued much more closely the feminine aspects of the Muse, which seem to have come to the fore in association with his physical dependence and banishment from worldly power.

The last sonnet Milton ever wrote, probably shortly after beginning the epic, recorded a dream of his dead wife Katherine (whose face he had never seen) returning, "like Alcestis from the grave", dressed in white and with her face veiled.

> Her face was veiled, yet to my fancied sight
> Love, sweetness, goodness in her person shined
> So clear as in no face with more delight.[5]

Then, as in the myth of Orpheus and Eurydice, she vanishes on the point of bending down to embrace him; his lack of faith is shown not by turning round, as in the myth, but by his awakening: "and day brought back my night". Milton generally composed his poetry, in his head, in the hours before dawn—this was so as far back as the "Nativity Ode", long before he needed an amanuensis to "milk" him. Elements of this dream—the whiteness, the bright spirit in the darkness and its intangibility, together with his Orphic insufficiency to recall it, recur in the invocations of *Paradise Lost*. The dream recurs as Adam's dream of Eve: "She disappeared, and left me dark" (VIII.478). Yet, as he had written in the sonnet on his blindness some years before, "They also serve who only stand and wait". The first invocation is an uneven mixture of Biblical reference, grandiosity (his intention to "justify the ways of God to men"), and intense pleading to a Spirit to make pregnant the dark field of his mind, faintly suggesting an identification with his heavily pregnant, dove-like, brooding wife:

> Instruct me, for thou know'st; thou from the first
> Wast present, and with mighty wings outspread
> Dove-like sat'st brooding on the vast abyss
> And mad'st it pregnant . . .

In the dream also, she "inclines" towards him, enforcing a certain passivity, nurturing his "fancied sight", the dream-vision contrasting with his waking self.

In the third invocation, beginning "Hail holy Light", he focuses specifically on his blindness. He is momentarily soothed by imagining that previous blind poets and prophets, such as Homer and Teiresias, sung "darkling" like the nightingale, feeding on their inner thoughts:

> Then feed on thoughts, that voluntary move
> Harmonious numbers; as the wakeful bird
> Sings darkling, and in shadiest covert hid
> Tunes her nocturnal note. [*Paradise Lost*, III.37–40]

He identifies with the nightingale that, in harmony with nature, "sings darkling", and for a moment his pain is soothed. When Keats refers back to this passage in his "Ode to a Nightingale", he writes: "Darkling I listen", reversing the perspective and the burden of responsibility for thinking. He understands (partly from Milton) that the Muse-qualities of the song must lie in the ear of the listener. For the natural analogy, of thoughts that "voluntarily" make music, does not in itself sufficiently comprehend "the weariness, the fever and the fret / Here, where men

sit and hear each other groan". Milton, too, finds that the nightingale
identification simply intensifies, by contrast, the bitterness of his human situation,

> from the cheerful ways of men
> Cut off, and for the book of knowledge fair
> Presented with a universal blank
> Of Nature's works to me expunged and razed,
> And wisdom at one entrance quite shut out.

The poet is isolated and imprisoned by "cloud" and "ever-during
dark", "Cut off", "quite shut out", "Presented with a universal
blank"—a bitter reversal of his early hopes for "universal knowledge".
As the passage progresses, the normal experience of light is almost
savagely excised, "expunged and razed", along with everyday existence and the "cheerful ways of men". For it is only when the poet's
darkness and isolation has been fully established "And wisdom at one
entrance quite shut out" that the entrance of wisdom in another sense
becomes imaginable. Thus the failure of the nightingale to embody his
emotional conflict leads him to seek another containing source of
knowledge:

> So much the rather thou celestial Light
> Shine inwards, the mind through all her powers
> Irradiate, there plant eyes, all mist from thence
> Purge and disperse, that I may see and tell
> Of things invisible to mortal sight.

"Purge and disperse" echoes "expunged and razed", but this time with
the emphasis of affirmation, not of bitterness. In the forceful, physical
image, eyes are planted within him; and the establishment of insight,
of a relation with celestial Light, culminates in the new regular rhythm
of the last line and a half, which triumphantly reinforces the first
invocation's "Things unattempted yet in prose or rhyme". It has become clear to Milton that these "things" are not heroic or even sacred
deeds, but things invisible, not picturable—their meaning not their
appearance. The new vision is not a *consolation* for the loss of mortal
sight. Rather, the achievement of a new knowledge has involved the
erasure of the poet's previous vision of reality, however dependent on
it he had felt himself to be. The elimination of daily sight—everyday
thinking—is a necessary prerequisite for the gaining of inner sight.
And knowledge brings not the sense of pleasure and power Milton had
envisaged in his early poems and prose essays, but—initially at least—

a painful and overwhelming impression of powerlessness and exposure.

This split between the spheres of operation of self and objects is essential to creativity. It creates the pathway, the cleft in the smooth surface of existing knowledge, in which, as Bion says, "an idea might lodge", as in the irregularities formed within the regularity of poetic metre.[6] In the invocation of Book IX, Milton describes how the Muse's thoughts slip into his mind in the form of dreams:

> If answerable style I can obtain
> Of my celestial patroness, who deigns
> Her nightly visitation unimplored,
> And dictates to me slumbering, or inspires
> Easy my unpremeditated verse:
> Since first this subject for heroic song
> Pleased me long choosing, and beginning late;

This "unpremeditated verse" is not the "unmeditated song" of Adam and Eve, as yet unfallen. The poet speaks already haunted by the knowledge of death and evil, and this context changes the quality of the song. The anxiety and effort and sense of his life passing away are vividly present in his anxiety about finding the right style, and in "beginning late"; this process of long choosing, research, and thinking-about is a function of his self and its achieved knowledge. But sandwiched in-between the words "answerable style" and "beginning late", in contrast, is the visitation of the Muse, whose movements are experienced as beyond the control of the poet: she comes "unimplored" and from a different world from that of effort and motivation and decay. The movement of the verse suggests the breathing of sleep; after the run-on line "inspires / Easy", the way is opened for the arrival of the "unpremeditated verse" unawares, slipped in between movements of sleep, "verse" being the last word to arrive. It is clear that the Muse brings the *verse* as opposed to the subject, and that the states of premeditation, and of being inspired, are as different as those of waking and sleeping, in that one accords with the values of the everyday world, while the other has laws of its own. This is the Muse's "answer" to "voluntary move / Harmonious numbers"—the spirituality beyond the natural voice of the nightingale. The invocation, the last of the series of invocations, ends with Milton explicitly separating off the powers of his selfhood from those of the inspiring Muse: he knows that his poetic "wing" will sink "Depressed . . . if all be mine, / Not hers who brings it nightly to my ear".

It was in the invocation of Book VII that Milton rediscovered unreservedly, again through the myth of Orpheus, the centrality of the poet's childlike dependence on his Muse–mother. This is the most poignant and haunting of the invocations, with no taint of the grandiosity that infiltrates the first ones, apart from a possible hint in the famous phrase "fit audience though few". Recalling the figure of Alcestis inclining towards him, this one begins by calling down the Muse from heaven, and she is given the name Urania, as if a name should make the link more intimate, even though it may not be the "right" name ("if rightly thou art called"): for he knows he is calling on the meaning, or abstract function, beyond the name:

> Descend from heaven, Urania, by that name
> If rightly thou art called . . .
> The meaning, not the name I call; . . .
>   Up led by thee
> Into the heav'n of heav'ns I have presumed,
> An earthly guest, and drawn empyreal air,
> Thy temp'ring . . .

The "empyreal air" is like the baby's first breath . . . is it death or life? It is "tempered"—mixed, alleviated, predigested—by the Muse–mother. The poet has been lifted out of his "native element". In the process, he encountered not the "night" of ordinary blindness, but the darkness of "the void, the formless infinite"; and in this context he had been "up led" by the Muse, "rapt above the pole". While Satan, museless, is one who "rides with darkness, full of anguish driv'n"; however far he travels, he cannot escape the claustrophobic confines of his self, for he carries hell within him: "Myself am hell."[7] Milton had visited Galileo, then old and blind, when in Florence; and one thing that distinguishes the Miltonic universe from the Dantesque is its sense of the astonishing potential of the concept of infinite space. The gruesome horrors and the rapture are not kept separate as they are in Dante: the cosmic world of the imagination, the "vast abyss", is pregnant with poetic ambiguities. Keats comments, in his notes on *Paradise Lost*, on

> the light and shade—the sort of black brightness—the ebon diamonding—the Ethiop Immortality—the sorrow, the pain, the sad-sweet Melody—the Phalanges of Spirits so depressed as to be "uplifted beyond hope"—[8]

This pathos of this "uplifting" is that it is self-propelled, so brings no real hope. By contrast the poet, though "fallen on evil days", finds the darkness of his solitude tempered by the Muse; her visitation comes when he is

> In darkness, and with dangers compassed round,
> And solitude; yet not alone, while thou
> Visit'st my slumbers nightly, . . .

Yet, like Plato's Cave-dweller who is "unsighted" by a transition from darkness to light, the poet may mistake and fall on the Aleian field, "Erroneous there to wander and forlorn", or like Orpheus be torn to pieces by the "barbarous dissonance / Of Bacchus and his revellers":

> nor could the Muse defend
> Her son. So fail not thou, who thee implores;
> For thou art heav'nly, she an empty dream.

The "empty dream" or false Muse is not specifically any rejected classical Muse such as Clio or Calliope, but a figure who—like Spenser's "Duessa"—imitates the external characteristics of the true Muse while being essentially self-generated and therefore leading to grandiosity. She carries the "name" only and not the "meaning". Reliance on this emptiness leads the poet into becoming the "dreaming thing" condemned by Keats in *The Fall of Hyperion*. The dangers of the field of Error consist not only in the delusions of omnipotence, as Milton first noted in "The Passion" and *Lycidas*, but also in the hint of potential madness, equivalent to that which Keats diagnosed in his lines after visiting Burns country: the possibility that "man may lose his mind on mountains bleak and bare". They are associated with journeying beyond the margins of everyday assumptions, like the knight in "La Belle Dame", foregoing the squirrel-mentality. The squirrels represent what Milton calls the protection of "custom and awe"; when the poet drops this, there is the possibility that they may transform, as in the Orpheus myth, into the "wild rout" that "drowns harp and voice". As Bion says, "Daylight is safer".

To avoid the disastrous-catastrophic potential of this isolation, the poet must intensify his dependence on the Muse. At this point of ambiguous catastrophe, a fledging-point in life, a compromise is not possible in the way that it is during the general course of events. Yet if the poet is not willing to enter this sphere of dark unknowing, the Muse does not speak at all; inspiration cannot find a pathway. *Paradise Lost* is permeated by the material of Milton's selfhood—the reasonableness of Christian Doctrine (he was writing his cherished *De Doctrina Christiana* at the same time) and the patriarchal hierarchy of the society of his time. He even formulated a distinction between the writing of his "left hand" (referring to his polemical prose) and the natural poetic vein of his right hand. The story of the poetic principle in the epic follows the rough-edged pathway left open in the doctrinal smoothness for inspiration to find. In the "Nativity Ode", the meek-eyed Peace slid down through the turning sphere; in *Paradise Lost*, likewise trailing clouds of glory, Satan falls dizzily from heaven, bearing with him a Promethean spark of divinity that, mixed with the obscurities of "bottomless perdition", immediately makes him interesting:

> His form had not yet lost
> All her original brightness, nor appeared
> Less than Archangel ruin'd, and th'excess
> Of glory obscured: as when the sun new ris'n
> Looks through the horizontal misty air
> Shorn of his beams, or from behind the moon
> In dim eclipse disastrous twilight sheds
> On half the nations, and with fear of change
> Perplexes monarchs. Darkened so, yet shone
> Above them all th'Archangel; but his face
> Deep scars of thunder had intrenched, and care
> Sat on his faded cheek . . . [I.591–602]

The ambiguities of this moment of change appear in the varying emotional aura that surrounds Satan, like a sun in mist or a moon in eclipse—the literary origin of the Wordsworthian mountain, whose fleeting storm-clouds, precipices, and sun-shafts reflect the gigantic godlike engravings that, like ancient runes, impress their meaning on Satan's "faded cheek".

The lesser devils, after their fall, fill the emptiness of their time in hell's "vast recess" with philosophical discourse, cultural activities, and games. They lament "with notes angelical" that "fate / Free virtue should enthrall to force or chance" (II.550–51). Satan likewise has his fine speeches of specious reasoning and self-deluding logic—"a mind not to be changed by place or time", etc. These represent his fruitless claustrophobic confrontation with "th'Omnipotent", "he whom thunder hath made greater": the tedium of an adolescent power-struggle whose parameters are limited by the notion of authority and rebellion—a mentality that new ideas cannot penetrate. But Satan has another aspect to his mind. He is greater than the other fallen angels because he has the imagination to conjecture that "Space may produce new worlds". He imagines in advance God's intention to create a new baby, "instead / Of us outcast, exiled", and is filled with burning curiosity to see him and his world, even "if but to pry".[9] After wading and winging his way through Chaos, he discovers the earth suspended in the blackness by a golden chain:

> And fast by hanging in a golden chain
> This pendent world, in bigness as a star
> Of smallest magnitude close by the moon. [II.1051–53]

The telescopic view, bringing "bigness" close to "smallness", suggests how the infant earth is protected by the heavenly bodies. God, disappointed in his first offspring, has had "second thoughts". This is his "new favourite".[10] Satan's inner anguish, the anguish of the "hateful siege of contraries", bursts forth:[11]

> O hell! what do mine eyes with grief behold!
> Into our room of bliss thus high advanced
> Creatures of other mold, earth-born perhaps,
> Not Spirits, yet to heav'nly Spirits bright
> Little inferior; whom my thoughts pursue
> With wonder, and could love, so lively shines
> In them divine resemblance . . . [IV.358–64]

Satan's curse, "O hell!", still has the original brightness of its meaning, full of hate and pain; it is not merely a four-letter word. It foreshadows "O earth! how like to heaven" (IX.99). In hiding on the edge of Paradise, his eyes and thoughts trace the forms of Adam and Eve before him; and the movement of the verse, following his thought, leads him through short interlinked phrases to "wonder" and then "love". The phrase "and could love" is irregularly stressed, in the middle of the line; it stands out, heralding a new world of possibilities. At such a moment we see Satan-as-hero, container for the emotionality of the aesthetic conflict. We feel on the pulses the "hot hell that always in him burns", and we sympathize with his failure to tolerate it, as he succumbs to his infantile envy—the feeling that these creatures have impinged onto his "room of bliss", squashing him out. He then justifies his feeling of hostility by means of political jargon and rationalization:

> And should I at your harmless innocence
> Melt, as I do, yet public reason just,
> Honour and empire with revenge enlarged
> By conquering this new world, compels me now
> To do what else though damned I should abhor. [IV.388–91]

Earlier, Milton-as-narrator had spoken of "necessity, the tyrant's plea" (I.394). Here the rhetorical proclamation of "public reason", etc., contrasts with the simple, halting phrase "Melt, as I do", which slips into the syntax in the same way as earlier, with Satan, "Words interwove with sighs found out their way"—or in the same way as the Muse's words slip in to the poet's mind between movements of sleep.[12] The Muse speaks in the gaps left between the smooth rationalizations of the selfhood. Milton's own definition of poetry, in fact, was language that is "simple, sensuous and passionate".[13] The simplicity of the "true voice of feeling", in Keats's distinction, contrasts with the "false beauty of art".[14] Through Satan, Milton explores the alternation between adolescent politician and infant emotionality that images his own deep-rooted dilemma as both preacher and follower of the Muse. It is a dilemma that, as Keats suggests, may belong essentially and eternally to the situation of the poet or artist, and therefore equally to the soul-making aspect of the individual mind. Bion describes it as the perpetual oscillation in orientation between the paranoid-schizoid and depressive positions.

In terms of Miltonic doctrine, Eve is more susceptible to Satan than Adam because she is the weaker vessel. In terms of the story told by the Muse, she welcomes Satan because she wants to become pregnant. Milton, foreseeing this interpretation, has carefully defended himself against it by his descriptions of prelapsarian sex, along with insisting that "younger hands" are part of the predetermined programme of life in Eden. Nonetheless, as book follows book and the pleasant monotony of the diurnal round of pruning and vine-tying begins to become a bit tedious, we empathize with Eve's desire for something to happen. "Domestic Adam" fears, not without reason, that she may be getting bored with him and his talk.[15] Indeed, Book IX—the narrative of the Fall of Man—opens with the words "No more of talk". Eve's dissatisfaction appears first in her disturbing dream of Book IV, a dream that prompts a rational and ineffective disquisition about "evil" from Adam, who has been schooled in doctrine by Raphael. Adam assures Eve that

> "Evil into the mind of god or man
> May come—or go, so unapproved, and leave
> No spot or blame behind" [V.117–18],

innocently employing a Satanic–Miltonic ambiguity: "come—or go". No spot takes root in Eve's womb so long as she and Adam, in their fleshly natural way, model their intercourse on the lines of the angels who, bodiless, mix "easier than air with air . . . nor restrained convey-ance need / As flesh to mix with flesh, or soul with soul" (VIII.626–29). The thoughts of the angels are in effect like those of the nightingale, moved "voluntarily" by principles of natural harmony. Milton, author of the revolutionary *Doctrine and Discipline of Divorce*, knew that mar-riage was not like that, any more than poetry. His depiction of Adam and Eve's idyllic state of "unexperienced thought" was a type of wish-fulfilment that his poetic self knew to be essentially impoverished (IV.457). The definition of happiness as "seeking to know no more" was contrary to his deepest nature (IV.775); and when he attributes the hunger for knowledge to Satan, as he does throughout *Paradise Lost*, it serves simply to enhance Satan's stature, not to condemn him. Thus, Satan's reaction to learning about the forbidden Tree of Knowledge is:

> Knowledge forbidden?
> Suspicious, reasonless. Why should their Lord
> Envy them that? Can it be sin to know,
> Can it be death? [IV.515–18]

Milton picks up Cleopatra's question "Can it be sin to rush into the secret house of death?", with all its complex premonitions of a forth-coming change that could be described—in the Bionic sense—as "death to the existing state of mind". It is a move to a new plateau of knowledge and self-knowledge. Indeed, Milton never does manage to justify this particular way of God to men. He tries to circumlocute the issue by spinning a web of sophistication over it, in truly serpentine manner. So, by the time we get to Book IX, the Tree of Knowledge has become the "tree of disobedience" or the "tree of prohibition". It is a mere test of obedience. Milton could have got out of the difficulty by presenting Eve as succumbing to Satan's wiles through mere vanity; but he does not do her this disservice—she is sufficiently mature to recognize "overpraising" and to rebuke Satan for it. Instead, he makes Eve's fall a type of classical hubris—sinful not in its search for knowl-edge, but in its temptation to become "like God who all things knows"—a false omniscience. But the narrator's hapless admonitions are in vain; we feel, with Eve, the progressive inevitability of her unconscious motivation—that she *must know* the meaning of her dreams.

   She has two dreams. (Adam also has two dreams before the Fall—of Eden, and of Eve.) The first, in Book IV, finds Satan "Squat like a toad, close at the ear of Eve", trying to "forge illusions, phantasms and dreams" (IV.800–803). He is caught in the act by "two fair angels", young breast-like Cherubs (attributes of Eve herself) who pretend not to "know" him:

> "Know ye not me? [he demands] . . .
> Not to know me argues yourselves unknown" [IV.828–30]

Even *Paradise Lost* has its comic interludes. The two Cherubs cheekily counter Satan's taunt by informing him the reason they didn't recognize him is that he is not as good-looking as he used to be in heaven. He is older and scarred by experience. The Archangel Gabriel comes to their rescue, threatening to chain him up before "all hell breaks loose", upon which Satan dubs him a "proud limitary Cherub". But Satan has been successful in his testing of the waters: by Book IX, the previously virginal Eve herself is ready to receive his dream. She appeared not to notice—not to "know"—him, the first time; for to Adam, Eve's beauty seems like an "angelic guard" placed around her, evoking "awe" (VIII.559). Satan's visitation nonetheless creates a subtle change in the nature of her inward attentiveness, toad though he was. Next time Satan, who has also learned a lesson, reappears less brashly as the beautiful serpent, subtlest beast of the field:

> In at his mouth
> The Devil entered, and his brutal sense,
> In heart or head, possessing soon inspired
> With act intelligential, but his sleep
> Disturbed not, waiting close th'approach of morn. [IX.187–91]

It is quintessential Milton that the word "possessing" reaches, simultaneously, backward to "sense" and forward to "inspired", binding the ethereal and the concrete; poetry can do this, whereas prose would have insisted on a grammatical choice—one or the other, not both together. His "angelic essence" is "constrained into a beast and mixed with bestial slime", just as in response to Eve's phantasy he "glides obscure" into her garden, "involv'd in rising mist".

Satan becomes Milton's dark angel of annunciation. His first step is to gain Eve's attention. Eve pays no heed to the many dumb beasts daily "gambolling" around her; they are commensal to her existence, familiar aspects of her mind-body. They form a parallel to the little devils who stay behind in hell, playing games, while Satan alone "wings the desolate abyss", vehicle of the poetic imagination. He is singled out from the rest of the "Circean herd" owing to his bursting inner speech. The words are a calculated deception; but the need to speak, and the music of communication, is real. Through it, Satan penetrates the narcissistic attraction to her own reflection that was Eve's first earthly act. He speaks "with serpent tongue / Organic, or impulse of vocal air"—language that evocatively suggests the strangeness of being spoken through, like the Pythia of ancient Greece (IX.329–30). It recalls the "first endeavouring tongue" of the "Vacation Exercise" years before. Milton's intention is to make Satan's fraudulence convincing, as he masquerades as the infant–poet. Instead, what happens is that a split is created between the sensuous sensuality of the serpent and the pseudo-logicality of Satan's arguments—serpentine in the coldly manipulative sense.[16] Keats, in his notes on Milton again, noted the "mysteriousness" of the type of mental operation that he called "describing in parts" in a way that enables the poet to go beyond the confines of his selfhood:

> One of the most mysterious of semi-speculations is, one would suppose, that of one Mind's imagining into another. Things may be described by a Man's self in parts so as to make a grand whole which that Man himself would scarcely inform to its excess.[17]

Eve has already intuited the presence of Satan—"evil", that attribute of God—and become aware of this foreshadow of the swelling of knowledge inside her. Her interest is held by the concentrated housing of projective-introjective tensions in the serpent's phallic undulations as he rises to the occasion and

>   toward Eve
>   Addressed his way, not with indented wave,
> Prone on the ground, as since, but on his rear,
> Circular base of rising folds, that tow'red
> Fold above fold a surging maze; his head
> Crested aloft, and carbuncle his eyes;
> With burnish'd neck of verdant gold, erect
> Amidst his circling spires, that on the grass
> Floated redundant. Pleasing was his shape
> And lovely, never since of serpent kind
> Lovelier . . . [IX.496–505]

The language that described Satan's plaints in his soliloquies is channelled into the body of the serpent: phrases such as "Then much revolving, thus in sighs began" (IV.31) or "Collecting all his might dilated stood", "recollect", "gratulate", "insinuate", "inspiring venom", all become part of his mental movement—tortuous, sidelong, oblique, fluctuating, intricate, "in himself collected", "involved in rising mist". The serpent–poet is a fit analogue for Milton's Latinate, caesura-led verse; it is characteristic of Milton to use the slight pause between linked clauses to cast associations both forwards and backwards, a concertina-like pulse of energy. The burnished serpent glows ambiguously through a cloudy haze like the will-o'-the-wisp with its "wandering fire, / Compact of unctuous vapour, which the night condenses" (language based on Ariel leading Caliban). The passage also echoes Shakespeare's picture of airy sexual emanations in Cleopatra's burnished barge, undulating on wave and wind to the pulse of the "serpent of old Nile". In aesthetic terms, the serpent is a match for Eve herself (the "fairest unsupported flower"); he is an avatar of Pluto who stole Proserpine with her poetic associations, "herself a fairer flower".[18] "Abstracted" Satan and "amazed Eve", at the heart of Eden's flora, "veiled in a cloud of fragrance", are both night-wanderers veiled in ambiguous spiritual mist. In this way Satan-within-the-serpent, a function so far split off from Adam—or, at least, not acknowledged by Milton as Adamic—finds the reciprocation it seeks in the desire of Eve to eat the apple—though she "knew not eating death".

To Adam, indeed, Eve *is* the serpent: "thou serpent!" he accuses her in Book X:

> Nothing wants, but that thy shape,
> Like his, and colour serpentine, may show
> Thy inward fraud . . . [X.869–71]

The ambiguous Miltonic syntax makes it appear that Eve's beauty is in fact serpentine, just as earlier it was her "angelic guard" of "awe". Later in Milton's career the serpent will reappear in degraded form— shorn of ambiguity—as the "viper" within Dalila in *Samson Agonistes*, who approaches the fallen hero–poet "like a fair flower surcharged with dew" to erotically tempt him when he is at the nadir of his existence and in need of "secret refreshings that repair his strength":

> But who is this, what thing of sea or land?
> Female of sex it seems,
> That so bedecked, ornate, and gay,
> Comes this way sailing
> Like a stately ship
> Of Tarsus . . .[19]

Instead of the poetic ambiguity always associated by Milton with visual beauty, there is a contemptuous caricature—"what thing of sea or land?" Nonetheless it is Dalila who awakens Samson from his torpor of depression and makes him realize that he is not in fact impotent—that his strength did not lie, narcissistically, in his hair, any more than his inner sight was housed in his eyes.

Milton never did forgive Eve for draining his serpent of its doctrinal stasis and in a sense stealing the ground from Adam, giving him "second thoughts" about the implications of his entire epic, which he could only see as weakness, "overcome by female charm". He insisted on the split between the sensual Adam—the Serpent—and the tender, loyal Adam. The sensuality was blamed on Eve and was coupled with a defence of doctrinaire logicality—as when Adam tells her: "Would thou approve thy constancy, approve / First thy obedience" IX.367–68), while the tender, dependent aspect has also a certain helplessness—"forlornness". Certainly the new sensuality of Adam and Eve complicates their relationship: "high passions" such as "anger, hate, mistrust, suspicion" shake "Their inward state of mind, calm region once / And full of peace, now tossed and turbulent" (IX.1125–26). Ultimately, however, Adam stands by his initial emotional response to Eve's fall:

> How can I live without thee, how forgo
> Thy sweet converse and love so dearly joined,
> To live again in these wild woods forlorn? [IX.908–10]

The word "forlorn" is used by Satan to ambiguously describe both Adam and Eve, when he meditates on the prospect of their loss of Eden and, at the same time, himself (owing to a grammatical twist): "To you whom I could pity thus forlorn" (IV.375). He is truly bound up with them in a "mutual amity so strait, so close" that they are an inseparable trio. It is the word used to convey the poet's fear of losing himself on his own journey, "Erroneous there to wander and forlorn" (VII.20). It is also Eve's word to describe the loss of intimacy with Adam (X.921). "Forlorn!" wrote Keats, at the end of the "Ode to a Nightingale": "The very word is like a bell / To toll me back from thee to my sole self."

Ultimately the integration of Adam and Satan really only happens within the mind of Eve. (It will be echoed, two centuries later, in Emily Bronte's poetic novel *Wuthering Heights*, in the form of the characters Edgar and Heathcliff.) It is what is necessary for evolution to take place. After the Fall, Satan's role as a developmental force is finished: he becomes the mere discarded shell of his former passionate and tragic self. The fundamental split, which has always existed, becomes evident. His doctrinaire selfhood continues in the role of "plebeian angel militant" (X.422) and is finally degraded into the form of a literal, non-burnished serpent, who is hissed to the floor by his parliamentary fellow-serpents in their last assembly (X.508). Whereas his function as carrier of the poetic spirit, the vitalizing spark of godliness, passes over to Eve. As hero, Satan simply fades away. Now that the "tree of prohibition" has been demystified, there is a new knowledge, contained in a new mist or mystery. Once again, Eve has a dream—this time of a conversation between Adam and the Archangel Michael, who promises "a paradise within thee, happier far". Satan's "perverted world" will "dissolve" into "new heav'ns, new earth" (XII.546–49); and the new "world all before them" will be that of time and history, not fairy-tale. The conversation is related, as an event, in the narrative of Book XII. But the fact that Eve *dreams* it indicates, simultaneously, that she is the one who understands the process of conception and internalization that is the crux of the Archangel's speech. It is she who points out that "God is also in sleep, and dreams advise" (XII.611). Later, disturbed by the Muse's implications, he wrote *Paradise Regained* to set the record straight with regard to Satan's relentless predominance as hero, and *Samson Agonistes* to quash the idea of Eve as heroine.[20] Yet only as Eve could Alcestis return from the grave. Like Proserpine, she partakes of the Muse's cycle of disappearance and return. Ultimately, Psyche will descend from her through the voice of another poet, emerging from the darkness of "neglect".

After the Fall, there are no more invocations. Instead, the poet pictures the processes of internalization and symbol-formation that result from the idea of the Muse becoming embedded in the world of circumstances—the womb of Eve. Cheered by the prospect of the new working life, breeding children instead of flowers, Eve finds herself no longer bored with "domestic Adam" as he had once feared and confirms her commitment to him: "But now lead on . . . thou to me / Art all things under heav'n, all places thou".[21] The beautiful ending of the epic echoes, and rewrites, the mist of contrary emotions that had originally enfolded Satan when he was "archangel fall'n". Eden, when empty, will later become "an island salt and bare". Its inner life is pictured in the aura that surrounds Adam and Eve as they descend its tiered terraces—a mist composed of minute, massed, fiery cherubim who descend in a vaporous stream:

> all in bright array
> The Cherubim descended; on the ground
> Gliding meteorous, as ev'ning mist
> Ris'n from a river o'er the marish glides,

And gathers ground fast at the labourer's heel
Homeward returning. . . .

In either hand the hast'ning Angel caught
Our ling'ring parents, . . .

Some natural tears they dropped, but wiped them soon;
The world was all before them, where to choose
Their place of rest, and Providence their guide;
They hand in hand, with wand'ring steps and slow,
Through Eden took their solitary way. [XII.627–49]

The "hast'ning Angel" who in *Lycidas* "looked homeward" now shows Adam and Eve the way "homeward". Now that Eden is no longer a mental state, the idea of "home" takes on a dual dimension: the outer world of their new daily existence, and, simultaneously but distinctly, the inner world of their mind. Instead of the decorative classical serenity of the original garden, they are led to a working English landscape of ploughed furrows and temperamental mists. The gardeners will become farmers. Like the poet "in solitude", their way is "solitary", yet "not alone". The solid reality of the new world is conveyed through the feel of the Angel's hands, which is literally transferred to Adam and Eve "hand in hand" to remind them that now they are responsible for holding the idea of Providence within them, an inner guide. Satan once glided into the Garden of Eden "involv'd in rising mist". Now, trailing clouds of glory, the misty swarm of cherubim still clings to the "labourer's heel", echoing the way the fallen angels at the beginning of the story "strowed the brooks of Vallombrosa" like leaves and streamed into the narrow entrance of Pandemonium like "fairy elves".

In Coleridge's description of the internal workings of such a symbol:

That most glorious birth of the God-like within us, which even as the Light, its material symbol, reflects itself from a thousand surfaces, and flies homeward to its Parent Mind enriched with a thousand forms, itself above form and still remaining in its own simplicity and identity.[22]

The thousand forms of these ethereal associations foreshadow the "innumerable" souls of future humanity, each one a spark of God's identity with potential to become—as Keats said—"personally itself". The infant-self establishes an ever-renewing contact with its object, the "Parent Mind". The aura of divinity that once accompanied the newly-fallen Satan now surrounds "our first Parents" as it did the child of the

"Nativity Ode", and constitutes their beauty. Now the mind really is "its own place", rather than a scion of heaven or of hell, there will be room for the "hungry generations", the future children of Eve, the thoughts of the mind to come.

NOTES

1. Keats, marginal notes on Milton, in: *Complete Poems*, ed. J. Barnard (Harmondsworth, Middlesex: Penguin, 1978), p. 518.
2. The words of Bion's character "Myself", in: *The Dream*, the first book of *A Memoir of the Future*, single-volume edition (London: Karnac, 1991), p. 56.
3. Blake, *The Marriage of Heaven and Hell*, plate 6, in: *Complete Writings*, ed. G. Keynes (Oxford: Oxford University Press, 1972). p. 150.
4. Milton's first wife, with whom he had no marriage-of-minds, had died after giving birth to their fourth child; the third child—and only son—had died in infancy.
5. Sonnet XXIII.
6. See Bion, *A Memoir of the Future*, p. 268.
7. *Paradise Lost*, IX.62–64; IV.75.
8. Keats, notes on Milton's *Paradise Lost*, Barnard, *Complete Poems*, p. 520.
9. *Paradise Lost*, I.650–56, IV.105–6.
10. *Paradise Lost*, IX.101, 175.
11. The "hateful siege of contraries", *Paradise Lost*, IX.121–22.
12. "Words interwove . . .", *Paradise Lost*, I.621.
13. Milton, *Of Education*, in: *Areopagitica and Of Education*, ed. K. M. Lea (Oxford: Oxford University Press, 1971), pp. 54–55; Coleridge, *Notebooks*, ed. K. Coburn (London: Routledge & Kegan Paul, 1957), Vol. 3, no. 3287.
14. Keats, describing his own problem with *Hyperion*, letter to Reynolds, 21 September 1819, in Gittings, *Letters*, p. 292.
15. See *Paradise Lost*, IX.318; and "But if too much converse perhaps / Thee satiate, to short absence I could yield, / For solitude is sometimes best society" IX.248–50.
16. Coleridge praised "that good and necessary word 'sensuous'", as distinct from "sensual, sensitive, sensible", etc.; Coburn, *Notebooks*, Vol. 2, no. 2442.
17. Keats, notes on *Paradise Lost*, Barnard, *Complete Poems*, p. 518. His comment on the passage in which Satan enters the head of the serpent is: "Whose spirit does not ache at the smothering and confinement—the unwilling stillness—the 'waiting close'? Whose head is not dizzy at the possible speculations of Satan in the serpent prison?" (p. 526).
18. See the passages relating Eve and Proserpine: *Paradise Lost*, IV.270, IX.396, 432, 792.
19. Milton, *Samson Agonistes*, ll. 665, 710–15, 728.

20. Milton, according to the testimony of his nephew, could not bear hearing that *Paradise Regained* was "inferior" to the first poem; H. Darbishire (Ed.), *The Early Lives of Milton* (London: Constable, 1932), pp. 75–76; *Paradise Regained* is a straightforward debating-society argument; *Samson Agonistes* is a more complex reaction and a work of great technical innovation. Where *Paradise Regained* is tedious, *Samson Agonistes* is, in parts, alluring; yet by comparison with *Paradise Lost*, they are both works of the selfhood.
21. Eve's lament for her home-bred flowers is in XI.273–79.
22. S. T. Coleridge, *The Statesman's Manual* (1817); in: *Lay Sermons*, ed. R. J. White (London: Routledge, 1972), pp. 23–24.

CHAPTER FIVE

Oedipus at the crossroads

Nothing is here for tears; nothing to wail
Or knock the breast, no weakness, no contempt,
Dispraise, or blame; nothing but well and fair,
And what may quiet us in a death so noble.

Milton[1]

The patients, for the treatment of whom I wish to formulate
theories, experience pain but not suffering. They may be
suffering in the eyes of the analyst because the analyst can,
and indeed must, suffer. The patient may say he suffers but
this is only because he does not know what suffering is and
mistakes feeling pain for suffering it.

Wilfred Bion[2]

The plays of Sophocles became available in print in the Western
world in the sixteenth century, and their influence on English
literature must be inestimable. Although Shakespeare is said
not to have read Sophocles himself, it is hard to believe that the author

---

An earlier version of this chapter was published as "A Man of Achievement: Sophocles' Oedipus", in the *British Journal of Psychotherapy*, 11 (2), 1994.

of *King Lear* was not aware of *Oedipus the King*. Certainly Milton's *Paradise Lost* is imbued with the Sophoclean preoccupation with the nature of the search for knowledge and its relation to "sin"; and his last work, *Samson Agonistes* (Samson suffering), is modelled directly in theme and form on *Oedipus at Colonus*, the final vehicle for the wisdom of Sophocles' old age. The three plays that tell the story of Oedipus span the second half of Sophocles' long life. They represent an inquiry into the nature of suffering and its potential for either creativity or soul-entombment. They dramatize, in effect, the distinction Keats made between the vale of tears and the vale of soulmaking. This is essentially the same as that formulated by Bion in terms of the kind of pain that causes "symptoms" while enclosing the mind in a sort of comfortable pessimism, as opposed to the pain that is truly felt mentally—which he calls "suffering". The first type of pain is non-developmental, repetitive, as in the revenge cycles of classical and neoclassical tragedy. It finds expression in the continually reiterated choruses about how "man is born to suffer", in the sense of meaningless, predestined persecution:

> As flies to wanton boys are we to the gods—
> They kill us for their sport.[3]

This pain is associated with the endless circularities of the Claustrum.[4] The second type of pain occurs at points of "catastrophic change" and derives from the tension between conflicting emotions in the face of new knowledge. The initial, infantile pain of guilt (as in the *Oedipus Tyrannos*) is superseded by the pain associated with the enigma of the bittersweet moment of contact between the self and its objects, whose goal is the internalization of meaning. As the Oedipus saga progresses, Sophocles focuses increasingly on the nature, quality, and implications of the suffering that is caused by the goodness of the internal objects, and on the struggle of the self to allow itself to be a vehicle for their knowledge, such that it becomes "generative"—to use Bion's term—or transmissible. The culminating symbol of Oedipus' life is when the "gift" of his "battered body" is received by the state of Athens as an act of grace.

Antigone, the earliest of the three plays, investigates the nature of the first type of pain and clarifies what is wrong with it—to what extent it is useless, like the "weakness and contempt" judged by Milton to be inimical to true heroic tragedy. The play concerns the trouble in the family after Oedipus has died, so it narrates the last part of the legend; but in terms of Sophocles' investigation into the nature of suffering, it takes place before Oedipus-as-hero has been born into literary form. The subject of the story is the conflict between Antigone and Creon over the burial of Oedipus' rogue son Polynices, after his unsuccessful attack on his home city of Thebes. Polynices comes to embody the hated, unwanted, defiling aspects of Oedipus—originally cast out, and now returning in the form of revenge on the Theban mind. Creon's solution is to ostracize this unwanted element in the family, by ordering that the body must remain unburied and therefore deprived of its proper route to Hades. In doing so he is, as the Chorus make clear, usurping judgement that should be left to the gods. Hades (associated in ancient Greece with women) is not only the home of the dead but the world of mystery and unknowing, of indecipherable patterns of morality, as Antigone insists:

> *Antigone*:   Death longs for the same rites for all.
>
> *Creon*:   Never the same for the patriot and traitor.
>
> *Antigone*:   Who, Creon, who on earth can say the ones below
> don't find this pure and uncorrupt?[5]

She does not attempt to extenuate her brother's sins but simply declares his right to be judged by a higher power. But Creon, with his rigid splitting of "patriot" and "traitor", limits his knowledge to that within the narrow bounds of his own authority. He has no conception of "the gods" in the sense of a mental *terra incognita*; his gods are merely a source of punishment. Antigone, who has the "passionate and wild" spirit of her father (ll. 525–26), represents for him the unmanageable element in the family mind that also took shape in Polynices and threatened to destroy the state.

In the argument with his son Haemon, who is betrothed to Antigone, it becomes clear how Creon's understanding of kingship is the tyrannical and authoritarian view in which the king "owns" the city and is the origin and justification of its laws: "Am I to rule this land for others—or myself?" (l. 823). This would make him, as Haemon points out, the "king of a desert island", an infertile mind. He cannot imagine how acceptance of the undesirable—oedipal—elements figured in different ways by Polynices and Antigone could contribute to the state's well-being: could in fact be essential to its ultimate progression and fertility. Afraid of development, he would like to fossilize the status quo and be on the safe side. This takes the form of his decision to entomb Antigone alive; it is only his superstitious fear of retribution by the gods that prevents him from killing her outright. Creon thus separates the Antigone–muse from his hopeful son–self, and in doing so strangles his own future as a king (imaged in the hanging). He fears these links with the unknown will deprive him of his masculinity:

> I am not the man, not now: she is the man
> if this victory goes to her and she goes free. [ll. 541–42]

His underlying terror is of "anarchy", which he blames on the infiltration of a "woman's" influence (ll. 750–58): "No woman is going to lord it over me" (l. 593). When Haemon tries to remind him that he too has a "woman" inside him—a soul—Creon accuses him of being on "the woman's side", to which he replies: "If you are a woman, yes—my concern is all for you" (ll. 829–30). Creon's stifling of his femininity puts an end to his prospects of mental growth as figured in the future of his son.

Yet Antigone's fanaticism is as lethal as Creon's authoritarianism; it complements and supports it. She is essentially a heroine of the barricades—hence her attraction for the early Romantics. There is a sense in which she barricades herself. When her father's "spirit", which she embodies, is cut off from the state and earthly fulfilment (marriage), she withers and dies. To bury Polynices properly, as Ismene emphasizes, would require the cooperation of the entire "state". Antigone alone cannot complete a process that belongs to the mind as a whole. As both she and Creon describe it, she becomes "married to death". For there is a certain truth in Creon's accusation that Death is the only god she worships (l. 875), shown by her denial of the love both Ismene and Haemon have for her, or at least her refusal to acknowledge that it could have any reparative power. Her statement that "no loved one mourns my death" is contradicted by the evidence; it merely demonstrates her lack of faith (l. 969). She rejects Ismene's desire to share her punishment and pre-empts Haemon's effort to pull her out of her tomb, scrabbling among the heap of stones—the mental rubbish responsible for her despair. Because she is unable to imagine that there could be another solution, she loses her own potential for pioneering a path towards the knowledge of the gods, her Muse-like function. Instead, she becomes adhesively identified with the dark and destructive spirit of Polynices and goes, she says, "to wed the lord of the dark waters" (ll. 908). She is unable to suffer the pain of surviving. Her false "marriage to death" is the end result of a process that began to happen long before her actual entombment: she says herself: "I gave myself to death, long ago, so I might serve the dead" (ll. 630–31). Through this resignation, which is very different from the strength of negative capability, she loses her desire to be intimate with the living. As the prospects for the state become shadowed by pessimism, Antigone slips gradually towards Hades, but in the sense of spiritual entombment rather than of mystery.

The mind-locked situation is welcomed by Teiresias, the prophet of doom: "the avengers now lie in wait for you", he exclaims gleefully (l. 1195), as the play nears its final denouement. Sophocles balances the sense of pessimistic inevitability against the false hope that surges up in the form of the last-minute attempt to rescue Antigone. The pathos of Creon's reliance on his delusory omnipotence is intensified by his change of tactic, which is not a genuine change of heart but merely a superstitious reaction to the foreboding injected by the prophet:

> Now—I'm on my way! Come, each of you,
> take up axes, make for the high ground . . .
>   I shackled her,
> I'll set her free myself. [ll. 1232–36]

The king who presented himself as the guardian of law and order and the enemy of anarchy and chaos rushes about the stage looking for a spade, while the vultures circling the city drop gouts of Polynices' carrion flesh on his head. The curse descends yet again on the mind–city, in the familiar repetitive pattern—the circlings of the Claustrum. Sophocles shows that a mind cannot be made by its own "authority", for it will suffocate in its own pollution, a victim of the fundamental lie-in-the-soul. Creon cannot "by himself" set free the Antigone–muse. Antigone's anguished cry over Polynices' desecrated corpse (like that of a bird returning to find its nest ravaged) is repeated by Haemon when he enters the cave–tomb too late, to discover she has hanged herself: it is a type of anti-marriage consummation, just as Antigone had sung in her farewell lament (an anti-Epithalamion). In imitative despair he too commits suicide, *Romeo and Juliet* fashion, and his suicide is followed by that of his mother, continuing the chain-reaction. Creon's attempt to play safe has resulted in the loss of his own nest of birds, his intimate inner life; it is the nearest he can get to identification with Antigone. At the same time it is also the lost future of Thebes, which would have been stabilized by the marriage of his son to Oedipus' daughter.

Oedipus Tyrannos [*Oedipus the King*] was written some ten or twelve years after *Antigone*. Oedipus takes over the quest from Haemon, the growing part of the personality whose forward-looking faith takes the form of a strong identification with the feminine. Unlike Haemon, Oedipus is firmly married to his mother, his internal Muse-figure, not in death but in life—they have a palace, children, prosperity—until the "sickness" appears that indicates some catastrophic change is on the horizon. The inhabitants are dying as a result of some unidentified pollution. The presence of an unpalatable idea, hanging over the city like a cloud of pestilence, has taken the somatic form of symptoms. There is no pathway for inspiration. The pain needs to be transformed into the developmental one of "suffering"—in the sense intended by Bion, something distinct from either stoicism or masochism. In this sense the story begins where that of *Antigone* came to an end: the mind is subjected to the claustrophobic pain associated with lack of access to knowledge of its emotional condition. If the play is appreciated for its phantasy content alone (as in the case of Freud), it appears to be a story about the "Oedipus complex". To empathize with this, we do not in fact need the play itself—a summary will do just as well. Jocasta herself formulates the universal "dream" of a man's marrying his mother—but as a matter for soothing lullaby, not for painful revelation. It is not the phantasy alone that has an impact but the way in which it is presented—the way in which it becomes real to us, in fact continually astonishes us with its reality, however many times it is read or performed. When we read the play *as a play*—that is, as a poetic structure—we see that it is really a story about weaning; and when we consider it in the context of the sequence of Oedipus plays, we realize that the overall drama concerns the nature of the mind's fertility, and the forces that help it to progress and "have ideas", versus the insinuating or bullying forces of negativity.

Oedipus Tyrannos is a minefield of linguistic puns and ambiguities, through which the Greekless reader has to stumble more blindly than Oedipus himself, led by the hand of scholarly exegesis.[6] The play's structure is so compelling, however, that even those of us who cannot read the original language can appreciate the flavour that this verbal dance imparts to the quest for the underlying pattern of the emotional experience. Sophocles' famous dramatic "irony" takes the form of the characters speaking more truly than they know, or unknowingly pressing towards revelations from which they would consciously withdraw in horror. It continually forces on us man's ignorance of the workings of *Tyche*—Fate, Chance, Destiny—and the greater knowledge of the gods. The clutch of words that refer to a leap or lunge, strike, violent entry reverberate with one another and link in our mind the moment Oedipus killed his father, his father's attempt to kill him with a double-pronged fork, the piercing of his ankles as a baby by his parents, the piercing of his eyes by himself, his sexual entry to his mother, and to the double doors of her bedroom at the end; and simultaneously, alongside all these, the rhythmic "lunge" of a *daimon* [immortal spirit] who pushes him towards the *catastrophe*, in the classical sense of climax and revelation. The *daimon* strikes from both inside and outside the protagonists; and the idea of "doubleness" recurs continually, impressing on us that there is more than one layer of meaning involved at each point. Another group of words links, and at the same time separates, different types of knowledge: matter-of-fact understanding, conscious investigation, oracular "seeing", and the type of knowing most characteristic of Oedipus—*gnome*, innate intelligence, or power of recognition (sometimes translated "mother-wit").[7] In addition, Sophocles frequently puns on another word for knowing, *eidos*, that through its sound echoes the name of Oedipus, who is thus both swollen-footed and knowing-footed—one who painfully pursues a path to knowledge. There are puns throughout on "feet" as stepping towards a truth and as being cruelly hounded by a truth.

We are introduced to Oedipus as one who has "laboured over many paths of thought";[8] his talents and "experience" in intellectual pursuits are well established. But now something different is to be put to the test: his capacity to think through an overwhelming emotional turbulence, which will shake the mental constitution to the core. The quest of Oedipus' selfhood is for the "facts" about his birth; the quest of his internal *daimon* or poetic spirit, is for the mystery of his growth and identity. Oedipus, unlike Creon, accepts from the beginning that his kingship has to be earned and proved continually; the city, in his view, contains his "children" (ll. 1, 69)—his mental fertility—not merely support for his own authority. He states his determination to "speak before all" in his inquiry and to put the good of the city—the mind as a whole—before his personal comfort and status. And the nature of his inquiry is also the nature of his suffering. He seems to guess instinctively from the beginning that Thebes' dis-ease has some intimate relation to his own birth and identity, as when he says, with the ambiguity characteristic of the play, that there are "None as sick as I" (l. 61). Now he considers what tools he has available for dealing with this sickness. He began as one who "knew" [*eidei*] the "famous riddle of the Sphinx". Solving the riddle is first statement of readiness to undergo life, from four-footed infancy to three-footed old age; this is his birthright, his natural intelligence. It is what seems to lie behind his otherwise strange assertion that he has a "key" to the mystery:

> Alone, had I no key
> I'd lose the track.[9]

The word translated "key" is *symbolon*, with its suggestion that the type of investigation he is undertaking is one of matching-up, finding a congruence with another source of knowledge.[10] The toppling of the Sphinx, that false Muse ("clawed virgin"), with its sexually teasing riddles in tripartite form, occurs near the killing of Laius at "the place where three roads meet", a narrow rocky passage beneath the mother–mountain of Cithaeron.[11] The double "toppling" images how Oedipus overcame his father's hostility to the idea of his birth: trying to bar his entrance to life with pessimistic phobias, which took the form of a curse on the city (the Sphinx), an enemy to fertility.

Now this hostility re-emerges in the person of Teiresias, whose knowledge, like all superstition, is always of "dreadful secrets" (l. 374).[12] His reading of bird-entrails is reminiscent of the filthy gobbets of putrid flesh that rain down on Thebes at the end of *Antigone*, burying the Antigone–muse aspect of the mind. He tells lies not about facts, but about their meaning. For Teiresias, any increase in knowledge must be turned into a misfortune. He tells Oedipus that his "birth-day" (the day he discovers the mystery of his birth) also marks the day of his death (l. 499), implying that, as the Chorus will say later, there is no point in facing life at all. It is better not to be born than to know the full extent of one's sinfulness. As in *Paradise Lost*, it is deemed better to "know no more". Oedipus retaliates by reminding him that his own methods of knowing had been unable to loosen the grip of the Sphinx—they had no healthful enlightening power:

> Did you rise to the crisis? Not a word,
> you and your birds, your gods—nothing.
> No, but I came by, Oedipus the ignorant,
> I stopped the Sphinx! With no help from the birds,
> the flight of my own intelligence bit the mark. [ll. 449–53]

"Oedipus the ignorant" reads like "I the knowing, not-knowing . . .". Because he has the mental strength to accept this doubleness (his certainty of his mother's love, together with his doubts that she may betray him through weaning), he overcomes the ill will of the prophet of doom and is not deflected from his quest. He is prepared, in fact, to face "death", the death that he has already pronounced for himself. The emotional vitality takes the form of his famous "anger" [*orge*], for which Creon and the Chorus admonish him. Yet this anger is a manifestation of his *daimon*, his Promethean fiery spirit, and is as essential a tool for his investigation as his *gnome*, his faculty of recognition. Creon's lack of anger is connected with his weakness and sterility. "You could provoke a stone to anger" Oedipus tells him (l. 335). Like Milton's "smooth-tongued" Belial, Creon speaks in glib, pompous generalities that disguise from himself and from everyone else his sullen but emotionless antagonism. His lying self-portrait as an unassuming, comfort-loving family man is a masterpiece of political rhetoric. Oedipus, in his rage, would like to kill him. However, he refrains from abusing his power in the usual political way. He recognizes, with his characteristic *gnome*, that in releasing Creon he is unequivocally turning the spotlight on himself. He drops his instinctive search for a scapegoat and—in contrast to Creon in *Antigone*—takes the burden of this polluting element within him. With a new clarity he accepts that this will mean "my ruin, my death or my disgrace" (ll. 742–43). He has begun to "suffer". His rule as king of his mother is over.

At this point, Jocasta comes on the stage. Now that Oedipus has overcome the temptations of "weakness and contempt" represented by Teiresias and Creon, he needs the guidance of his mother–Muse, whom, he says, he respects more than "all these men here". The sensitive relationship with Jocasta is instrumental in the process of "remembering" that constitutes the central section of the play and is essentially (as Jocasta suggests) a dream-analysis, a memory that comes to life and takes its meaning from the present. It is the beginning of Oedipus-the-poet taking over from Oedipus-the-king.[13] Jocasta is engaged by Oedipus in unearthing features of his history that stir his unconscious memory:

> Strange,
> hearing you just now . . . my mind wandered,
> my thoughts racing back and forth. [ll. 800–802]

The emotional power comes from Jocasta really *being* his mother, not from Jocasta being his wife and at the same time the container for infantile projections ("every man dreams he has married his mother . . ."). That is the false dream, the soothing lullaby—the one that is "only a dream", as she would like it still to be, with part of herself. Responding to the urgency of his need, however, she conjures back into his consciousness two old "shepherds" who had fed him in his infancy. She summons the first directly, and the second appears on cue when she puts out suppliant branches to Apollo. They are attributes of Jocasta-as-muse, a function that she is about to relinquish (when she "recognizes" Oedipus at last to be her baby). This revelation is as painful to her as to him and is guided not by her will but by the sense of overseeing Destiny that governs every sequential step towards knowledge. Each step is a surprise; nothing is intentional (from the human point of view), but nothing is accidental (from the view of the gods). We see clearly in this central section of the play how the communication is between the internal objects of the protagonists. Jocasta does not leave the scene until she sees that Oedipus, the baby, has learned to internalize the meaning of his breastfeeding experience.

The story that she helps him to "remember" is as follows: Oedipus, a child of two cities—Thebes and Corinth—once had a "drunken" dream of parents he had once had (tempestuous and passionate in character), before he had abandoned them as an infant for more equanimical foster-parents who then brought him up in princely comfort, with doting indulgence. They could not bear to tell him the "truth" themselves, but they gave him the strength and independence to leave them and return to his first home, via the disturbing "crossroads" where he triumphed over his father's hostility. He interpreted this as meaning he should be his mother's husband and king of her city. Ousting his father recalled the moment of his difficult birth through the narrow passage—from which he still bears the "dreadful marks" on his knowing-feet ("I've had it from the cradle", l. 1134). They are also the scars of his sojourn as an infant on Cithaeron, the wild and "trackless" mountain–mother, where he was passed from one shepherd to another. Now, to his horror, he begins to learn that his devoted mother was instrumental in his original "expulsion": it wasn't simply that he chose to exchange a Theban breast for a Corinthian one; in fact, they both belonged to one mother (they both tended the sheep on the high pastures of the same mountain)—"her own child!" And now she seems to be demanding yet more work from him (was it not enough that in his "greatness" he had saved the city?) He and she both experience "sickness" at the possibility that is in the air. Nonetheless the investigation has to continue, propelled by both the *daimon* within and the daimonic world of divine knowledge inexorably drawing into line with one another. Polybus of Thebes, says the first shepherd, was "no more your father than I am" (l. 1115). "You didn't find me yourself?" demands Oedipus—"No sir, another shepherd passed you on to me". The second shepherd has to be squeezed (his arms twisted behind

his back) before he will blurt out the second half of the truth, concluding with—"you were born for pain!" When Oedipus fits together these
two facets of his experience, symbolized by the meeting between the
two old shepherd–breasts, he recognizes that the truth is as the baby
had always feared—"all come true, all burst to light!" (l. 1306)

In between the messages of the first and second shepherds, Jocasta
leaves the scene, her farewell cry: "man of pain!" At this point Oedipus
transfers his allegiance to *Tyche*—Fortune, or Chance. Despite her well-
known vicissitudes, he is determined to find her a "good" mother:

> I must see my origins face-to-face . . .
> I count myself the son of Chance,
> the great goddess, giver of all good things—
> I'll never see myself disgraced. She is my mother!
> And the moons have marked me out, my blood-brothers,
> one moon on the wane, the next moon great with power.
> That is my blood, my nature—I will never betray it,
> never fail to search and learn my birth! [ll. 1185–94]

The Chorus add their imagination to his song of affirmation—was he
perhaps the son of Pan, or Apollo who loves the upland pastures?
Whatever god fathered him, Mount Cithaeron is his "birthplace, nurse,
his mountain-mother". This joyous duet transforms and re-evaluates
the earlier picture of the unknown murderer running through rocks
and caves "like a wild bull", pursued by "dread voices" that surround
him like "dark wings beating", "ringing out of the heart of Earth"
(Earth's navel, at Delphi; ll. 545–48). The "horrible" sins and dark
thoughts (the "anger") of the stranger-within-himself now find their
home and resolution in these wild aspects of his god-traversed mountain–mother, but as a child of nature, not of perversion. Oedipus' mind
is suddenly irradiated by this possibility, in pre-Wordsworthian fashion. It appears—as with all oracular knowledge—that there is another
way of hearing those "dread voices of Earth". The song is a sort of
Tychean Magnificat, an exhilarating moment in the play, since it is
spiritually true even though factually a "wild surmise".[14] It takes place
precisely when Jocasta is hanging herself in her chamber within the
house, offstage. She is no more his *internal* mother than she is his wife.
The phase of motherhood in which she was split into good and bad, in
the infant's kingly possession, has been completed; Jocasta has demonstrated to Oedipus that she was both the one who fed him and the one
who caused him pain. She was party to the rivets in his ankles, the
sharp nipples in the caring breasts—the wild, dark powers of

Cithaeron who co-exist with the homely shepherds, sharing their territory, like the good and bad daughters of Lear. Through a triumph of integration, these opposing attributes or agents of Oedipus' internal mother have been returned to their source in *Tyche*, a well that will never run dry. Oedipus' "discovery" of his mother in Tyche and Cithaeron is the beginning of his internalization of the *idea* of his mother as internal object.

The significance of the image of a woman hanging by her own hand is thus diametrically contrasted with that in *Antigone*. Antigone's death is an image of soul-destruction, the fruit of despair; she is blockaded by the heap of stones, the mental rubbish that also takes the form of pestilence dropping from the sky—the plague. She will be followed, later in poetic history, by Samson pulling the temple of the philistines down on his head (the first suicide bomber?). Jocasta's death, like that of Cordelia in *King Lear*, is one of fulfilment: it is the end of a particular function, a specific service to the baby that is now completed, and it takes place in the bedchamber. Together with the baby, she experiences "death to the existing state of mind" (in Bion's term). The weaning process has been painful for her too, and there were times when she would have liked to reverse it—to "call off this search! / My suffering is enough"—yet knowing all the while that Oedipus' desire to discover the "mystery of his birth" is by now overwhelming and will carry him through to the end. She does not have to do much, simply allow the facts to appear before him—her experience, like his, is essentially one of "suffering". His self-blinding, like her hanging, and like the birthmark of his ankles, is an act of recognition. He uses Jocasta's doubleness—her two-pronged brooch (recalling the two-pronged fork of Laius)—for this stab of recognition, reinforced by his parents as combined object. It is described as "digging the twin points down into the sockets of his eyes" (l. 1405), and the word used for sockets [*arthra*] is the same as that for the joints of his ankles. Fusing these historical moments into present significance, he repeats the movement "over and over, the stabbing daggers, stab of memory / raking me insane", affirming his courageous taking of the knowledge within him (l. 1455). The pattern of his life is taking shape:

> O triple roads—it all comes back, the secret,
> dark ravine, and the oaks closing in
> where the three roads join . . . [ll. 1530–32]

He "drank his father's blood" at the crossroads of his birth, then he "came here" to the house of his kingship, the "harbour" of his mother's body,[15] and "did it all again"—drinking his mother's milk. "Apollo ordained it"—he says—"but the hand that struck my eyes was mine . . . I did it!" (ll. 1467–71). At last the self-*daimon* has made contact with the object-*daimon* and brought itself into line with this evolutionary principle—the "evolution of O" as Bion calls it.

The Oedipus–baby now understands that the nature of "death" for himself will not consist in some easy release from the turbulent emotions of life; it is not the type of death predicted by Teiresias, or wished on him by Creon. Though no longer *Tyrannos*, he has, he feels, been "saved from death"—in the literal sense—in order to fulfil some further unknown, "strange" destiny (l. 1595). Indeed, as if foreseeing this, he had earlier in the play commuted his prospective sentence, as the polluter, to that of "exile". Now he accepts—in a sense welcomes—the double knowledge that

> My troubles are mine
> and I am the only man alive who can sustain them. [ll. 1547–49]

The next phase of his "suffering", as the idea continues to grow inside him, is the period of confused searching, expressed by his many years of blind wandering, an outcast, searching for "the haven where I am destined to live on".[16] His innate power of recognition, his *gnome*—the inner "oracle"—tells him that he will find it if he perseveres. It is the equivalent of Keats's "straining at particles of light in a great darkness". As before, it is some fifteen years before Sophocles writes the next phase. *Oedipus at Colonus* was in fact produced posthumously, during the final throes of the wars that would end the golden age of enlightened Athenian imperialism. Like *Paradise Lost*, it was produced in response to an inner compulsion to make the concept of the "paradise within" a living reality, a demonstration for subsequent generations of the process that no external violence can destroy.

Milton's *Samson* opens with the words:

> A little onward lend thy guiding hand
> To these dark steps, a little further on, . . .
>   Here I feel amends,
> The breath of heav'n fresh-blowing, pure and sweet . . .

This opening is modelled closely on that of Sophocles, with the blind and faltering man full of trouble asking to be led onwards to a sacred grove of olives and nightingales, away from the scorched and dusty road of the everyday world where he is assaulted by thoughts of the Claustrum: "eyeless in Gaza, at the mill, with slaves". But Samson has no guide, beyond the shadowy one in the first two lines who then seems to fade away: the Eve of *Paradise Lost* has been degraded to the Dalila–viper, a punishment imposed by his selfhood in an attempt to correct the epic's revelations. His thoughts become increasingly persecutory, tormenting him like bee-stings; and he blames bitterly his dependence: "in power of others, never in my own". His lament, though directed towards his blindness, is essentially for the loss of inspiration—"inward light"; and the most poignant and striking passages are those that evoke this absence:

> The sun to me is dark
> And silent as the moon,
> When she deserts the night,
> Hid in her vacant interlunar cave. [ll. 79–89]

No matter how closely he follows his classical model, he cannot, without remaking the relationship with his Muse, pull himself out of this type of hell, this "vacancy". Through his "own power" he cannot reestablish the link with "intimate impulse" that he has lost. In the terms of Keats's distinction, he leaves the realms of the "poetic dream" and enters those of the "fanatic".

Oedipus, however, has a different type of dependence: one on his daughters. Like the poet of *Paradise Lost*, he is "not alone" while the Muse visits his nightly slumbers. The origin of the intimate relationship with Antigone and Ismene is pictured at the end of *Oedipus Tyrannos* in his desire to "touch" the two small girls who had always eaten at his table and shared pieces of food with him. Creon allows them to approach him temporarily, tantalisingly, then has them removed ("No more!"). However the idea has been established that his daughters have come to symbolize the breast–eyes that need to be made a part of his internal equipment now that Jocasta and her shepherds exist for him no longer.[17] They are, literally, the fruit of that relationship. This symbol-making power has been transferred through the sense of touch. Like Gloucester in *Lear*, he comes to "see feelingly". And although Antigone has more to say than her sister—owing partly to the fact that Greek drama allows for only three speaking actors at a time—Ismene is given a full complementary role: acting as Oedipus' "guard" or "outpost" in the world while Antigone sees to his immediate needs—his feeding and footsteps. In the final scene they are locked together, "all three as one", awaiting the voice of the god that, in the ensuing silence, calls Oedipus to his death. In *Tyrannos* they were young children, themselves dependent on Creon (the worldly king); but by the time of *Colonus* they have matured and have strength of their own, and they have established a system of communication—imaged by Ismene riding towards her father and sister on her pony, in a wide-brimmed sun-hat, having successfully found their whereabouts despite a difficult journey.

Oedipus, contrasting his daughters with his sons, repeatedly affirms that they are "like men", while his sons are "like Egyptians" in their addiction to an easy life. It is the total picture—of daughters and sons—that constitutes the nature of Oedipus' "suffering" at this point. In a sense his sons represent that part of the Tyrannos-baby which would like to continue forever on the throne of its mother-city and cannot see beyond the values of power, possession, and competition. It is a type of mental blinkering that he discards at the end of that play (when he tells Creon not to concern himself with his sons—they are old enough to look after themselves). Yet only in *Colonus* does the significance of this become clear, in his final poignant interview with the hapless Polynices. In contrast to this, Antigone and Ismene, in different ways but without rivalry, come together to facilitate Oedipus' contact with his Muse. Creon, contemptuous as always, calls them his "sticks". Creon's portrait is expanded from that in *Antigone*, to specifically include features of the false poet, the mere rhetorician, with his "wicked way with words" and a "double-edged" tongue that expresses "some twisted ingenious justice of your own" (ll. 906, 867). Possibly he has some affinities with the word-gamester aspect of Sophocles himself. Through his verbal bullying he attempts to "blockade" Oedipus' haven of truth (ll. 928–29). Polynices, more pathetically—and to the distress of Antigone—also constitutes a blockage. Oedipus does not curse his sons until he is quite sure they are bound up in the self-obsessed political mentality of Creon. Polynices' marriage is one of political convenience, not love. In trying to recruit his father to his cause by stirring feelings of rivalry, he shows damningly that he has no conception of the driving force of love that Oedipus invokes at the end of the play. He and his brother represent the youthful egotism that must be cast off if the Oedipus–baby is to mature into a man. Oedipus says, "my dead body will drain their hot blood down" (l. 705). His "body", in its final form, becomes a vehicle for the daimonic necessity of evolution. Only when Polynices feels the full force of his father's "rage" does he accept that his own mentality must come to an end, and he goes bravely to meet his fate. He is superseded by Theseus, Oedipus' adoptive "son", who is (as later in *A Midsummer Night's Dream*) the pattern of an ideal philosopher–ruler. Oedipus' feminine identification leads him onwards; his boyish one looks backwards. Theseus is tested against both Creon (which he finds easy) and Polynices (which he finds difficult). He proves himself strong enough to rescue Oedipus' daughters, his feminine parts, by means of the Athenian cavalry—he will not let them be taken away from him.

The other feature of *Colonus* that is equally fundamental to its symbolization of the relationship between the poet and his Muse is its sense of place. In this play, instead of the relentless wordplay that was used to build up tension in *Tyrannos*, we find poetic ambiguity. Colonus—then a small rural community nestling amidst woods and "white rocks" just outside the city of Athens, its beauty "little known" except to those who lived there—was in fact Sophocles' birthplace. Now this place comes to gather within its bounds all the significance of the internal landscape of *Tyrannos* and all the power and glory of the lost Athenian empire, with its enduring vitality imaged in Athena's ever-renewing olive trees and in Poseidon's sinewy racing horses and ships with their flashing oars. These are all celebrated in the beautiful choral ode at the centre of the play, beginning:

> Here, stranger,
> here in the land where horses are a glory
> you have reached the noblest home on earth
> Colonus glistening, brilliant in the sun—
>   where the nightingale sings on,
> her dying music rising clear,
> hovering always, never leaving,
> down the shadows deepening green
>   she haunts the glades, the wine-dark ivy,
> dense and dark the untrodden, sacred wood of god . . . [ll. 762–70]

The beauty and sacredness of Colonus is literally at the heart of the play, counterbalancing the painful confrontations of the dialogues, irradiating their significance. Its "swelling breast of earth" takes over from Cithaeron as the home of the Muse, the internal mother. The ambivalent characteristics of that first Muse with its cruelty and "wildness" (like Keats's Belle Dame) were associated with the "drunkenness" of the passionate baby ("angry", *orge*), gorging himself on blood–milk. Here (as in *Psyche*), they are enriched by the overwhelming vision of fertility and modulated by the cyclical dance of nature. Here the "springs will never fail, quickening life forever, fresh each day"; here the "reveller Dionysus" (god of wine) is free to express his nature, dancing in the woods, surrounded by his "wild nymphs"— "nymphs that nursed his life".

For the woods of Colonus enclose the shadowy life of those inner gods or goddesses, the feminine deities who preside over man's entrance and his exit to life, the crossroads of catastrophic change. Oedipus recognizes immediately that he has arrived at his final home when he hears the grove is sacred to the Eumenides, who are both the Furies and the Kindly Ones. Close by is the hill of Demeter [Ceres] and the "brazen threshold" to the underworld. His intuition tells him this is the place for which he has been searching all those wandering years: a place of contemplation, in which he can "brood on the old prophecies, / Stored in all the depths of my being" until they quicken into life (ll. 509–10) The sacred grove recalls the crossroads beneath Cithaeron, likewise associated with female divinities of the underworld—Hecate and Persephone [Proserpina]. At the end of the play Oedipus is guided onwards by Demeter and Persephone, who by implication restore his strength such that he can lead everyone else—including Theseus—to the place of his death by means of his inner vision. The goddesses supersede his daughters at that point—it is the point of Milton's "eyes plant inward" (in *Paradise Lost*) or Keats's "I see and sing, by my own eyes inspired". Initially, however, on his arrival at the grove, Oedipus appears to repeat his polluting function: yet again, to the horror of the Chorus, he "sets foot where none may walk". But with the aid of Antigone, whom he asks to show him the "way of wisdom", he slowly feels his way down through the rocks (of obduracy) to a position in which the superstitious terror of the everyday mind is modified, such that it does not block out the message that he knows he carries within him:

Oedipus: Oh dear gods—

Antigone: . . . step by step, our steps together,
   lean your aged body on my loving arm.

Oedipus: Oh so ruined, doomed. [ll. 217–19]

Antigone facilitates the mental movement that is governed by the Muse–Furies, the "queens of terror, faces filled with dread", whom Oedipus feels have "led my slow steps home to your green grove" (ll. 102–20). The epithet "kindly ones" had been coined by the common mind merely to avert the evil eye. But Oedipus will be the one to show that the Furies who guard man's most primitive emotional needs—

those "sweet daughters of primeval Darkness"—are indeed kindly as well as angry. He has already learned to integrate within him the double emotionality of the breast as internal object, cruel and caring, and now he comes to clarify its dual function as both nurturing and cleansing.[18]

This takes the form of his dawning realization of his "innocence"—something that intensifies and expands his "suffering" still further. His culminating insight in *Tyrannos* was: "Apollo ordained it—and I did it!" The exultation of recognition was followed initially by guilt. But now he has emerged from that phase and becomes more and more convinced of his innocence. Repeatedly he says: "I am innocent." When the Chorus assume he has "sinned", because he did the deeds and suffered the consequences, he contradicts them, saying that he "received as a gift, a prize to break the heart" (l. 605)—the gift of his mother. The ambiguous quality of the daimonic "gift" was a function of inspiration. As in *Tyrannos*, he relives the past in the present, a form of dream-remembering that revises its significance. This results not in less suffering, but in more. "I come as someone sacred" (l. 310), he states in response to this new feeling inside him, which will increasingly dominate and dispel the remnants of his sense of pollution (guilt). Later he insists emphatically, "there is nothing criminal deep inside me" (l. 1105). He brings "vision", he retorts, when the Chorus express doubts about the usefulness of a blind man. He has this new feeling even before Ismene arrives with the news that the Theban family who had originally cast him out now have a use for him:

> *Ismene:*   Their power rests in you.
>
> *Oedipus:*   So, when I am nothing—then I am a man! [ll. 430–31]

It appears that he has finally become a kind of celebrity in the outside world. But the various characters have differing views of the nature of the power he embodies. The warring relations—Creon, Eteocles, and Polynices—don't value his knowledge, attained by suffering. They do not intend to incorporate his body within the city–mind; they merely want to paralyse his effectiveness (burying him just outside the city wall where he "cannot help anyone else"). It is a form of iconization—described by Bion as "loading with honours and sinking without trace".[19] They want him as a mascot. This would enshrine his pollutedness like a fly in amber, preserving him for ever as an object of superstition, blocking his cleansing knowledge from entering into the outside world.

Throughout the play we have seen the way in which Oedipus has fiercely protected himself—not alone, but with the aid of Theseus and his daughters—from this form of abuse. To Theseus he said:

> I come with a gift for you,
> My own shattered body . . . no feast for the eyes,
> But the gains it holds are greater than great beauty. [ll. 649–51]

He seeks a "burial"—a form of mental incorporation—that can see the beauty of his innocence through the ugliness of his body. He knows he has it within him to become "useful" and proceeds to feel his way towards this possibility. The old mind (Thebes, the sparring city "sprung from the Dragon's teeth") will be discarded and the new mind—Athens—take its place. This can only happen when the sense in which his "acts" have always been "acts of suffering" (l. 285) becomes completely clear. Its basis is the rock-like endurance that Oedipus has proved he possesses:

> Like some great headland fronting the north
> hit by the winter breakers beating
> down from every quarter—
> so he suffers, terrible blows crashing over him
> head to foot, over and over
> down from every quarter—
> now from the west, the dying sun
> now from the first light rising
> now from the blazing beams of noon
> now from the north engulfed in endless night, [ll. 1401–10]

This image of his rage, which is also his passion and his poetic spirit—his *daimon*—suggests the way in which his body will become welded into the landscape, at the same time as vanishing into thin air. The moving ending of the play images, in concrete terms, a process of abstraction: the final stage of the evolution of an idea in the poetic mind. As Oedipus' new friends turn their backs and Theseus shields his eyes, his body simply disappears from earthly view—"snatched away by the fields unseen" (l. 1909), they do not know whether heavenward or downwards. The final judgement of the imagination is that the rocky birth-passage of Cithaeron has become a "kind" one: the Earth "bursting open in kindness / To receive him" (ll. 1885–86). There is no grave, no funeral pageantry; nothing remains to incite worship or idle curiosity: only the idea in the mind, the feeling in the heart.

Sophocles recognized, as did Aeschylus before him, that those "dread goddesses"—the "Furies" of man's primeval nature—needed metabolizing, not expelling after the manner of the standard revenge tragedy, as they are in *Antigone*.

But the judgement of Athena, which concludes Aeschylus' *Oresteia*, is an intellectual solution, balancing the needs of the civilized and the primitive sides of humanity. As such, it perpetuates the placating or propitiatory element—hence the common mind's fear of the Eumenides at the beginning of *Colonus*. This goes with Plato's idea of the theatre as sublimation, a way of indulging man's "evil dreams"— giving these dark unwanted elements the type of worship that will keep them within the confines of respectability, so they will not take the form of action and pollute civic life. Sophocles, however, saw the theatre as a means of dramatizing the "truth" about essential steps in man's development, which involved confronting the dark and fearful features of the Muse, not seeing them with eyes averted. The Furies must be integrated not just intellectually—brought within the rule of law—but through an intimate emotional link, on the pulses. The truth is *in itself* noble and civilizing, whatever its content, if it can only be endured, "suffered". And unless it can feel and know this truth, the mind's development is thwarted: it will ultimately take revenge upon itself. The Sophoclean "idea" is not one of apportionment of blame or reward, but one of identification and integration. There is no balancing, no compromise, none of the bargaining represented by the Creon and Polynices aspects of the mind. By the end of the play there is a new conception of innate nobility ("kingliness"), founded on Oedipus' opening words that "suffering" together with "nobility, my royal birthright" had taught him patience (ll. 6–8). "Be brave as you were born to be", is Oedipus' last message to his daughters. His famous rage, we now realize, is the same thing as his love:

> It was hard, I know,
> my children, but one word alone repays you
> for the labour of your lives—love, my children.
> you had love from me as from no other man alive,
> and now you must live without me all your days to come. [ll. 1830–34]

Sophocles' new definition of a king is not someone with authority, but someone with the power of love. Oedipus' daughters have served to reunite him with his Muse; now he is teaching them the process of internalization—he will become their Muse. Because he clung fast to his rage-love, the gift of his daimon–mother, while "the horrors" beat over the shore of his mind, he has repulsed the temptation to become an icon and transformed his selfhood into an Idea, available like Milton's Genius of the Shore to those in "days to come". As the spirit of Sophocles ascends to the Elysian fields, his descendants Theseus, Antigone, and Ismene express their faith in it, not by sticking together, as he had hoped, but by going their separate ways. The two girls insist they must return to Thebes, to try to prevent their brothers' mutual destruction. On the surface, the drama appears to be returning full circle, because we know what happens next.... Or do we? After Sophocles, tragedy was never again doomed to be merely *revenge tragedy*, the curse man seems to have pronounced on himself from the moment of his birth. But it took Shakespeare to rediscover that fact.

NOTES

1. John Milton, *Samson Agonistes*, ll. 1721–24.
2. W. R. Bion, *Attention and Interpretation* (London: Tavistock, 1970), p. 19.
3. Shakespeare, *King Lear*, IV.i.36–37.
4. As in D. Meltzer's term: *The Claustrum* (Strath Tay: Clunie Press, 1992).
5. *Antigone*, in: R. Fagles (Transl.), *Sophocles: The Three Theban Plays* (Harmondsworth, Middlesex: Penguin, 1982), ll. 584–87; subsequent line references are to this edition.
6. For explication of the language see Thomas Gould (Transl.), *Oedipus the King* (Englewood Cliffs, NJ: Prentice-Hall, 1970), pp. 46ff.
7. See E. F. Watling (Transl.), *Sophocles: The Theban Plays* (Harmondsworth, Middlesex: Penguin, 1947), p. 38; D. Taylor, *Sophocles: The Theban Plays*, (London: Methuen, 1986), p. 21. On the significance of *gnome* [thought] and its relation to *gignoskein* [recognition] see Gould, *Oedipus the King*, p. 63; on its contrast with the *phronein* [prudence] preferred by Creon, see pp. 80–81. Gould writes: "Oedipus' *gnome* is a mystery to the Chorus. They do not really know how he arrives at his decisions" (p. 74).
8. *Oedipus the King*, in Fagles, *Sophocles*, 1. 79; subsequent line references are to this edition.
9. Gould, *Oedipus the King*, l. 221.
10. A symbolon was a small item broken into two pieces and divided between friends as a memento and mode of recognition at some future date; Gould, *Oedipus the King*, p. 42.
11. The Sphinx was said to have sexually violated young boys; Gould, *Oedipus the King*, pp. 72–73.
12. One story was that Teiresias was castrated or blinded after watching snakes copulating; another that he was blinded by Hera after saying that

women enjoyed sex more than men. His blindness is thus associated with knowledge-as-castration; Gould, *Oedipus the King*, p. 50.

13. The verb meaning "to do", often used in the earlier part of the play (he will "do" all that the oracle tells him), is replaced in the second half by the verb "to suffer", predominating over the story. See note on line 77; Gould, *Oedipus the King*, pp. 24–25.

14. To borrow Keats's phrase in "On First Looking into Chapman's Homer".

15. The metaphor of a ploughed field or harbour is used frequently in the play for Jocasta's womb, home to father and son.

16. *Oedipus at Colonus*, in Fagles, *Sophocles*, l. 929.

17. The second shepherd, foreseeing the *catastrophe* to come, had "touched the queen's hand"—a very intimate gesture—pleading to be given a different job.

18. Meltzer's concept of the "toilet breast": see *The Psychoanalytical Process* (Strath Tay: Clunie Press, 1967).

19. Sophocles himself had been awarded this type of honour, not for his plays but for his military achievements; see B. Knox, introduction to *Oedipus at Colonus*, in Fagles, *Sophocles*, pp. 257–58.

CHAPTER SIX

The weavings of Athene

Then felt I like some watcher of the skies
When a new planet swims into his ken

John Keats[1]

Many heroic liars existed before the many-wiled Odysseus
was saved by his dog from everlasting night.

Wilfred Bion[2]

The thought-wanderings of Oedipus in his search to know himself—to find the symbol of his identity—had their literary origin three hundred years earlier in the story of the homecoming of Odysseus, sung in the "shadowy halls" of the Achaean kings by the blind bard known as Homer, and his followers. This "song for our time" emerged at the crucial, fluid point in history when the rhetorical patterning and acute audience-sensitivity associated with the oral tradition was enhanced, rather than replaced by, the new potential of the

---

An earlier version of this chapter was published as "Conversations with Internal Objects: Family and Narrative Structure in Homer's *Odyssey*", *British Journal of Psychotherapy*, 20(2), 2003.

written word to fix and hold meaning. It was also the historical beginning of the sea-empire, the civilization marked out by the criss-crossings of Poseidon's ships, as celebrated in the swansong of *Oedipus at Colonus*. The actual poem of Homer's *Odyssey*, as distinct from the legend that circulated during the medieval period, had a profound influence on Milton and other English poets following its rediscovery in the early Renaissance.[3] It is the sensuous reality of the poem, not the paraphraseable sequence of events, that embodies the "weavings of Athene", the poet's Muse. The poem is an extraordinarily complex narrative structure of flashbacks and enfoldings.[4] These relate, on one level, a straightforward adventure story; on another level, making use of the emotional juxtapositions suggested by the structure, they convey an internal network of family conversations taking place through the mediation of Athene. The main protagonists in this narrative web are Odysseus and his wife and son, though other household characters are also included. Eventually it results not only in Odysseus regaining his earthly home, but in the remaking of his troubled marriage and the maturing of his son, symbolizing the new mentality of the king of Ithaca.

Like Oedipus, Odysseus is a "man of pain" or "trouble", and this is written into his name, branding his identity like the scar on his thigh or the one on Oedipus' ankles, the mark of his passionate identity and capacity for suffering.[5] He is a man of "many twists and turns" (*polymetis, polytropos* being his standard epithets), in the sense of a master storyteller as well as an addicted wanderer. He weaves his way over the sea, borne by its waves and currents, for years on end, unwillingly fighting, lying, and philandering; while Penelope, at the same time yet apart from him, weaves and unweaves her "shroud" for Laertes, Odysseus' father—by implication, for Odysseus himself. Meanwhile Athene, who is also a tale-spinner and goddess of weaving, concentrates on trying to weave husband and wife together into regaining a marriage of *homophrosyne* [like-mindedness].[6] This is the glory of the home [*oikos*] as distinct from the glory of battle [*kleos*] that was celebrated in the *Iliad*, the focal symbol of which was the marriage with death at the moment of utmost heroism.[7] With the power of Zeus behind her, Athene comes close to the internal "combined object" of Kleinian theory; she investigates the human necessities and does the groundwork, enabled by Zeus' support.[8] Odysseus is known, by tradition, to be a favourite of Athene; she stood by him for ten years during the siege of Troy and planted the stratagem of the wooden horse in his mind, clever yet ruthless. It is recognized that, whether or not the same poet was responsible for both epics, they have different "gods"—not in name, but in quality.[9] The gods of the first epic are appropriate to a story of siege [*nous*], while the gods of the second epic facilitate an intimate tale of homecoming or return [*nostos*]. The relationship with Athene in the *Odyssey* is humorous, affectionate; it operates by making links with other family members rather than by instructions; and it is evolutionary—her presence or absence responding to Odysseus' state of mind. The *Odyssey* tells the story of how Odysseus regains contact with his Muse after a period of nine years' shipwreck and wandering, during which (as he complains in Book 13) she had never appeared or advised him. They are the years in which he had been subject to the wrath of Poseidon, the sea-god and "earthshaker", as punishment for putting out the eye of his son, Polyphemos the Cyclops, on his voyage home after the sack of Troy.

The epic begins with a Freudian-style division between civilized or intellectual gods and instinctual ones, like that in Aeschylus' *Oresteia*, with Odysseus persecuted by his own Poseidonesque passions, hounded over the sea between one type of female monster and another—for Odysseus' "adventures" involve predominantly female adversaries; even the Cyclops has feminine traits. During the opening council of the gods, Athene takes the opportunity of Poseidon's temporary absence from Olympus to discuss how to effect Odysseus' return to civilization, since at the moment he seems stranded beyond its reach. For the past seven years he has been held prisoner on an island at the edge of the Western world by the possessive and immortal nymph Kalypso, whose name means "engulfing, concealing". Her cave-care had initially saved him from the sea but has now become emasculating.[10] At the same time, Penelope is likewise entombed in her inner chambers on Ithaca, in a frozen depression; her marriage has not been happy since Odysseus went away to "see Troy" (which she terms *kakoilion*: bad-Troy)—a venture of pointless curiosity, in her view, an emotional black hole. She has surrounded herself with suitors, a crowd of parasitic adolescent children, who flaunt their sexuality but in an essentially impotent way and fail to fulfil her need.

It is their son, Telemachos, whose desire for change on the threshold of manhood instigates Athene's process of revivifying the marriage of Odysseus and Penelope. At this point, back on Ithaca, he is lounging at home among the suitors, in passive collusion with their scavenging and extravagant ways, such that everyone looks on him (aged nearly 20) as still a boy. He feels engulfed by the gang of suitors, just as Odysseus feels engulfed by the Kalypso–claustrum. And Penelope also, in Odysseus' absence, seems to collude with this—overprotecting her son in a way corresponding to Kalypso's cave. Now, however, Telemachos shows an inner need to grow up and make contact with an inner model of a father. The possibility of "finding" Odysseus becomes real for the first time, as Telemachos' need is reciprocated by his sudden awareness of Athene's presence in the house. He sits,

> a boy, daydreaming. What if his great father
> came from the unknown world and drove these men
> like dead leaves through the place, recovering
> honour and lordship in his own domains?
> Then he who dreamed in the crowd gazed out at Athene.[11]

Athene is visiting the house as a stranger in disguise, yet Telemachos unconsciously recognizes her, noticing this stranger who seems to have arrived in response to his daydream. He "gazes out", just as his father, at that point in time, is sitting on a rock gazing seawards at the tip of Kalypso's island. Indeed his simile of the "dead leaves" echoes Odysseus' first night on Phaeacia, when Athene showers sleep over him in his bed of leaves to keep his smouldering spark of vitality alive for the next day's work (VI.486–93). The smotherings of the Claustrum are about to be thrown off, revealing the fiery spark of developmental potential. "Ah, bitterly you need Odysseus then!" exclaims Athene to Telemachos. His own spark of discontent is what marks him out from the other suitor–children as being Odysseus and Penelope's "true son" (as Athene puts it); he is ready to emerge from his chrysalis. Yet he has no internal image of his father—he was a baby when Odysseus left for Troy. He explains to his new visitor that, though his mother says he is Odysseus' son, it does not mean much to him—he knows nothing of his own engendering (I.216). This is one of several indications of his suspicion of his mother's sexuality. Athene, who is generally disguised as "Mentor" or "Mentes" ["thinker"], puts the seeds of thought into his mind, and he thanks her for the "fatherly" advice for which he hungered—or, more precisely, for the "father to son" feeling she has given him. When she disappears, Telemachos recognizes that a god has been his guest; he has been inspired and set on a new course:

> And all night long, wrapped in the finest fleece,
> he took in thought the course Athene gave him. [I.437–44]

Tenderly he is put to bed like a child by the old nurse Eurykleia, epitomized by the detail of how she catches his carelessly thrown tunic, smoothes and folds it, and hangs it on a bar beside his bed.

Athene thus reinforces the "nursing" aspect of his mother; her dreams enfold him like the "finest fleece", "all night long". It is the starting point for his sexual inquiry.

The first long lyrical passage in the epic describes the ship that carries Telemachos on his voyage of discovery, borne by Athene's inspiring wind:

> Grey-eyed Athene stirred them a following wind,
> soughing from the north-west on the winedark sea,
> and as he felt the wind, Telemachos
> called to all hands to break out mast and sail . . .
> until the wind caught, booming in the sail;
> and a flushing wave sang backward from the bow
> on either side, as the ship got way upon her,
> holding her steady course. . . .
> And the prow sheared through the night into the dawn. [ii.418–28]

The exhilaration of the sailing, with its sense of being moved by a higher power, is echoed by the description of Odysseus' final sea-voyage (XIII.84–93), as he is carried home asleep by the Phaeacian sailors, likewise on wings of thought. The Phaeacian ships cross the seas "like a flashing thought" (VII.35) and have no need of steersmen or steering oars, for the vessels know their way instinctively and un-erringly (VIII.558–64). Odysseus' emergence from his depression on Kalypso's isle takes place contemporaneously with Telemachos' emer-gence from the claustrum of the group. For the first time he "feels the wind". Athene gives the inexperienced Telemachos the practical help he needs: outfitting his ship and gathering a crew for him, consisting of a more suitable group of friends (II.382–412). Odysseus, on the other hand, is quite capable of escaping from Kalypso by building a raft with his own hands; what was lacking, in his case, was the inspiration, the message from the gods (V.35). Now he too feels the wind. Both sea-voyages are part of the same mental movement, unknown to each other, yet orchestrated by Athene. The fact that they happen at the same period (in terms of the story) yet are placed far apart in the narrative (one in Book IV, the other in Book XIII) is characteristic of the telescopic timing of the narrative, which evokes mental or dream-events, layered by the Athene–Muse to enrich their significance.

The first four books of the *Odyssey* in fact comprise the *Telemachy*— the story of Telemachos' quest for an internal image of his father. In story-time they cover the week or two of his preparation for the sea-voyage and his brief sojourn in Pylos and Sparta at the homes of his father's old work-colleagues, Nestor and Menelaos. In mental time this comprises his schooldays and his initiation into the adult world—speaking out at home, speaking in assembly, speaking as his own ambassador to the mainland kings. When Telemachos rejoins the suitors in the hall at home, they are surprised to find that he has grown up, despite their plots to "kill" this unwelcome example: he has discovered his father. For Odysseus has, like Athene, materialized on Ithacan soil in response to his need—in particular to the clearer idea taught by his travels of what he wants in a father. During the meeting with Nestor—like Odysseus, a famous orator—he learns not to speak like Nestor who, in his old age, has become garrulous and superfluous. Initially he was worried about his lack of training in rhetorical speech (by implication, Odysseus' failure to formally educate him). But Athene (disguised as Mentor) advises him to rely on his "heart and reason" for clarity of communication, together with any inspiring aid from a spirit (III.28). Telemachos wants an internal father who can speak meaningfully, who can discard the rubbishy rhetoric of political persuasion that prevailed during the siege of Troy.

The visit to Menelaos of Sparta is even closer to the bone, since it concerns the nature of the marriage for which the war was fought in the first place—the mental orientation that underlies his father's prolonged "absence". Menelaos, like Nestor, claims that he and Odysseus were intimate friends, alike in feeling and desire. If only Odysseus returned, he says, he would clear out one of his own rich towns in Argos and install Odysseus there, so that they could banquet and reminisce continuously about the war at Troy—the good old days (IV.176–80). Clearly, Menelaos has no conception of Odysseus' longing for home; his idea of Odysseus is a nostalgic projection. His detachment from reality is emphasized when he offers to give Telemachos gifts of horses; Telemachos has to remind him that rocky Ithaca is an unsuitable land for horses. Menelaos' nostalgia is complemented by Helen putting an anodyne—an anti-Odysseus—into the wine, "mild magic of forgetfulness" that (in a familiar pattern) will banish all pain associated with losing a family (IV.221). Their attempt to make a protégé of Telemachos reflects their colonizing attitude to Odysseus, which has been elaborated into a post-war fiction, generated by their own marital disharmony. They each have a tale to tell about Odysseus, vying with one another, as it were, in their assertion of intimacy. Helen describes how she alone "knew him" when, during the siege of Troy, Odysseus entered the city disguised as a beggar; she bathed and anointed him; he was naked in her hands, literally and metaphorically, though, as she proudly points out, she did not betray him to the Trojans (IV.252). His father, she demonstrates to Telemachos, was not impervious to her charms. "An excellent tale, my dear, and most becoming", comments Menelaos (IV.271). In retaliation, he tells how Helen, with yet another lover (Deiphobus) in tow, tried to lure the Achaeans out of the wooden horse to their destruction by calling to them (Siren-like) in the voices of their wives. One was on the point of replying, but Odysseus saved them by clamping his hands over his jaws. Helen may have taken possession of his body, implies Menelaos, but not of his wits.

Telemachos thus learns the kind of temptation that has divided his parents and alienated his father from home. He has had a glimpse of the "dread goddess" of his father's adventures in the world of phantasy, with the associated temptation that recurs in various form of seeking forgetfulness, becoming "nobody",[12] succumbing to the overwhelming effect of glory or beauty. Its relevance is emphasized by the family ties—the brothers Agamemnon and Menelaos, married to sisters Clytemnestra and Helen, cousins to his mother Penelope. The three queens encompass "womanhood" between them, and Penelope's enigmatic quality stems from the possibility of containing elements of her cousins: she is not a straightforward contrast to them. Telemachos, in hearing from Menelaos the history of Agamemnon's return, to be murdered by his wife, learns also how the nature of the woman's pull dominates the "homecoming" [nostos] of the man. This story also presents him with a model of the "heroic son" in the form of Orestes—a model that, he says, he hopes to live up to. Helen and Menelaos, however, exemplify the kind of marriage that will not restore the health of the oikos on Ithaca. They belong to the old heroic world and, because of Helen's semi-divine origin, they are destined—or condemned—to an eternal Elysium in one another's company.[13] Politely Telemachos compliments the King and Queen on their "marvellous tales", saying: "I could never be homesick here" (IV.597). But we know the dangers of not feeling homesick, of the anodyne they offer. His characteristic epithet is "clearheaded", but here is a place that befuddles values and desires. Telemachos sees instinctively (with the help of Athene in a waking dream) that he must get out of Sparta as soon as possible. His business is not here, but in Ithaca. Now he knows the direction of his quest for manhood.

Telemachos has learned that neither the melancholic Menelaos, entrammelled by his prize of Beauty, nor the pious Nestor is his "father". But in fact, when he does encounter his father, he discovers that changes need to be made to that model also. It is not simply—as he complains—that he is not given the opportunity for an heroic, single-handed feat of revenge like Orestes; rather, the roles and requirements are different. A "dead" father requires a simple type of revenge, and Telemachos and others—including Penelope—often say how much easier things would be if Odysseus' death were a known fact: he could be revenged, canonized, and replaced, all at once. The problem with Odysseus is that he is not dead but out of communication. The protagonists cannot reopen the lines of communication by themselves: that can only be done by Athene the master-weaver, serving each of them individually and putting their internal objects in touch with one another. At the beginning of the epic, the poet, conscious of this fact, had invoked his Muse in an untraditional manner, asking her to begin the story not at any particular point, but wherever she chose:

> Launch out on his story, Muse, daughter of Zeus,
> start from where you will—sing for our time, too.[14]

Athene-as-Muse then enters in to the oral-formulaic woof of the epic fabric and uses her freedom to interdigitate the stories of Odysseus and Telemachos, with their traditional patterning. She weaves them together into an internal story of mental evolution: a "song to generations", as Milton expressed it, a song "for our time", whenever that may be. This can only happen when the Muse *constructs* the poem.

Telemachos having put out a feeler in the direction of his father and demonstrated his commitment, Athene now turns to the situation of Odysseus himself, in order to forge the reciprocal link. While Telemachos was seeking information (really ideas) about his father, Odysseus, having escaped from Kalypso in his home-made raft, has been recounting the story of his adventures to the Phaeacians. The two processes are not just simultaneous in story-time, but parallel in significance. For again, this is not merely a narrative of facts, but a process of digesting his experiences so that they can exist as dreams rather than taking the form of action (somatic persecution). This is where Odysseus tells of the Cyclops, Circe, the Lotus-eaters, the Sirens, and Aeolus, whose bag of winds is a failed attempt at the type of journey that the Phaeacians themselves can offer, on "wings of thought". The various episodes suggest the underlying principles of his flawed relation with the world-as-woman, when under the dominance of Poseidon unmitigated by Athene. Broadly, they image a gradual progression from the deeply primitive realms of machismo, beginning with the Trojan-war "wooden-horse" mentality of intrusive penetration. Odysseus recounts in a matter-of-fact way how the first thing he did after setting out from Troy was to attack the peaceful city of Ismarus, slaying the men and enslaving the women. This would have been standard behaviour of its era, and therefore not worthy of particular condemnation. However, the Muse has been given the task of structuring Homer's epic and presents us with a different view. A few lines later, Odysseus is himself vividly described as weeping "like a wife mourning for her lord", killed in battle fighting to defend his children, and she "feels the spears, prodding her back and shoulders" as she is led into slavery (VIII.531). The juxtaposition of the two passages enables us, without any authorial comment, to gauge the improvement in Odysseus' emotional aware-ness (feminine identification) over the period of his sea-story. After the sack of Troy–Ismarus, Odysseus enters his nightmare phantasy world—Troy's revenge. He encounters Polyphemos the Cyclops, son of Poseidon, described as "a shaggy mountain reared in solitude"—a Romantic mountain-man who milks and tends the flock within his cave-body. Odysseus' intrusive curiosity and greed for spoils results in his homecoming being delayed by nine years. His verbal poking (like the stake in the Cyclops' eye) is a delusory triumph, since calling himself "Nobody" merely accentuates the loss of his internal family. The hero of the wooden horse, who escapes from the Cyclops' cave by the belly of the ram, appears "small, pitiful and twiggy" in the view of this part-feminine giant, and it is Cyclopean "rough justice" to find Odysseus repeatedly, after this, clinging to a mast or spar stripped of the appurtenances of civilization—ships, men, clothing, etc.

The key figure in Books 10–12, the mid-point of the epic, is Circe, the sensual fairy-like enchantress. The cold sensuality is indicated by the way the relationship is conducted, by means of magic wands and swords, or drugs and antidotes. Odysseus does not enter her "danger-ous bed" from lust, or even from coercion. Rather, he negotiates, until she swears a binding oath that will establish a power balance between them, a type of perverse marriage vow: then, "being a man, I could not help consenting". So long as he is sure of not appearing a pig, he has no qualms about wallowing in the bed indefinitely, while his crew "bump and bawl" around their captain "like calves in tumult". Eventually they demand to go home—"shake off this trance!" We begin to see the origin of the children–suitors wallowing in the sty of the great hall. Circe, however, when she accepts his wish to move on, opens a win-dow for him on the world of "the dead"—the state of those who can no longer grow and develop; she informs him that he cannot set out for home without first visiting Hades and learning its lessons. There his attention is immediately seized by the piteous youth Elpenor ["hope"] who died by mistake in Circe's house. Elpenor requires his burial-rites, and Odysseus returns to Circe's isle to fulfil them, such that the spirit of hope may still continue for him on earth. He also sees his mother, Antikleia ["against-fame"], who has faded away in his absence; and Agamemnon, who tells him "the day of faithful wives is gone forever" and so awakens doubts about his own marriage. His meeting with Achilles, who dispels his "smooth talk" about the value of undying glory, helps him to survive the Sirens' song of Iliadic seduction, which lures him to stay and listen forever to his own praises: their flowery meadow offers, on closer inspection, nothing but a dried-up heap of bones. His crew, he knew, would not be able to resist this temptation, even "tied to the mast". Indeed, even before the loss of his last ship, Odysseus, owing to his increasing knowledge, has become separated in spirit from his crew. While his desire to return home strengthens, theirs is waylaid by the "belly"—imaged in their delinquent slaughter of the cattle of the Sun, mimicking the suitors' depradations in the hall. "I am alone, outmatched", he says to Eurylochos, his second-in-command, who accuses him of being made of iron. They are not sufficiently iron-hearted. (Later, Odysseus, Eurykleia, and Penelope are all described as having "iron" in their make-up.) Alone, Odysseus is swept back past Scylla and Charybdis, clinging to twigs, and comes to Kalypso's isle.

It is made clear that his final passage home, in one of the magical Phaeacian thought-ships, depends on the quality of his story-telling. If he does not capture their hearts, he will have to remain there forever, a victim of his own narcissism (figured in the false romance with the young princess Nausicaa—which needs to be, and is, gradually relinquished as a lie). Odysseus' hardest test so far is to transform his proverbial wiliness and lying trickery into a tale that contains the truth of his emotional experience—in other words, a work of art. He has to become a bard, like the poet who is at that moment singing his story, and tell it "as a poet would" (XII.370). During the central books of the epic, there is a story-within-a-story-within-a-story that must hold its audience (like the Phaeacians) "spellbound in the shadowy hall" (XIII.2). If it does not, the bard may suffer a fate worse than death: not only will he lose his supper and his lodging, but he may be trampled like Orpheus among the debris (as nearly happens to Phemius at the end of the epic). It is his daily task to put his listeners in touch with their dreams—a task of humble status (unlike that of the war heroes) but as vital as bread, wine, and shelter. Athene, having rescued

Odysseus' body from somatic pain (drowning), now sets about making him suffer—the process of apparent humiliation that will culminate in his becoming the beggar in his own hall. The Phaeacians are relatives of the gods, and of the Cyclops. Alcinoos, the Phaeacian king, is described as one who "knows thoughts from the gods, intuitions"; and his judgement is: "You speak with art, but your intent is honest" (XI.369). He and his queen, Arete (to whom Odysseus—instructed by Nausicaa—makes his first appeal) function together as a receiver for the transference of Odysseus' dream-story; and eventually this transference status must be relinquished (internalized) lest it become a claustrum in itself.

Odysseus manages to achieve this poetic orientation because he has finally, after nine years, renewed contact with Athene. He prays to her for the first time since the war when he is shipwrecked on the Phaeacian coast—"and Pallas Athene heard him" (VI.331). At this point, in story-time, Athene sends a dream to Penelope (in the form of her sister) to reassure her that her "little one" (Telemachos) will escape the sea-ambush of the suitors and return safely to Ithaca. At the same time she prompts Nausicaa in a dream to go to the river to wash clothes in preparation for her wedding. The encounter with Nausicaa becomes Odysseus' re-living of Penelope as a girl-bride, before she earned the epithet "wise" as a result of her experience. In the throes of Poseidon's last storm as he approaches the island of Phaeacia (or Scheria), Odysseus throws off the heavy drowning weight of Kalypso's cloak and accepts instead the light veil of the sea nymph Ino, heralding the arrival of Nausicaa and her washing (the veil of her virginity, to which she is preparing to say farewell). This life-preserving veil enables him to swim back away from the flesh-tearing rocks and to discover the pull of the river-mouth just at the moment of the turning tide, sucking him gently onto the beach. The virginal associations of this vaginal pull exorcize the death-trap of Scylla with her voracious mouths and the lethal vortex of the whirlpool Charybdis. Nausicaa–Penelope, looking forward to marriage, is the only one of the group of girls not to shrink from the vision of Odysseus' lust, as he emerges from Athene's bed of leaves. Like a hungry lion prowling round the homestead "with burning eyes", his "rough skin ... streaked with brine, and swollen, he terrified them", despite the olive-branch he clutches (VI.139). His appearance avows the "hunger" of his sea-streaked Poseidonesque depths—the "hungry belly" of which he will frequently speak when he is a beggar. The next time Odysseus is described as a "mountain lion" is after the battle with the suitors, when they have, indeed, become a heap of dead leaves. At the same moment, in story-time, Telemachos himself is feeling "lion-hearted" after foiling the suitors' plot to assassinate him.

It is Nausicaa who elicits from Odysseus his vision of a happy marriage—one of *homophrosyne,* a marriage of true minds (VI.181). Yet this very definition makes it clear why marriage with Nausicaa would be a lie. Penelope is no longer young and idealizing; she, like Odysseus, has years of weaving-and-unweaving behind her. She herself feels "like a cornered lion" when imagining the suitors' trap closing on Telemachos, until soothed by Athene's dream. When Odysseus left Kalypso, he explained, as tactfully as possible, that he would prefer a Penelope, though she must grow old. For the same reason he must leave Phaeacia: it is an idealized world, whose sumptuous art and craftsmanship is mirrored in the country's eternal fruitfulness. It reflects meaning but cannot be lived in—staying forever constitutes a narcissistic delusion. The spirit of the place is embodied in the "undying dogs that never could grow old" that stand at the doors of the king's palace (VII.95), in contrast to Odysseus' own dog Argos, who holds death at bay at the threshold of his house until he is released from his vigil by his master's return (XVII.290). Where there is no power to die, there can be no faithfulness. Argos guards the threshold where Odysseus will test his own faith and discover Penelope's. Ultimately Phaeacia itself becomes a work of art, for men to "marvel at" in times to come—when the sailors' ship is turned into a rock, in mid-oarstroke, and their city ringed with mountains by Poseidon. It is the archetypal Grecian Urn, embodying a message that will speak to those who want to know. As such, it contrasts with the floating wind-island of Aeolus that was intolerant of Odysseus' inner turbulence—its bag of winds like the "bottomless bag of tricks" Athene tells Odysseus he is himself (XIII.290). The meaning of the Phaeacian dream will be anchored to the seabed for ever by the storm-god's stroke. And Nausicaa's last words to Odysseus, as she stands by a pillar (in the posture often associated with Penelope), looking at him with "wonder", are:

> Farewell, stranger; in your land remember me,
> who met and saved you. It is worth your thought. [VIII.461–62]

Odysseus promises to remember her "as a goddess"—an idea. At about the same time, in Sparta, Telemachos bids farewell to Helen with the same words, while she gives him clothing for his future wife, fine fabric woven by her own hands, to be kept in his mother's room until

that time (XV.179). Telemachos' eyes are now awakened to that possibility. The sting is drawn from Helen's archetypal beauty when it
becomes a symbol mediated by his mother, an idea in the mind of the
beholder. For both Odysseus and his son, this is the end of the false
romance of Elysium; the adventurer's fear and desire to be swallowed-
up by art and beauty is readjusted to make room for contemplation.
The Cave-dweller returns to the Cave.

The dream-world is superseded only when Odysseus awakes on
Ithaca in Book XIII. The Phaeacians have deposited him in an out-of-
the-way cove sacred to an ancient sea-god (a relative of Polyphemos)
and filled with features suggestive of Odysseus' phantasy world: stone
looms, separate entrances for mortals and immortals. We might imagine he has been sleeping here all the time. Athene wraps the island in
mist (prolonging the moment between sleeping and waking) and for
the first time has a direct conversation with him, unique in its affectionate intimate quality. She teases him about his own disorientation and
its relation to his identity (echoing Odysseus' language to the Cyclops
at IX.252) and confirms the identification between herself and him—
"contrivers both". This is where she terms him a "bottomless bag of
tricks", a "chameleon". We now know that there are many varieties of
"trickiness", many types of acting and disguise; and the forthcoming
battle to win his own home will be more tricky than any of the battles
at Troy. Athene promises that, provided he has faith in her, she will
help him to achieve the impossible: namely, the killing of the suitors
without recrimination, and the regaining of Penelope. "Weave me a
way", says Odysseus. In this conversation there is one point of conflict,
one quarrel, and it concerns Telemachos. Odysseus is angry that
Athene has sent him off to sea on a wild-goose chase to find his father,
at the very moment that his father has come home. Why does she play
tricks with him, too, rather than simply telling him the truth? Athene
points out that this is no casual trickery, but necessary for Telemachos'
experience; he needs to make his own voyage of discovery (XIII.421). It
is not enough simply to tell Telemachos that his father is coming home,
just as it is not enough simply to tell Odysseus that his wife is faithful.
Domestic *kleos* has to be won, not just stated. From this point the
Odyssey and the Telemachy interdigitate. Their parallel mental quest
takes the form of a united action of "revenge" against the forces that
have been paralysing the household.

The first step in this quest entails that Odysseus establish himself
organically as a presence within the household—not as an authority,
but as a suppliant, who is at the same time a Socratean "pest" goading

the suitors—a position in some ways equivalent to a king's fool, his trouble-making protected by Zeus's dictates about hospitality. Before entering his own home, he is told by Athene to go and live with Eumaeus the swineherd, disguised as a beggar. This disguise is not a trick in the old omnipotent Odyssean sense; instead, it is a necessary viewpoint, a means of learning on the pulses. Indeed, his old trickery is metaphorically stripped from him at the start, when he approaches the house of Eumaeus and is almost torn to pieces by the dogs, despite applying his "beggar's trick" of dropping his stick and sitting on the ground (XIV.31). His trick does not save him—he is saved only by Eumaeus' intervention. Living with his swineherd, depending on his unpretentious hospitality, is a step in Odysseus' remaking his identity. A genuine intimacy develops between the two men. It is confirmed by the return of Telemachos, who has been summoned home urgently by Athene in a dream. Telemachos beaches his ship during the long autumn night while the older men stay awake talking, then heads directly across country to the swineherd's stockade, reaching it by first light.

> But there were two men in the mountain hut—
> Odysseus and the swineherd.

These are the opening lines of Book XVI, indicating Telemachos' new understanding that he has two fathers. He is at home in the swineherd's hut (as shown by the dogs—the spirits of the place—fawning on him). By now Odysseus is also at home, helping to cook breakfast and send out the lads with the pigs. Eumaeus speaks in a sense for Odysseus when he greets Telemachos joyfully like a long-lost son. "I am with you, uncle", says Telemachos simply (XVI.34). He comes to knowledge of Odysseus in the first instance as a friend of his swineherd-father. This is Athene's way of introducing father and son, gradually, by indirections (unconscious links) that have an emotional reality—indeed, necessity. Gradually the web of internal conversation expands.

Even so, when Athene arranges for father and son to be left alone, revealing Odysseus' identity, there is not a simple reunion but an emotional crisis, taking into account Odysseus' guilt, Telemachos' fear and anger. Telemachos resists the recognition until Odysseus acknowledges his failings as a father, insisting he is not a god, and that, for better or worse, he is the only Odysseus Telemachos will ever know:

> "I am that father whom your boyhood lacked
> and suffered pain for lack of. I am he." [XVI.76–77][15]

At the same time he rebukes Telemachos for his dismay—it is "not princely" to recoil from his father just because Athene has changed his appearance from beggar to godlike king; he should not be so confused by a mere "change of skin" but focus on the identity beneath the surface (XVI.202–15). His appearance may fluctuate at the will of the gods, according to infusion by internal objects; in fact, he is neither a god nor a dog but a father. Telemachos must learn to accommodate these fluctuations within the new image of a father that he is construct-ing if he is to play his part in the battle with the suitors (the forces of degradation). He needs to stand his ground when assailed by internal aesthetic conflicts and tensions—this is something only Odysseus the king, not Eumaeus the swineherd, can teach him.[16] Thus Telemachos, unlike the simpler characters, instinctively resists the recognition of Odysseus, until he finds an internal congruence.

The process in which Penelope comes to recognition is complex and long drawn-out; it necessitates a network of internal dialogue between herself and Odysseus—or, rather, via their internal objects. Books XVII–XX are flooded with portents and signs of Odysseus' presence. Unlike the suitors, who are deaf to their significance, Penelope has ears to hear what is going on in the hall below her. As readers have pointed out, the poet suggests in various ways how she unconsciously recog-nizes him from the moment of his appearance as the beggar in the hall.[17] The drama lies not in the mere fact of recognizing, but in the meaning of the recognition—what does it mean that Odysseus has come back, and who is Odysseus anyway, twenty years on? "Or did I dream him?" she asks herself (XIX.317) when she calls Eurykleia to come and "bathe—bathe your master, I almost said" (XIX.358). Mean-while her public movements and announcements seem intended for the attention of Odysseus more than the suitors—in particular the time when she is prompted by Athene to relate how Odysseus "enfolded her hand and wrist" the day he left for Troy and advised her to wait for the beard to grow on Telemachos' cheek before she should remarry (XVIII.260). She needs to demonstrate her predicament, but also to gauge his commitment to the marriage: she does not want another "bitter marriage", "deprived of the sweets of life" (XVIII.261). Tracing the lines of this implicit or unspoken conversation, we may also guess at her own degree of responsibility—her ambivalent encouragement of the suitors' parasitic mentality—especially in the dream of the geese, where she seems at first reluctant to accept that this mentality (embod-ied in the suitors themselves) must be destroyed in order for a fresh start to be made.[18] Like Antigone in *Oedipus*, she wishes there were a

way of retaining the Polynices element at the same time as transcending it.

Penelope's inspired plan for the contest of the axes (formulated in
Book XIX) appears to be the result of two dreams: the dream of the
geese, which she relates or possibly dreams up spontaneously for
Odysseus, and the dreamlike situation in which she sits back in the
shadows, "bemused" by Athene, while Odysseus has his feet washed
by his old nurse Eurykleia in the famous episode of the revelation of
the scar on his leg. The action of the narrative is frozen in mid-move-
ment, and there is a long film-like flashback to Odysseus' childhood,[19]
from the moment Eurykleia held him as a newborn baby (as she is at
that moment holding his leg, bending over the bath) to the initiation
ceremony of the boar-hunt when the leg receives its wound of identity,
a non-erasable core of personality that will underlie all the transformations and disguises of Odysseus' tales and travels. When his thigh was
gored, Odysseus became irrevocably Odysseus, man of pain and trouble, encountering his own Poseidonesque traits in the form of the boar
and fulfilling the name given by his grandfather when he was a baby—
the primitive ancestor of his own cunning and trickery.[20] Eurykleia
recognizes him, not so much through sight—which is uncertain—as
through feel, her fingers tracing the indentation of the scar:

> *You are Odysseus!* Ah, dear child—I could not
> see you until now—not till I knew
> my master's very body with my hands! [XIX.474–76]

Odysseus' reaction is explosive (he seizes her by the throat), striking
deep and primitive chords—associated with the powerful women of
his sea-adventures, including Helen of Troy, when she also bathed him
at a dangerous moment within enemy territory—that time, preparing
for a conquest of intrusion. Odysseus is sometimes criticized for a
failure of forethought at this point; he is caught off his guard in a way
that could have been fatal to his plan. Indeed, he sees the danger
coming and turns his body into the shadows—but shadows are irrel-
evant to the sense of touch. The fact is, this type of primitive and
sensuous recognition is necessary to Odysseus' discovery of his own
identity and relation to his internal objects; in a sense he unconsciously
engineers it when he asks for some faithful old servant to wash his feet,
"old and wise"—none of the brash young maids. The reunion with
Eurykleia, his earth-mother, purges and realigns the primitive links
with all those chthonic goddesses, daughters of Poseidon, in a way that
is complementary to the intellectual and sophisticated relationship

with Athene. We remember how Eurykleia complemented Athene for Telemachos at the beginning, when she wrapped him in bed in the "finest fleece" so that he could digest the thoughts Athene had given him. As her name indicates, she is a more robust version of Odysseus' mother Antikleia—the mother who, like Argos, has faith in his power to return and be himself. *"You are Odysseus!"*

This struggle within Odysseus, imaged in the episode with Eurykleia, is mirrored in a quiet way by Penelope as she sits "bemused", charmed by Athene so that she notices nothing of the drama over the bathtub (XIX.479). Instead, everything sinks in unconsciously—"My heart within me stirs, mindful of something" (XIX.375). When it is over, she relates to Odysseus her dream about her pet geese being killed and compares herself to Pandareos' daughter, who sang like the nightingale about the child she killed in her madness. Part of her mourning is for the suitors, the naughty children who seem incapable of learning, whom she would like to remain forever children (the Phaeacia temptation). The meaning of the dream is evident, yet she wants to have it confirmed by Odysseus himself. "My dear, how can you choose to read the dream differently?" says the beggar to the queen. On Odysseus' part, he needs her approval and support before risking his life in purging the house of the suitors. Their tacit agreement on this, in their private conversation this night before the battle, is really a consensus of internal objects. It happens because the queen finds she can confide in the beggar, whoever he may be, about her intimate problems; their objects have a language in common. He reminds her of the "close-fitting tunic, like dry onion skin", which she had put on him with her own hands before he sailed for Troy, clasped by a brooch bearing the motif of a hunting-dog seizing a deer in agony (the "lover's pinch", in Cleopatra's words). Through this lying-but-true tale about himself and the pain he has caused, the beggar relieves the queen's frozen anguish, so she weeps like snow melting, though he weeps only inwardly, retaining eyes of "horn or iron" (XIX.204–17). After her weepy, nostalgic mood has ended, Penelope speaks to Odysseus with a new determination. Mirroring the cooperation between Athene and Zeus, it is she who conceives the initiation of the action; Odysseus is the instrument. In short, incisive phrases she says that she will marry the man who can string the bow and shoot through the axes, "whoever he may be" (XIX.68–79). She will take the bow out of its inner sanctum (a cave-room in the house), guarded and concealed by her in a way that reflects its sexual significance. It is not an instrument for warfare but for "hunting", an essentially domestic activity. Its disuse has found a parallel in the way her own loom weaves fabric in the day that is unravelled during the night, finding no aesthetic reciprocity—no body to enwrap. The "shroud" is the work of Penelope-as-Kalypso, with her drowning "cloak". But Penelope has now "remembered" the onion-skin penis, with its configuration of deer and hunting-dog. This memory is in itself a reciprocation of the emotionality aroused in Odysseus by seeing Argos on the threshold. Just as Odysseus threw off Kalypso's cloak in order to reach Phaeacia and renew his courtship, so now Penelope decides to take a chance on the bow and bring it out of concealment, in a direct challenge to the beggar to prove his identity, to become the Odysseus of her imagination. It is not a plot in the usual sense—certainly not a mechanical plot in the sense interpreted later on by the suitors in their complaint to Agamemnon after death, in the halls of Hades, saying that Odysseus used his deceitful queen as bait (XXIV.167). They have no conception of *homophrosyne*, of the male-female relationship as a fitting-together not simply of body-shapes but of minds.

Odysseus has no plan, because no plan is possible; it is not possible for one to fight one hundred—"not even a hero could", as Telemachos said to the beggar in XVI.89. While Odysseus turns on his bed like a sausage on a spit, trying to conceive a battle-plan for the next day, Athene teases him for his lack of faith in her; she can inspire victory whatever the odds (XX.46). The situation is the reverse of the wooden horse, when he was the master-schemer who designed the sack of Troy. Here, his victory depends on the emotional cooperation of the family within—Penelope, Telemachos, Eurykleia, the swineherd and cowherd. Until they place the bow in his hands, he is helpless; and the emotional tension of this procedure is analogous to the muscular power entailed in stringing and loosing the bow itself. Antinoos, chief suitor and false son, says he remembers from childhood how Odysseus used the bow—"I can see him even now" (XXI.95). Yet Telemachos (whose name means "Far-fighter"), without claiming this literal memory, astonishes everyone by knowing precisely how to set up the axes for the contest and is the only one who from sheer determination comes near to stringing the bow ("he meant to string that bow . . .") and has to be stopped by a warning sign from his father (XXI.126–29). On the level of the plot, he must not interfere with Odysseus' use of the bow. But in the internal story, Telemachos' drawing-back at this point expresses his awareness that what he needs to grow up is not a spirit of competition with his father but, rather, a reinstatement of his internal parents—a source of strength. Oedipal vestiges fall away as the prospect of becoming a lover appears a real possibility. He relies on identification while the other adolescents, by contrast, try heat and grease, to no avail (XXI.183). In a sense the cleansing of the house from the suitors does itself portray the emergence from adolescence into manhood, with Telemachos shaking off the debris of his old identity—the gang—like the pile of dead leaves, his chrysalis. He has found the spirit of his father, which he desires to follow—expressed by the song of the bow that replaces Odysseus' verbal facility—and sings out after his superhuman, extended silence during the shufflings in the hall:

> Like a musician, like a harper, when
> with quiet hand upon his instrument
> he draws between his thumb and forefinger
> a sweet new string upon a peg: so effortlessly
> Odysseus in one motion strung the bow.
> then slid his right hand down the cord and plucked it,
> so the taut gut vibrating hummed and sang
> a swallow's note. [XXI.405–12]

The "swallow's note" is the song of inspiration, musical–sexual, indicating the identification with Athene who, in the shape of a swallow, sits on the rafters and in spirit governs the ensuing battle in the hall. It dominates and organizes the crises of the confrontation—such as the moment when Telemachos, in childish ambivalence, leaves open the armoury door, and it appears that all might be lost, but instead it becomes an opportunity for realignment between father and son: as Telemachos clear-headedly confesses his fault while, reciprocally, Odysseus is indebted to Telemachos for preventing him from murdering the bard himself, Phemios, in his rage.

To Penelope, the battle with the suitors and the hanging of the faithless maids (the embodiment of sexual teasing) appears as much a dream as her dream about the geese. Athene ensures that she sleeps through it all, and when she comes down afterwards to view the "strange one" who has cleansed the house, she shows no curiosity about the battle itself (XXIII.84). Her attention is reserved exclusively for the problem of analysing the inner nature of the stranger—in other words, for the meaning of the battle, not its action. Even when Athene restores his appearance, Penelope is not convinced this may not be a trick—such as that which deceived Helen, the tricky side of the gods—rather than an infusion by internal objects (the gods' inspiration).

Odysseus, even if it is he, may not match the internal image of the qualities she desires in a husband. The beautifying of Odysseus is Athene's last literal action in this section; after this, she becomes internalized within Penelope herself. She is now the weaver, the poet—no longer engaged on a shroud but a marriage-bed. Penelope and Odysseus sit quietly, scrutinizing one another. They call one another "strange", and Odysseus accuses her of having a "heart of iron"—an epithet usually applied to himself (XXIII.174). He tells Telemachos to leave them alone, to let his mother test him in her own way. Again she silently muses, as she did during their previous conversation under the influence of Athene, and finally, during the split-second hesitation when she says "But all the same ..." (XXIII.180), she comes up with her ultimate inspired initiative—the test of the bed to follow the test of the bow.

Strictly speaking, neither of these is a test in the crude sense—there is no preconceived answer that will prove anything; rather, these are opportunities for revelation. Odysseus passed the test of the bow, not because he could string it, but because he remained silent until the bow was in the right position, handed to him, to "sing"; he found the "swallow's note". He passes the test of the bed not because he knows how the bed was built, having built it himself round the trunk of the olive (a mechanical fact that any deceiving god might know) but because he responds to Penelope's "breaking point", the tautness of her probing. This time it is she who is the bowman—not in the sense of conquest, but in the sense of performing a service for him, equivalent to that which he performed for her, in relieving her frozen condition. Her tension makes him let fly at last; he reveals his jealousy at the thought that another man might have moved his bed in his absence:

"Woman, by heaven you've stung me now!
Who dared to move my bed?" [XXIII.87–88]

He drops his earlier language, of the courtly beggar–suitor (when he called her "my lady", not "woman"), and becomes the fiery, impulsive Odysseus who has pain and anger in his name and who killed the boar in the thicket. He is the same man she met years before at the rivermouth when she was Nausicaa. For the first time since then, Odysseus is tested by his own passions, sprung upon him by Penelope, and finding aesthetic reciprocation. In this way she releases Odysseus from his own frozen state, his own suspicion and caution, his own heart of iron,

       and he wept at last,
his dear wife, clear and faithful, in his arms,
longed for as the sunwarmed earth is longed for by a swimmer
spent in rough water where his ship went down
under Poseidon's blows, gale winds and tons of sea.
few men can keep alive through a big surf
to crawl, clotted with brine, on kindly beaches
in joy, in joy, knowing the abyss behind:
and so she too rejoiced, her gaze upon her husband,
her white arms round him pressed as though forever. [XXIII.233–42]

At last, through this earth-and-water metaphor that gathers within it the entire journey of the poem, we see how the crossings of Poseidon have suffered a sea-change as a result of the weavings of Athene. Penelope does not "recognize" her husband until, guided by Athene-within-her, she discovers the Poseidon in him. In this revision of Odysseus' arrival on Phaeacia to meet Penelope–Nausicaa for the first time, Poseidon is no longer antagonistic but the foundation for the richness of the relationship and its capacity for endurance. It is not a Freudian–Aeschylean balance of intellect and instinct, but a Sophoclean integration achieved by "suffering" in the full aesthetic sense.

However well-rooted his olive-tree bed, there is a sense in which Odysseus will always remain a man of the sea. He has found his home, including the pears and apple-trees that were given him as saplings by his father Laertes. But he has not retired. That night he and Penelope discuss, and accept, their future trials—including his prophesied journey carrying an oar to inland countries that know nothing of the sea and assume it is a winnowing-fan. They know, or imagine, that their home will be peaceful and fruitful, and that ultimately,

      Death will drift upon me
from seaward, mild as air, mild as your hand,
in my well-tended weariness of age,
contented folk around me on our island.

But Odysseus cannot escape the mission ingrained like a scar with his name and character, to plant his sea-knowledge in areas of the mind that are still ignorant of such turbulence. The bed is immovable, like Penelope's loom or the pillar against which she stands; but the oar is a movable shadow of all these icons of his marriage. It also serves to remind him of the history of his voyage—the twigginess of his omnipotence (the mast to which he clung like a straw), the fragility of his hope (the oar which marked the grave of young Elpenor), the power of Poseidon (the Phaeacian rock-statue)—as necessary as Athene to the foundation of his character. When Odysseus plants his oar in the country of ignorance, it is a sign [*sema*, also "seed"] of knowledge yet to come—a reminder of the ship-loom-bed of the combined object, no longer erratic and twiggy but firmly rooted.[21] His role as omnipotent verbal trickster, at the mercy of sideways currents, has now been superseded by his identification with the wandering bard, who relies on internal rockfast support by the Muse. The meaning of being "Athene's favourite" has changed—as indeed, Athene herself has evolved. Odysseus is no longer the architect of the wooden horse: instead, he has become, like Bottom in *A Midsummer Night's Dream*, one of Athene's weavers.

NOTES

1. Keats, "On First Looking into Chapman's Homer"
2. W. R. Bion, *A Memoir of the Future*, single-volume edition (London: Karnac, 1997), p. 130.
3. For the history of the legend of Odysseus, see W. B. Stanford, *The Ulysses Theme* (1954) (Oxford: Oxford University Press, 1983).
4. On the archaic device of "ring composition" see R. Hexter, *A Guide to the Odyssey* (New York: Vintage Books, 1993), pp. 124–25.
5. In the sense of both causing and suffering pain. On the significance of Odysseus' name see G. E. Dimock, "The Name of Odysseus", in: G. Steiner and R. Fagles (Eds.), *Homer: A Collection of Critical Essays* (Englewood Cliffs, NJ: Prentice-Hall, 1962); and J. S. Clay, "Odysseus: Name and Helmet", in: H. Bloom (Ed.), *Homer's Odyssey* (New York: Chelsea House, 1988).
6. On the association of weaving and poetic composition see L. Slatkin, "Metis and Composition by Theme", in: S. L. Schein (Ed.), *Reading the Odyssey*, (Princeton, NJ: Princeton University Press, 1996).
7. See "Kleos and Its Ironies", in: C. Segal, *Singers, Heroes and Gods in the Odyssey* (Ithaca, NY: Cornell University Press, 1994).
8. Zeus with his thunderbolts, and Poseidon with his earthquakes, both constitute the male component of the combined object. They are in disagreement at the beginning of the epic but in agreement by the end.
9. On the "theology" of the *Odyssey* see Hexter, *Guide to the Odyssey*, p. xliii.
10. M. M. Nagler describes how the "dread goddess" figure of mythology links to the "axis mundi" (delving backwards in time) and forwards, to

Penelope's struggle to remain a pillar of the house: see "Dread Goddess Revisited", in Schein, *Reading the Odyssey*.

11. Homer, *The Odyssey*, transl. R. Fitzgerald (1961) (London: Collins Harvill, 1988), I.113–17; the following book and line references are to this edition.

12 Odysseus' famous pun by which he saves himself from Polyphemos the Cyclops in IX.367, stressing that he is "nobody" to all his family—"mother, father, friends". As a result of the Cyclops' curse he returns home alone, having lost all the men under his command (a failure as military leader and father) and has to rebuild his identity.

13. Helen was the daughter of Zeus—hence destined for the Elysian fields together with her husband.

14. Robert Fagles' translation (Harmondsworth, Middlesex: Penguin, 1996), ll. 11–12. This contrasts with *The Iliad*—see introduction by Bernard Knox, p. 10.

15. These words contain a pun on Odysseus' name, as do those of Eumaeus when he says he is sheltering the beggar not for his *tales* but for his "trouble", and for the duty of hospitality imposed by the gods (XIV.385–86).

16. As Eumaeus says himself, Zeus takes half a man's manhood away the day he makes him a slave (XVII.327–29). For this reason Eumaeus is not let into the secret of Odysseus' identity until the last minute, at the beginning of the battle; it is said he would not be able to keep it from the queen.

17. See A. Amory, "The Reunion of Odysseus and Penelope", in: C. H. Taylor (Ed.), *Essays on the Odyssey*, (Indianapolis, IN: Indiana University Press, 1969); U. Holscher describes how in this scene Penelope's folktale cunning, from the legend, is transformed by Homer into epic majesty as a result of superimposing different layers of meaning and consciousness: "Penelope and the Suitors", Schein, *Reading the* Odyssey.

18. H. Foley writes that Penelope "finally breaks her almost enchanted attachment to the past, to the stopping of change which was her central weapon": "Reverse similes" and sex roles in the Odyssey, Bloom, *Homer's Odyssey*, p. 98.

19. The subject of Auerbach's seminal essay, "Odysseus' scar", in: E. Auerbach, *Mimesis: the Representation of Reality in Western Literature*, trans. W. Trask (Princeton, NJ: Princeton University Press, 1953).

20. The name of Odysseus' grandfather, Autolycus, was taken up by Shakespeare in *The Winter's Tale* to similarly represent a trickster type of poet, a word-peddler.

21. Indra K. McEwen explains how the structure of the classical temple, with its core building [*naos*] and surrounding columns [*pteron*], was founded on that of the tall loom and the ship, with its oar-wings. "The city became a ship, its *naos* a *naus*, with well-fitted oars like wings": *Socrates' Ancestor: An Essay on Architectural Beginnings* (Cambridge, MA: Massachusetts Institute of Technology, 1993), p. 104. She combines "the notion of the peripteral

temple as a ship" with "the *pteron* as a linked series of looms that bodied forth the political interdependence of households" (p. 120) These tools of civilization, the foundation for the strength and productivity of the *polis* [city-state], had an aura of sanctity that became formalized architecturally in the religious house: in psychoanalytic terms, a symbol for the combined object.

CHAPTER SEVEN

Cleopatra's monument

> Looking for and hasting unto the coming of the day of God,
> wherein the heavens being on fire shall be dissolved, and the
> elements shall melt with fervent heat . . . we, according to his
> promise, look for new heavens and a new earth, wherein
> dwelleth righteousness.
>
> Peter II.3.12–13

> There is a qualitative aspect of sincerity that has to do with
> richness of emotion. Clinical work strongly suggests that this
> aspect of the adult character is bound up with the richness of
> emotion characterizing the internal objects. It can be
> distinguished from other qualities such as their strength or
> goodness. It is different from their strength or integration. It
> seems perhaps most coextensive with their beauty, which in
> turn seems related to capacity for compassion.
>
> Donald Meltzer[1]

Shakespeare's search for "the noblest Roman of them all"—ideal-ized in Brutus, undermined in Hamlet, begun again in Lear, incomplete in Othello, eventually finds fulfilment in Antony, the archetypal pattern of the heroic or great-souled magnanimous man.[2]

149

And his magnanimity finds its ultimate expression in the achievement of a marriage of *homophrosyne*, like Odysseus—an equal love. It is the "new heaven, new earth" heralded in the Bible and referred to by Antony, half-jokingly, at the opening of the play when Cleopatra demands to know "how much" love he has for her:

> *Cleopatra*:   If it be love indeed, tell me how much.
>
> *Antony*:   There's beggary in the love that can be reckoned.
>
> *Cleopatra*:   I'll set a bourn how far to be belov'd.
>
> *Antony*:   Then must thou needs find out new heaven, new   earth.[3]

The goal of the match between them, and of the play itself, is to qualitatively transform a quantitative experience; it is not enough to "stretch every minute of their lives with pleasure", locked in a claustrum of indulgence that will eventually pall, like that with Circe, Kalypso, or the Belle Dame—"and nothing else saw all day long". In this process of transformation there are strong hints of the Christian concept of redemption, infiltrating unobtrusively Shakespeare's portrayal of pagan abundance and primitive life-forces: "The elements shall melt with fervent heat". And yet the quantity, abundance, richness is the necessary foundation for love's purging through the refiner's fire—Antony's "bounty" is, for both Cleopatra and Enobarbus, his crowning characteristic. There needs to be sufficient emotional fuel to propel the aesthetic conflict through the refining phases to redemptive knowledge.

This emotional fuel derives from what Meltzer terms the "beauty and richness of internal objects" and is the foundation for "sincerity", something that does not apply to a particular emotion but, rather, to the state of mind within which emotions interact, a bringing-together of emotions. It has to do, he says, with Wittgenstein's category of "meaning it". It has an "aspirational quality", conveying the possibility of an ethical realm or existence beyond the self. It is something that Hamlet shied away from when he meditated on "To be or not to be" and that Shakespeare, interested in the particular quality that Hamlet lacked, seems to have first investigated in *Othello* when he chose a hero who is non-intellectual—the "noble Moor"—but who is likewise believed by his lover to have gone mad as a result of some fault, not in themselves, but in the love between them. The non-intellectuality allows him to focus on the emotionality that cannot be paraphrased by words and to ignore the confusing blanket of virtuoso wordplay that dazzles and disguises the emotional "sickness".

In *Othello*, such wordplay is taken to its most degraded degree in the mouth of Iago, with his stock fund of second-hand epithets and aphorisms that give the illusion of integrity and profound earthy wisdom: "I am not what I am" (I.i.65), "'tis in ourselves that we are thus, or thus" (I.iii.319); "no, let me know, / And knowing what I am, I know what she shall be" (IV.i.72–73).[4] His impoverished language is the vehicle for his so-called "honesty", the casual cynicism defined by Coleridge as "motiveless malignity". This "honesty" is the precise opposite of "sincerity" and thereby helps to define it. It derives from envy, not in the "hot" Satanic sense of Milton, bursting with pain and admiration, but in the cold sense of Bion's "Negative Grid", devoid of emotion. It functions less through calculation than through opportunism: seizing on the chance dropping of Desdemona's handkerchief to perpetrate its destructiveness. "Chance"—and yet, Desdemona drops the handkerchief when she is disturbed by Othello's own disturbance, after Iago has started to set him "on the rack" with the obsessive repetitions of his "honesty". For the man whose "noble nature . . . passion could not shake" has lived as a soldier until now and has as yet no idea of the perturbation of love (IV.i.261–62). He is, he says, "not easily jealous"—but, then, he has not had the opportunity to get to know such a feeling. At such a time, when they do not yet "know" one another sexually, some opening for the intrusion of opportunistic cynicism is liable to present itself—the equivalent of Cassio's susceptibility to alcohol; it does not require any psychological acuity on Iago's part to engineer it.

The strawberry-spotted handkerchief was Othello's "first gift" to Desdemona. Cassio—and Emilia—would like to "copy" it, in the sense of expressing admiration. But when brought into the public domain, it becomes like the wedding-sheet displayed in primitive societies as proof of the bride's virginity. Iago capitalizes on this and by a process of repetitive insinuation makes it not a reminder of, but a substitute for, that "essence that's not seen"—Desdemona's own "honour" or "honesty"[5]: namely, her genital:

> Her honour is an essence that's not seen,
> They have it very oft that have it not:
> But for the handkerchief—[IV.i.16–18]

He takes advantage of Othello's dazed state of mind as he transfers from soldier to lover, to awaken his primitive superstitions about the female witchcraft that put "magic in the web" (III.iv.67). When Desdemona places the handkerchief on Othello's forehead to cool his "headache", it has for him a tantalizing sexual significance, as if covering his cuckold's horns, while at the same time awakening desire. "They have it very oft"—who has it? Unable to tolerate these suspicions, he throws off the aggravating touch of the material; it falls to the floor and into Iago's possession. It is a pseudo-symbol, its concreteness disguising its meaninglessness. Its fabric comprises not the weavings of Athene but the clouds of superstition.

Iago genuinely believes that all women are whores, all friendships are political alliances, anyone who desires anything is a fool. It is simply his nature to believe so; his imagination is so limited that he cannot see things any other way. Likewise, he assumes that Othello, despite his status in society, must secretly feel inferior on account of his blackness and must secretly prefer the homosexuality of the battle-field—the "puffing of the cannon-ball"—to the strawberry-spotted bed. He discovers, however, that Othello accepts, and is not disturbed by, his own strangeness in this refined and courtly Venetian culture ("black and begrimed as my own face", III.iii.393). This is not a point of vulnerability, so Iago cannot attack him here. Along with the history of his fantastical adventures through which he wooed Desdemona, it represents his primal inheritance of emotional richness, the fountain-head of the stories of his inner life. He believes in his worthiness not in itself, but owing to his faith in her judgement: she pitied his dangers, "and I loved her that she did pity them" (I.iii.193). Even in the midst of his jealous torment, he reaffirms to Iago that "She had eyes, and chose me" (III.iii.393). There is no defect in his sincerity, so he is unassailable through the usual route of the selfhood—he has no vanity. Similarly, Desdemona holds fast to her vision of his spiritual qualities, originally revealed via her own compassion: she "saw Othello's visage in his mind" and retains this vision of what he was to the moment of her death, when she believes that he has lost his mind ("I have no lord"). Their mutual attraction was one of internal objects, seeking sensuous expression—"the rites for which I love him".

Nonetheless Desdemona is foreign to him in terms of both her culture and her sex: "O that we can call these delicate creatures ours and not their appetites!" The marriage consummation marks his initiation into the process of *knowing Desdemona*. But the intervention of Iago prevents this from developing. The pseudo-symbol, because of its concreteness, filled the mental space where "conception" should have occurred, resulting instead in mis-conception, substituting a tantalizing secrecy for a mystery. Othello becomes, quite simply, a fool ("O

fool, fool, fool!"). When he finally recognizes this, he regains his nobility, as "one that loved not wisely, but too well". The fault was not in his
love but in his knowledge; this constituted his vulnerability to undermining. And his failure to achieve knowledge was associated with a
lack of emotional strength. "On the rack", he insisted on the concrete,
"ocular proof" of anti-knowledge, which would relieve him of the
unbearable tension of not-knowing: "Villain, be sure thou prove my
love a whore". Desdemona's purity or "chastity" is finally revealed to
Othello by her spiritualizing capacity to internalize her dream of him
in a way equivalent to religious faith, transcending concrete representation, while insisting on her will to live: "Cold, cold, my girl, even as
thy chastity". It was the only way she could get him to know her.

Shakespeare places a single profound statement in the mouth of
Iago, near the end of the play, as if to clarify what he himself has
discovered through his dramatic investigation. This is when Iago says
that Cassio has "a daily beauty in his life / That makes me ugly"
(V.i.19–20). Othello has it too, and it is the beauty not of themselves,
but of their internal objects. It is, in fact, sincerity. Cynicism is ugly in
itself, since it exists only to block off the possibility of truthful knowledge; sincerity is beautiful because it indicates this contact with objects.
Having established this, when he comes to *Antony and Cleopatra*, he
takes up the story where Othello had end-stopped it. What happens
when a hero of similar "nobility", likewise a soldier, likewise non-
intellectual, acts intelligently in accordance with the dictates of internal
objects, rather than stupidly under the sway of cynicism—in other
words, when his objects are not only rich but also strong? What happens when the energies of the battlefield are transferred to the field of
love, and mutuality consists in having the opportunity to develop in
stages, through alternating phases of union and division, rather than
love being strangled at birth by the forces of negativity? Also, what
happens when the "blackness" (richness, strangeness) of Othello is
transferred to being part of the woman's equipment, focusing attention
on the aura of ambiguity that came to envelop Desdemona in Othello's
eyes? It is the ancestral "magic" that, owing to his intolerance of doubt,
became perverse and vengeful, like the Greek Furies, clouding his
mind with superstition. In *Antony* (uniquely in Shakespeare), the idea
of physical feminine beauty is given a secondary role, in the person of
Octavia, in order to focus on the beauty of objects, operating through
the protagonists. For it is the internal objects who generate the ambiguity. Shakespeare rearranges the various emotional elements of *Othello*

in order to clarify how "loving too well", and hating the enslavement, can be transformed into knowledge in the sense of "new heaven, new earth".

For the daring goal of the next play is to establish that the world will be a better place as a result of the love of Antony and Cleopatra.[6] There is throughout Rome and Alexandria—the "sides o' the world"— an intensifying pressure for the lovers to embody some definitive statement, to model the match that in spirit rather than by force of arms will rule the world. The world-imagery, with its vastness, exuberance, and propensity for mingling of elements, becomes a metaphor for the feelings of the protagonists. Alexandria, with its female space and population of women, children, and eunuchs, frames the action of the play and engages in a dramatic conversation of contrapuntal play with the visiting qualities of Roman masculinity. Rome's military might, spanned by its "triple pillars of the world", interdigitates with Egypt's richness in treasures and natural fertility governed by the overflowing Nile. The action of the play flashes from one side of the world to the other in a multitude of short scenes; battles are fought and dismissed in moments, in characteristic Shakespearean disregard of the classical unities of time, place, and action. The effect of this, together with the exalted world-imagery, is to evoke a sense of cosmic scale, both geographically and in terms of the abundance of powerful energies. Yet on another level the entire drama takes place within Cleopatra's bedroom: there is a very precise location of internal action, and everything that happens sheds some light on the developing sexual relationship between the hero and heroine.

At the outset, the shape of the drama is sketched as in an overture:

Cleopatra: I'll seem the fool I am not; Antony
    Will be himself.

Antony: But stirr'd by Cleopatra.

Antony, who in the eyes of Rome is "not Antony" at such times, will lose and remake his identity "stirred by Cleopatra" (in the ambiguous sense of inspire and trouble). It will require an out-matching of Caesar in which Cleopatra will seem the fool she is not. It remains for these prophetic or playful words to be filled with meaning through the operatic body of the work. Although Shakespeare follows history in telling us that Antony and Cleopatra are mature lovers, in their behaviour with their peers they come across as young, rewriting the story of *Romeo and Juliet* without its erotic narcissism—the rush to lose virginity and commit suicide. They are on the point of expanding out of their native groups—the predominantly single-sex societies of Rome and Egypt. The values of imperial Rome—as usual, in Shakespeare, the forerunner of the British public school—are those of decorum, competition, and domination. This makes its humour of a subversive, unofficial type (as in Enobarbus' asides). While in Egypt, it is assumed that love is a "trade" (music is "moody food of us that trade in love"), and its humour is at the expense of the captive male, as in the scene with the hysterical girls and the soothsayer, or in Cleopatra's list of conquests when she was a "morsel for a monarch", etc. Her pre-eminence derives not from her purity or virginity, but from being "wrinkled deep in time" (I.v.29); she has outlasted them all: they have been ploughed in to her rich and fertile soil—just as Pompey "plough'd her, and she cropp'd". Her humorous view of her own voracious appetite is a match for Rome's obsession with colonization. The existing values or basic assumptions of each world are the elements that need to be melted and dissolved in the refiner's fire; and Shakespeare does not disguise the ugliness of the process—the dishonour of the jealous rages when both Antony and Cleopatra abuse the messengers who bring unpleasant news—any more than he modifies the inventive catalogue of insults heaped on Cleopatra. The phrases "gipsy", "boggler", "triple-turn'd whore" are all Antony's own; Antony himself incurs nothing worse than "womanish", as if to imply that to Roman eyes, nothing could be worse.

There is hate, ugliness, and humiliation in the play, but there are essentially no enemies to love. All the main characters in the play are lovers of some type. Caesar is no Iago with power to undermine; he is, in fact, a beneficial goad and ultimately a facilitator of the final act, love's triumph. He is seen by Antony and Cleopatra as "the Roman boy", "the young man", "scarce-bearded Caesar"; his rigid phantasies of omnipotence embody the pressure of a younger generation that forces Antony to emerge from its confines and commit himself to his new identity. We should not doubt Caesar's love for Antony, however competitive his spirit towards this older-brother figure—"we two could not stall together in the whole world". In his "stag" speech he expresses his vision of Antony-as-hero:

> Yea, like the stag, when snow the pasture sheets,
> The barks of trees thou browsed. On the Alps
> It is reported thou didst eat strange flesh,
> Which some did die to look on: and all this—

It wounds thine honour that I speak it now—
Was borne so like a soldier, that thy cheek
So much as lank'd not. [I.iv.65–71]

His words echo those of Cleopatra describing the Caesar who anchored his eyes in her brow and "died with looking on his life":
suggesting how simple is the transition from stag or soldier to the lover
who eats this strange female flesh, and how the language of asceticism
merges into that of eroticism. The different types of love have one well
or foundation. Likewise, we are in no doubt of the genuineness of the
love between Antony and Enobarbus (most movingly expressed by
Antony in the single word "Enobarbus" when he hears of his deser-
tion), or between Cleopatra and her "girls", or of Eros, whose very
name means love. Octavia also is loved by her brother and belies her
reputed coldness in her speech about the split between Caesar and
Antony—"as if the world should cleave"— (III.iv.31); her feeling goes
beyond duty, and she partakes of the cosmic force. She is even loved in
a sense by Antony, who sees her as a "gem of women", something
more than his reputation for never being able to "say no to a woman".
Her brief experience with Antony gives her the courage to strip herself
of the political trappings for which Caesar pawned her and to return "a
market-maid to Rome", expressing her own desires and foreshadowing Cleopatra the "milkmaid"; only after this does her brother truly
appreciate her. She inherits not only Desdemona's beauty, but her
absence of recrimination and independence of spirit; she returns to
Rome not to seek protection—any more than Desdemona seeks refuge
in her maiden Venetian culture—but to try to reconcile her loves. Even
Mardian the eunuch "has affections" and has a place in the affections
of Charmian and Iras—figuring the husband whom they could totally
command.

To emphasize all this, Shakespeare introduces a single character for
whom love is not so much a mystery as a vacancy—this is Lepidus, the
"third pillar of the world". His vacancy is pinpointed in the comic
dialogue between him and Antony during the party on Pompey's
galley: Lepidus enquires, "What manner of thing is your crocodile?",
meaning that "strange serpent" the Egyptian love-monster, which, in
bawdy caricature, in Antony's lengthy satirical reply, has "wet tears"
and "transmigrates . . . once the elements are out of it" (II.vii.40–48).
After this Lepidus becomes incapacitatingly drunk (symbolizing his
inability to hold any emotion) and has to be carried off. The fault that
caused Cassio's downfall is split into Lepidus and caricatured. It is not

a case of losing the world for love[7]—in this play of adolescent ferment the world *is* the world of love; those who are not in it fall off the edge of the world altogether.

Cleopatra, the primary "stirring" power, is Antony's "serpent of old Nile"; she of the "tawny front" takes on the exotic characteristics of Othello—his blackness ("with Phoebus' amorous pinches black") and associations with the strange and monstrous, crocodiles and Anthropophagi (later to be found in Caliban). Her monstrosity, like the "dread goddesses" of the Greeks, lies in her power and its potential abuse, her association with Fury-like primitive emotionality. She can threaten jokingly to "unpeople Egypt" and identifies with the goddess Isis, a force of nature, in her jealous fury ("Some innocents 'scape not the thunderbolt"). Her tantrums are part real, part acted ("though I am mad, I will not bite him"); at the same time they can be alleviated by a brand of humour shared with her girls—though never with Antony—as in "O that brave Caesar!" "Say the brave Antony! . . . I will give thee bloody teeth" (I.v.70). And indeed she has teeth to cut through the polite excuses and prevarications of Roman formality: "Mine ear must pluck it thence", "I know by that same eye" (I.iii.19) . . . "Ram thou thy fruitful tidings into mine ear" (satirizing sexual domination): though, as with Caesar later, she can play the Roman game of courteous submission if she pleases. She is never described as beautiful, unlike Octavia or Desdemona; and there is much ugliness in her behaviour. So where, then, lies her attraction? It is not Antony alone who feels it; we see it in the line of lovers and in the loyalty of her women, and most poetically, in the analysis of Enobarbus. It is he who describes, to his fellow-Romans, what Antony never seeks to explain to himself—the quality of Cleopatra's sexual attraction:

> I will tell you.
> The barge she sat in, like a burnish'd throne
> Burn'd on the water: the poop was beaten gold;
> Purple the sails, and so perfumed that
> The winds were lovesick with them; the oars were silver,
> Which to the tune of flutes kept stroke, and made
> The water which they beat to follow faster,
> As amorous of their strokes. For her own person,
> It beggar'd all description . . .
> Her gentlewomen, like the Nereides,
> So many mermaids, tended her i' the eyes,
> And made their bends adornings. [II.ii.190ff]

The baroque picture, foreshadowing Milton's "burnished serpent", is not a description of Cleopatra's "person", which is indescribable, but of her sexual emanations, invisible airwaves from "burning" through "beating" and "stroking" to "adorning". The "burning" barge and the "gazing" air prefigure Cleopatra at the end saying she is made of "fire and air". The purple sail, like a pulsating heart or vagina at her core, directs the symphony played by air, waves, oar-strokes, and the "adorning" (like the religious adoring) feminine bends. Antony, sitting in the marketplace, does not see the picture—his herald Enobarbus sees it for him—but he feels its emanations in the air's disturbance ("whistling to the air"). Enobarbus' knowledge at this stage is in advance of Antony's (still believing he is married to Octavia for his "peace"); for on the basis of his own poetical analysis, he can state emphatically that Antony will never leave Cleopatra:

> *Maecenas*: Now Antony must leave her utterly.
>
> *Enobarbus*: Never; he will not:
>   Age cannot wither her, nor custom stale
>   Her infinite variety. [II.ii.233–36]

The partnership between Antony and Enobarbus continues through the central body of the play like a bass-and-tenor duet on the lines of thought-and-feeling. They are both involved in the enigma of Cleopatra (in so far as she is the Idea of womanhood)—to discover why she has held the Roman interest for so long. Antony has the role of the "noblest of men", Enobarbus that of scientific and artistic inquirer. He is Antony's intimate lieutenant and supporter in his quest. Between these two vertices, Shakespeare believes that surely the "truth" about womanhood, and the possibility of a marriage of true minds, can be discovered. Othello's lieutenants were Iago, the voice of cynicism, and Cassio, the contrasting voice of sincerity, who had, however, no strength—his legs are taken from him by alcohol, and at the end of the play he appears on stage in a wheelchair. Enobarbus, however, represents the voice of the poet, in the sense of the craftsman and analytical observer for whom Cleopatra with her infinite variety is "a wonderful piece of work". He is the descendant of Mercutio, wedded to reality not in spite of but because of his fertile imagination. The Mercutio–poet, like a king's Fool, is dedicated to reminding his master of the truth when he appears to be out of touch with it; "I had forgot that truth should be silent", says Enobarbus during the Roman council, and when Antony tells him to keep quiet, calls himself "your considerate stone" (II.ii.110). And invariably, from the analytical point of view,

Enobarbus is right. But as the play progresses, and Antony follows tenaciously the instructions of his internal objects, given in the form of "feelings", there gradually evolves a sense in which Antony, in parting from Enobarbus' advice, becomes even more right.

Antony does not attempt to understand Cleopatra in the intellectual, analytical sense of Enobarbus. He makes a serious response to Enobarbus' satirical account of Cleopatra's "celerity in dying" (I.ii.141). While Enobarbus savours her "variety", like a fine wine, Antony feels that this same quality makes her "cunning past man's thought"; he senses that her mystery is beyond the reach of his own—or anyone else's—mere cleverness. Iago would get nowhere with him, because he is not impressed by "oracular proof", any more than Penelope trusts the concrete evidence of the bed until the symbol becomes permeated by Odysseus' spirit. Antony relies instead on his capacity for feeling, in confronting the burnished-serpent qualities of Cleopatra; and ultimately he is vindicated, against the odds, while Enobarbus falls at the last hurdle. Essentially, he pursues a form of knowledge that participates in the turbulence of catastrophic change, whereas Enobarbus simply observes and tries—though, as it turns out, unsuccessfully—to refrain from "throwing his heart at the horns" (in the words of Garcia Lorca, describing the creative spirit, the *duende,* in terms of a bullfight):

> The bullfighter who alarms the public by taking risks is not bullfighting, he is absurdly *playing with his life,* which any man can do. But the bullfighter bitten by the *duende* gives a lesson of Pythagorean music, and makes us forget that he is constantly throwing his heart at the horns.[8]

The "bullfight" comprises the central section of the play, when the hitherto inviolate world of martial masculinity is invaded by the "puzzling" presence of Cleopatra, interfering in Antony's wars. ("Puzzle" is Enobarbus' term (II.vii.10), an unusual word used also in *Hamlet* at a turning-point: "puzzle the will").

In the tempestuous mixing, exchanging, and "melting" of roles and elements that begins with Antony resigning his generalship to Cleopatra and following her whims—to fight at sea—against all military sense, Enobarbus sees only Antony's loss of this type of reality—which he calls his "brain", his capacity to think. The soldier within Antony is represented by the common soldier who twice appears to him, displaying the scars of his experience, to protest against his absurd decisions. Antony does not try to explain his actions to himself or his friends—just says "Well, well, away!"—but it is clear that he is aware that he is giving himself up—as Enobarbus says—"to chance and hazard / From firm security". He is not blind to the likely consequences; therefore he is not brainless. He is playing a different game, fighting a different war: following the higher instructions of his internal *duende*. Enobarbus is unable to see that Antony is shifting the focus of his military capabilities to the point when he will say to Cleopatra, "my heart / Makes only wars on thee" (IV.xii.14–15). She is the bull, not Caesar. Earlier he said he could not "snaffle" the lead of his previous warmongering wife Fulvia, who was more of a male impersonator than a female infiltrator. Now he *knowingly* consents to hazard himself to Cleopatra's lead, allowing the imagery appropriate to war to become polluted—in military eyes—by a feminine viewpoint. Thus the flight of the fleet's sails is reminiscent of women's dresses, as Cleopatra, with

> The breeze upon her, like a cow in June,
> Hoists sails, and flies. [III.x.14–15]

It is a situation that, from the soldier's point of view, violates "experience, manhood, honour". It is in line with this insidious domesticity that they together send their "schoolmaster" as ambassador to Caesar when in the past either Antony or Cleopatra, on their own, would have sent "superfluous kings".

Antony's intuitive, non-analytical tactic in his "war" with Cleopatra has worked. Through the seriousness of the defeat, Cleopatra for the first time becomes aware of Antony's seriousness towards her.

> *Cleopatra:*   Forgive my fearful sails! I little thought
>   You would have follow'd.
>
> *Antony:*   Egypt, thou knew'st too well,
>   My heart was to thy rudder tied by the strings,
>   And thou shouldst tow me after. [III.xi.55–58]

It is a different aspect on the playful "fishing" image in which, assuaging her hatred of Antony owing to his departure for Rome, she had enjoyed the idea of her mastery over him:

> I will betray
> Tawny-finn'd fishes, my bended hook shall pierce
> Their slimy jaws; and as I draw them up,
> I'll think them every one an Antony,
> And say, "Ah, ha! y'are caught." [II.v.11–15]

Her possessiveness has been refined by his freely showing his dependence on her. She "knew too well", says Antony; but in a sense she had not known before—indeed, she had believed that he might use his freedom to get away, hence her need for a fantasy of control—"y'are caught". Now that she realizes her "hooks" are not necessary, a sense of responsibility devolves on her for the first time, and she asks "pardon" for her part in the disaster, despite Enobarbus' assurance that it was solely Antony's fault for following her example.

Antony, meanwhile, can stand the humiliation of the military defeat; but he cannot stand the idea that, as a result of this, Cleopatra might desert him and "mingle eyes" with Caesar. Hence his explosive rage when he sees Caesar's messenger kissing her hand—abusing, he believes, "your hand my playfellow". He orders a physical whipping for Thidias—thereby demeaning his own Roman honour, like his Roman generalship—and delivers a verbal whipping to Cleopatra, in a series of long paragraphs that amount to "roarings", on the lines of: "you have been a boggler ever". Cleopatra accompanies the crescendo of these recriminatory flights with a series of half-line interjections— "O, is't come to this?", "Wherefore is this?", "Have you done yet?", and "I must stay his time", and, finally, "Not know me yet?" This last question penetrates, and Antony's tirade abruptly ceases, enabling him to pinpoint the correct formulation of his distress:

Cleopatra: Not know me yet?

Antony: Cold-hearted toward me?

Cleopatra: Ah, dear, if I be so,
From my cold heart let heaven engender hail . . .
Dissolve my life; the next Caesarion smite
Till by degrees the memory of my womb,
Together with my brave Egyptians all,
By the discandying of this pelleted storm,
Lie graveless . . . [III.xiii.157–67]

After her passionate avowal, Antony concludes the dialogue with a simple half-line: "I am satisfied". No more is said; immediately the conversation turns to political practicalities. The reversal of long and short speeches between them pivots on their mutual questioning, two halves of the single line "Not know me yet? Cold-hearted toward me?", as in a musical duet. The abrupt ending of this quarrel echoes Cleopatra's early, stagey outburst:

Cut my lace, Charmian, come,
But let it be, I am quickly ill, and well,
So Antony loves. [I.iii.71–73]

In this way, according to the pattern of the play, early passages in their relationship, which were light, humorous, or hyperbolic, are instilled with the rhythm and music that will refine their meaning in the direction of sincerity.

The new music is seen in the language of the play, which is infused with imagery of the intermingling of elements of water and air (and, later, fire).[9] Cleopatra is the first to use the word "discandy", in the above description of an emotional storm; the concept is reiterated throughout the second half of the play, beginning with Enobarbus' fear that Antony will makes all his followers weep, "onion-eyed", and "transform them all to women" (IV.ii.35–36), and proceeding with Antony's sense that he is losing his "visible shape" and his identity is vaporizing like a cloud:

> That which is now a horse, even with a thought
> The rack dislimns, and makes it indistinct
> As water is in water. [IV.xiv.9–11]

"Authority melts from me", he said when he ordered the whipping of Thidias. Later, when Antony dies, the "crown o' the earth doth melt", on the "varying shore of the world", "beneath the visiting moon". It is the mistiness and fluidity of boundaries that often in poetry accompanies a change of state, the "cloud of unknowing"—Satan's mistiness on entering Eden, or Keats's on the top of Ben Nevis, or Bion's speculations using the metaphor of the "caesura" of birth for the type of knowledge that is born on exchanging a "watery medium for a gaseous one". Later Cleopatra will pass through an analogous change of state when she becomes a "milkmaid". The image of "the rack dislimns" succinctly expresses Antony's disengagement from his worldly fortunes after the Battle of Actium—encouraging his followers to take his gold and leave him, for his course is now a solitary one and "has no need of you" (III.xi.8–9). He, also, uses the term "discandy" for this process (IV.xii.22).

Enobarbus provides a running commentary, in operatic style, debating at the end of each scene whether he, too, should desert. Ultimately, believing that Cleopatra is also playing a double game, he decides that Antony is "leaky", brain-washed, and he does not wish to be part of his wateriness. Enobarbus cannot bear to melt "onion-eyed"; yet he melts away himself while the music of the god Hercules plays beneath the stage, signifying that Antony's martial god "now leaves him". He then discovers that it is impossible for him to resume a purely Roman status: his thinking without feeling has merely earned him

Caesar's contempt (for no "honourable trust" is accorded the desert-ers)—that is, it was not real thinking; and, moreover, he finds that he is pursued by the "treasure" that Antony has sent after him and that confirms his mistake. The treasure is Antony's "bounty" of spirit, coming from the "mine of bounty"—the beauty of his internal objects. It embodies the type of thought that "kills" Enobarbus, as distinct from the type of thought that is merely pragmatic calculation (as in Cleopat-ra's earlier satirical "a Roman thought hath struck"):

> This blows my heart:
> If swift thought break it not, a swifter mean
> Shall outstrike thought, but thought will do't, I feel. [IV.vi.34–36]

Enobarbus thus enters into a new realm of knowledge, caught up in the powerful reverberations of Antony's world of love, though he had tried to avoid it. The old sensible Enobarbus dies, and he is reborn as Eros, Antony's new intimate companion or "squire" in the final stage of his own story—the poetry of love itself. The implicit metamorphosis of one character into another is peculiarly Shakespearean, as with Cordelia and the Fool, or the old statesman Antilochus when—denied by his courtier's role the fulfilment of his fatherly instincts—he is eaten by a bear in *The Winter's Tale* and re-emerges without his courtly shell as the old shepherd who nurtures the abandoned baby.

Antony's last movement in the play requires that he abandon Hegelian "consideration" (the old Enobarbus) for a Kierkegaardian "leap of faith", attended by Eros. This new freedom gives him his one day of personal victory, between the two fatal sea-battles. First he comforts his weeping followers with a balanced optimism: "Grace grow where those drops fall, my hearty friends", for "I hope well of tomorrow . . . .Let's to supper, come, / And drown consideration." (IV.ii.38–45). (The religious word "grace" is not casually used: it reoccurs with the death of Cleopatra.) No longer under the aegis of Hercules, he becomes part of a tableau of Venus, Mars, and Cupid, as suggested in the armouring scene when Cleopatra and Eros prepare him for the coming battle. This demonstrates that the source of his optimism is the new trust and solidity of his relationship with Cleo-patra—buckled within his breastplate rather than flying loosely after her sails, restoring his masculinity from within. Introjecting her faith in him, he goes to war "a workman", giving her "a soldier's kiss", for the first time uniting his own qualities as soldier and lover, and is re-warded with the day's victory:

> Leap thou, attire and all,
> Through proof of harness to my heart, and there
> Ride on the pants triumphing!
>   ... My nightingale,
> We have beat them to their beds. [IV.viii.14–19]

This day of victory confirms Antony's masculinity in the sense of fighter as distinct from policy-maker: the unwanted dross, the political manipulation, is left to Caesar's type of Romanness—he who, as everyone acknowledges, is not a swordsman. Caesar's claim afterwards that Antony was "my brother, my competitor, my mate in empire ... the arm of my own body" (V.i.42–45) is a type of homosexual wish-fulfilment, with some similarities to Iago ("from his very arm puff his own brother"); though, unlike Iago's, it is also an expression of admiration, albeit reflected back onto himself. But the grandiosity of the claim is demonstrated to us on this day, when it becomes clear that Antony's true companion in his war is the plain soldier Scarus—he of the scars— who had previously called Cleopatra a "ribaudred nag" and hoped that she would die of leprosy, and who now is embraced within Cleopatra's new family in the suit of "king's armour" that she gives him. Scarus proves himself Antony's true Roman "partner"—not Caesar. The plain Roman soldier within Antony is the one who both loves and hates (insults) Cleopatra but, unlike Enobarbus-the-sensible, does not desert. At the same time, Cleopatra emerges from her previous ignorant disregard of the practicalities of warfare and becomes more of a helpmate, a wife. Othello, unable to tolerate the intrusion of the foreign emotion "hate" into his view of Desdemona, does not give their relationship the chance to reach this stage.

Then, according to the prevailing pattern of the play, the same emotional movements are repeated with an intensification: Antony's love and hate for Cleopatra are soldered together by his rage at yet again believing that she has betrayed him. The emotions are so close, in time, that they are felt not consecutively but simultaneously, as the aesthetic conflict itself. Within moments (it appears—though in story-time it is the next day) Antony veers from "triumphing" to "All is lost". The cause of the change appears to be (from the way the drama is presented) that swallows have built their nests in Cleopatra's sails (IV.xii.3), another image of domesticity. Those few lines are all we know of the "battle"; then Antony enters with his final passion of anger against Cleopatra or, rather, at the power of the emotion she arouses in him:

> All is lost:
> This foul Egyptian hath betrayed me . . .
> . . . Triple-turn'd whore, 'tis thou
> Hast sold me to this novice, and my heart
> Makes only wars on thee . . .
> O this false soul of Egypt! this grave charm,
> Whose eye beck'd forth my wars, and call'd them home;
> Whose bosom was my crownet, my chief end,
> Like a right gipsy, that at fast and loose
> Beguil'd me, to the very heart of loss. [IV.xii.9–29]

It is a declaration of love as much as of hate: he will be "revenged on his charm", which then becomes his "grave charm", with its ambiguous connotations: showing how close love and death, triumph and loss, have become. Meanwhile, when Cleopatra briefly enters during this tirade, he paints for her the picture that will dominate her final act: of the Roman triumph, where she will be shown "most monster-like" to the vulgar curiosity of the plebeians. Cleopatra says nothing—she listens and leaves; but this picture is instrumental in strengthening her own resolve to exchange the vulgar triumph of life for the queenly one of a death "fitting for a princess / Descended of so many royal kings".

Cleopatra then on the spur of the moment draws forth the one weapon she knows will be effective in this war of love: the news of her death. She repeats, but with a difference, what was once a form of play-acting—the "celerity in dying" satirized early on by Enobarbus. Her urgency, approaching desperation, indicates that this time her message is not a manipulation but a form of inspiration. It immediately melts Antony's vengefulness, as he experiences the relief of knowing that he can no longer hold off "the battery from his heart". In his eyes this reported act of concentration instantly redeems the sexual "looseness" (the flying sails, "fast and loose"); it was the one signal he was waiting for, to tip the unbearable emotional contraries into the resolution of knowledge, as expressed by his vision of the new heaven and the new earth:

> Unarm, Eros, the long day's task is done,
> And we must sleep. . . .
> Eros!—I come, my queen:—Eros!—Stay for me,
> Where souls do couch on flowers, we'll hand in hand,
> And with our sprightly port make the ghosts gaze: [IV.xiv.35–52]

At this moment the presence of Eros, the spirit of love, merges into that of Cleopatra, as indicated by the interweaving of his calls to each of them, and by shortly saying that his queen and Eros jointly have instructed him how to become "a bridegroom in my death" (IV.xiv.100). Together they become the inspiring force, the summons of his internal object to "death". The note of resolution modulates the dissolution imagery that surrounds Antony's last battles with Cleopatra (from "Authority melts from me" to Cleopatra's "The crown o' the earth doth melt"). The fact that Cleopatra was not dead, only pretending, does not undermine Antony's feeling, which is essentially a form of self-knowledge, about his feelings for her. He has not been deceived; rather, he embraces an opportunity. He dies like Desdemona, pursuing an inner vision, but not before he has made clear to Cleopatra what he is doing and warned her of the consequences—for her own honour—of wavering in her resolution. As Antony followed Eros, Cleopatra will follow her handmaid of similar name and spiritual simplicity, Iras, who likewise "teaches the way to die" and who echoes Antony's words of transition with:

> Finish, good lady, the bright day is done
> And we are for the dark. [V.ii.192–93]

—a musical refrain that accompanies the reciprocal poetic duet that makes up the last movement of the play.

The death of Cleopatra is more complicated and protracted than that of Antony, owing to her character, sex, and situation. Despite her declaration immediately after Antony's death to "do it after the high Roman fashion / And make death proud to take us" (IV.xv.87–88), she lingers throughout the whole of the last act. Does she really retain some hope of conquering Caesar by the usual means? Is it only when it becomes absolutely clear that the only alternative to death is the disgrace of a Roman triumphal procession, that she commits herself—and does this mean that it is an egocentric fear of disgrace, rather than love, that is predominant?

> The quick comedians
> Extemporally will stage us, and present
> Our Alexandrian revels: Antony
> Shall be brought drunken forth, and I shall see
> Some squeaking Cleopatra boy my greatness
> I' the posture of a whore. [V.ii.215–20]

The complications of the process of Cleopatra's being true to herself begin even when she is confronted with the dying Antony and says she "dare not" come down from her monument to receive his last kiss, "lest she be taken" by Caesar. Has she brought him unnecessarily to his death through telling lies, yet is unwilling to make reparation by endangering, or demeaning, her own person? Shakespeare's answer is to show us, through another tableau, the poetic necessity for her raising Antony up into her monument. The scene revises the earlier images of fishing Antony up with her hook and of discovering him tied to her ship's rudder. The lazy luxuriant queen who could not "hop forty paces through the street" without getting out of breath now manages to heave up Antony's dying weight, with the words "Come, come. And welcome, welcome! Die when thou hast liv'd" (IV.xv.37–38). Her faint, after he dies, is a foreshadow of death ("She's dead too . . .") and symbolizes her new responsibility, the introjection of the weight of Antony.

When she awakens from the faint, she has undergone a profound change. Iras calls, "Royal Egypt: Empress!" But Cleopatra corrects her; now she sees herself as being

> No more but e'en a woman, and commanded
> By such poor passion as the maid that milks,
> And does the meanest chares. [IV.xv.73–75]

We remember how Octavia rid herself of the unwanted pomp of her situation and returned "a market-maid to Rome". Something of Roman Octavia with her previously reviled "patience" and endurance now enters into Cleopatra. She sheds the tyrannical and hysterical aspects of her regal role and begins to explore a new definition of queenliness, corresponding to Antony's new soldiership (based on "friends") after abandoning his original commanding role. Cleopatra's new royalty will fulfil itself, not in the mere fact of her death, but in its manner. Her absorption of masculinity is more complicated than Antony's melting into femininity and is associated with the place or space into which associations are gathered. Her "monument" is the female space in which Egyptian energies are concentrated: it is womb, tomb, and was also, in Shakespeare's day, a common term for a poem. It is the "cave of Nile" in which mysterious procreativity takes place, marked by the "aspic's slime" like the fig-leaves in the farmer's basket, or the place where fish are hooked or heaved in from the river. It is like Keats's garden, Oedipus' crossroads, Odysseus' cave of dreams. It contains the long history of the race of Ptolemy and their gods; Cleopatra is descended of "many royal kings", and, like a poem, it will contain the meaning and memory of her death, to be transmitted to future generations. Her internal objects, in their ancestral richness and fertility, have expectations of her, and they have now been joined by Antony in his Romanness. Her need to *know Antony*, to match up to the quality of his death, becomes in fact her means to knowledge of herself, the new regality. The new, thoughtful Cleopatra asks,

> Then is it sin,
> To rush into the secret house of death,
> Ere death dare come to us? [IV.xv.80–82]

She has a duty not just to Antony but to her sex, race, and religion to enter the house of death poetically, at the moment that will make it meaningful, not "sinful": sinful being connected with "rushing"—the overflow of powerful feeling, grief or desire. She must avoid the temptation of Antigone, "married to death", because she has lost faith in life. Her death must be a response to the call of internal objects, not the impatient escapism of despair or erotic indulgence. The goal of knowledge that she needs to attain becomes clearer, step by step, during the final phases of the drama.

Before she can enter the house of death, the relationship with Caesar has to be sorted out, and this occupies the entire fifth act. Caesar will be the future ruler of the world—the "universal landlord" (III.xiii.7 2)—and, he says, "the time of universal peace is near" (IV.vi.5). In his view this will happen when everybody obeys him at last and submits to his reasonable and well-organized rule, the model for the British–Christian empire. In Cleopatra's view, as she digests Antony's warning about the triumph, Caesar needs to be educated to honour the gods who are greater than his infantile narcissism. "'Tis paltry to be Caesar", thinks Cleopatra; there is "a better life"; he is not Fortune but "her knave" (V.ii.1–4). In order to purge Rome of its obsession with imperial domination, she must herself become a kind of warrior, fighting the one-to-one match that Caesar had declined to fight with Antony. To do this, she carries her knowledge of Antony one stage further, not just bearing his weight, but introjecting his military capacity; and Caesar himself is well aware of the martial nature of their encounter: he knows that in order for him to triumph, Cleopatra must first be outwitted,

> Lest in her greatness, by some mortal stroke
> She do defeat us. For her life in Rome
> Would be eternal in our triumph. [V.i.64–66]

If Cleopatra cannot be deceived, her own innate greatness will triumph instead of his victory procession. To be victorious, he must prove that

Cleopatra is a whore—as, said Antony at the beginning, she was "named in Rome". The coarseness of his mode of deception is demonstrated early on in the way his soldiers burst in to the monument from behind and seize Cleopatra while Proculeius is having a polite conversation with her—imaging the two-faced nature of their well-mannered civility. "O Cleopatra—thou art taken, queen!" her women cry out. There are echoes here of Othello's demand to Iago—"be sure thou prove my love a whore". From this violent episode Cleopatra draws her lessons: that the monument is not a safe haven, and that Antony was wrong in advising her to "trust none about Caesar but Proculeius" (IV.xv.48). Instead, she must trust her own wits and her internalized idea of Antony, not his practical advice. She must create a monument that will rise above the reach of such crude physical assaults, impregnable in its spirituality alone.

Proculeius' insistence that she rely on Caesar's "bounty", however, in "sweet dependency", gives her a cue as to how to proceed. For in her negotiations with Caesar, she needs to find one Roman to whom she can convey her idea of Antony—the meaning of Antony's bounty as opposed to Caesar's paltriness: someone who can understand the difference between Caesar's idea of "eternal life" and her own. Her knowledge will be incomplete, not fully internalized, unless she finds a means of transferring it to the outside world of continuing existence: as in the nature of a poem, it is both expression and communication. This is the point at which, relying on an instinctive moment of feminine inspiration, she chooses Dolabella and transfixes him with her "dream" of Antony's bounty, and the way it transcended the elements of everyday life:

> For his bounty,
> There was no winter in't: an autumn 'twas
> That grew the more by reaping: his delights
> Were dolphin-like, they show'd his back above
> The element they lived in: . . .
> Think you there was, or might be such a man
> As this I dreamt of?
>
> *Dolabella:*   Gentle madam, no. [V.ii.86–97]

She asks the same question as Penelope: "or did I dream him?" Dolabella is conquered by the impact of her vision, by its poetry. Despite his logical demurring, he admits its "weight", and, as with Enobarbus, his heart is "struck":

> I do feel,
> By the rebound of yours, a grief that smites
> My very heart at root. [ll. 103–5]

Through this "rebound" (transference) a conversation take place between their internal objects. Cleopatra has discovered one other Roman who would like to be the kind of man about whom a woman might "dream" in this way. He participates in the love-story by reflection and becomes Cleopatra's agent, relaying the truth about Caesar's plans for the triumph and thereby ensuring that Caesar loses the match.

Thus Cleopatra uses her dream or internalization of Antony to outwit Caesar's hypocritical smoothness, with its brutish undertone of degradation. He is willing to believe in the caricature of her former self that she presents to him—as in the scene with Seleucus, pretending she has been hiding her treasure, repeating ironically the words she knows Caesar want to hear: "my master and my lord". In his complacency he is not alert to the opportunity of getting to know her. She, on the other hand, flashes quick as thought, surveying the military potentialities of the scene. In this she incorporates something of Enobarbus, whose opinions she respected and with whom she could always converse. Her new thinking process is conveyed by Shakespeare in the briefest of communications between herself and her women:

> He words me, girls, he words me, that I should not
> Be noble to myself. [V.ii.190–91]

By returning worthless "words" to him while she makes her preparations—sending Charmian for the asp, at this moment—she exorcises the Roman end that she is about to make from the taint of conquering and submission:

> My resolution's placed, and I have nothing
> Of woman in me: now from head to foot
> I am marble-constant: now the fleeting moon
> No planet is of mine. [V.ii.237–40]

She selects out the worthwhile aspects of masculine Rome—courage, resolution—and discards the political hypocrisy, together with the fable of female vacillation. All the energies of her infinite variety are channelled into constancy. This is her new sincerity. Now she knows that the true monument must consist not of "marble" but of herself.

For Cleopatra, like Desdemona, would perhaps like to live "half an hour more" if this could be done without betraying her internal objects—but at this stage, it cannot; the symbol is approaching closure, as with Gawain and the Green Knight. By clinging to life, and at the same time not flinching from her inner vision of his noble mind, now lost, Desdemona finally made Othello "know" her and know his folly. The desire to live is essential to the transformative potential of faith. It is what makes Cleopatra's death meaningful and brings out all the rich implications of queenliness. The preparations for the death ceremony are a re-working of the "burnished barge" poetic description, as she states herself:

> Show me, my women, like a queen: go fetch
> My best attires. I am again for Cydnus,
> To meet Mark Antony. [ll. 226–28]

She is going to Cydnus again but with a difference, for this time she wishes to match the concept of being "noble to herself" with Antony's approval of her "noble act":

> Give me my robe, put on my crown, I have
> Immortal longings in me. Now no more
> The juice of Egypt's grape shall moist this lip.
> Yare, yare, good Iras; quick: methinks I hear
> Antony call. I see him rouse himself
> To praise my noble act. I hear him mock
> The luck of Caesar, which the gods give men
> To excuse their after wrath. Husband, I come:
> Now to that name, my courage prove my title!
> I am fire, and air; my other elements
> I give to baser life. [ll. 279–89]

She hears Antony "call", as if in response to his earlier "Call all my sad captains" (III.xiii.183). Antony's arousal from his deathly sleep images her knowledge of reciprocity, of fitness. Meanwhile she has received the basket of figs from the countryman, accepting the superstitious ambiguities with which he warns about the "devilish" quality of "the worm" along with the "joy" it brings: "I know the devil himself will not eat a woman". She purges their significance, as she purges her own nature of its Egyptian serpentine temptress quality when she takes the asp, selecting the phrase "his biting is immortal" and elevating it to "immortal longings" ("the stroke of death is as a lover's pinch"). This, together with the new Roman courage, will "prove her title" to Antony as "husband", her words "I come" reflecting her "come . . . welcome" when she heaved him up into the monument.

In the final movement of the play the ideas of sexual consummation, childbirth and breastfeeding, the sacredness of the marriage ceremony and its religious history are all gathered together in the tableau
of Cleopatra's death, not through heavy analogy but through evanes-
cent poetic implication, as she herself prepares to become "fire and
air". As she says to the asp–baby at her breast (who is at the same time
Antony):

> With thy sharp teeth this knot intrinsicate
> Of life at once untie: poor venomous fool,
> Be angry, and despatch. O, couldst thou speak,
> That I might hear thee call great Caesar ass,
> Unpolicied! [ll. 303–7]

The emotional fuel is termed "anger", as in Oedipus. The change of
state is suggested in the word "intrinsicate", with its concentration of
light, sharp sounds (*i*'s and *t*'s), scattered through the surrounding
words as if about to become unwound from their sensuous existence
and released into the ether. This "untying" parallels the "unpolicing"
of Caesar, the other type of baby or "fool"—one who depends too
much on words, balanced against the other who cannot yet "speak".
He, too, receives a "call", from asp to ass, containing within it the
debris of Othello's folly—the ignorant lover.

For a tincture of the light-hearted quality of the girls' earlier games
and experiments in love remains, even as they are raised to a higher
power. It was Iras who died first, and Cleopatra uses this to prompt her
own act, lest she reach Antony first and he, as always, would not be
able to say no. Then, after Charmian's (the charming one) last "chare",
Cleopatra gives her leave to "play till doomsday", and Charmian faithfully pursues the metaphor:

> Your crown's awry,
> I'll mend it, and then play. [ll. 317–18]

Her last play, work or chare, as she bends charmingly over her dying
mistress, recalls the burnished barge, with "all their bends adornings".
The bending and adorning, tracing serpentine curves around a crown
or heart, indicate the religious implications of adoring that existed
potentially even in the burnished barge. "It is well done", says
Charmian emphatically, in response to the guardsman who sees her
doing it—making sure that he understands its regal significance, before she speaks her last words, "Ah, soldier!" as she falls into his arms,

following her mistress to new heaven, new earth. They do not go on alone, as did Desdemona. Together they have relayed the true meaning of Egyptian charm, with the serpent of the aesthetic conflict at its core, in a way that gets across in its triumphant finale to its essential recipient, Caesar himself:

> She looks like sleep,
> As she would catch another Antony
> In her strong toil of grace.

The "knot intrinsicate" is raised to a higher power, the "strong toil of grace". Caesar's poetic words of admiration are the final vindication of the work Cleopatra has undertaken during the last act, intertwining being true to herself with knowing Antony. It is Caesar who perceives—and felicitously finds the right words to express—how the old serpentine identity, strengthened by its new work-ethic—the double meaning of "toil"—has become elevated and refined to a state of "grace". As a true Roman, Caesar can accept, even embrace, being vanquished by one who has outmatched him in a fair fight—not Antony, who had long lost interest in him, but Cleopatra, "bravest at the last". His acceptance is founded on his own love for Antony and for Octavia, however flawed. For a while, during the complacent period when he felt assured of his own triumph, he had appeared to be ineducable. Traces of narcissism still remain (he believes he is the "maker" of this "high event"):

> High events as these
> Strike those that make them . . . [V.ii.358–59]

But now the word "strike" applies to him also, as it did to Enobarbus and Dolabella before him—the serpent that strikes to the heart, the symbol that closes irrevocably the emotional pattern of the experience. He appreciates the "solemnity" of the event and prefers it, in fact, to the omnipotent triumph. He, the wordster, has finally made contact with the poetic principle, in the form of the new Romanized Cleopatra—the powerful impact of the combined object. It is up to him now to read the poem of Cleopatra. In this sense he is himself the might-be "other Antony"—ready, like ourselves, to "counter-dream" (in Meltzer's term). Cleopatra, in becoming her own monument, has been successful in her attempt to ensure that there will be more Cleopatras, beyond the reach of political pawning, rape, and whoredom, free to exist in a state of grace in the new Roman world.

NOTES

1. D. Meltzer, *Sincerity*, in: A. Hahn, ed. *Sincerity and Other Works* (London: Karnac, 1994), p. 204.

2. As in the Aristotelian "magnanimous man", described by D. Krook, *Elements of Tragedy* (New Haven, CT: Yale University Press, 1969), p. 201.

3. Shakespeare, *Antony and Cleopatra*, ed. M. R. Ridley, Arden edition (London: Methuen, 1954, 1971), I.i.14–17. Subsequent references in the text are to this edition.

4. *Othello* is quoted from the Arden edition, ed. M. R. Ridley (London: Methuen, 1958, 1971).

5. "Honour" and "honesty" are words with the same root, used more or less interchangeably in the play.

6. *Othello* was written in 1603–4, *Antony and Cleopatra* in 1605–6.

7. Dryden's play *All for Love* was based on *Antony and Cleopatra*.

8. Federico Garcia Lorca, "Theory and Function of the *Duende*", in: *Poems*, transl. M. Williams (Bala, Gwynedd: Bloodaxe Books, 1992), p. 229.

9. G. Wilson Knight describes how "we now ascend from water and air to air and fire . . .": "The transcendental humanism of *Antony and Cleopatra*", in: *The Imperial Theme* (London: Oxford University Press, 1931), p. 240.

CHAPTER EIGHT

Creativity and the countertransference

Donald Meltzer

On creativity

I am going to speak about creativity not in a descriptive or behavioural sense, as when we say: "this person is very creative"; but, in a more precise and definite mode, I am going to talk of creativity as a phenomenon of the personality, of the family, and of the culture. I will speak of Bion as a genius who in a certain sense produced everything that he did produce as though in a dream. I will describe him as someone who struggled, who made some errors, who corrected himself and often did not know where he had arrived. A creative genius is someone who permits his own internal objects to give him new ideas—even if he does not understand them or cannot use them: his function is to receive them, and he possesses the art of transmitting them. There is a distinction between invention and discovery. Invention is a function of the self—discovery, a function of the creative self.

I will start with Bion's theory of thinking and his particular formulation of the grid. The grid was a means chosen by Bion to describe the

---

The talk "On Creativity" was given by Donald Meltzer at Biella, Italy, in 1993 and has been translated by Adrian Williams from the Italian transcript. One or two paragraphs have been added from my notes on Dr Meltzer's talk on the same subject given at Stavanger, Norway, in 1992 (MHW).

processes by which thoughts evolve and the method of thinking. Bion made a very precise distinction between mental processes of an adaptive, contractual, or quantitative type, which, he said, made part of the exoskeleton of the personality, and the processes founded on emotional experience—creativity, symbolic representation, and dream thought. This emotional and symbolic aspect of the formation of the personality was considered fundamental by Bion for its development. He thought that the formation of symbols to represent emotional states was something initiated between the tiny baby and the mother. He believed that the maternal reverie, the dream thoughts that the mother transmitted to her little baby, was something the baby can internalize in such a way as to form the endoskeleton of the personality that would then permit him to think in his turn. The structure of the personality, according to Bion—and in agreement with Money Kyrle's view—was something that built up step by step while undergoing cognitive development. Every point in development involves the acquisition of new ideas or concepts placed on top of already existing ones. The impact of the new idea on these pre-existing concepts involves an experience of catastrophic change.

In order to give form to this, to be able to think about thought and to describe these processes, Bion has proposed a grid[1] similar to the periodic table used in chemistry, with two axes—a horizontal axis, and a vertical one—to indicate the development of the personality. To describe the processes that take place following the emotional impact, he has used the concept of alpha function. The formation of symbols is considered a function of an external parental object, possibly also internal; and it takes place while undergoing the impact of these emotional elements, forming them into a pattern. The vertical axis proceeds with an ever-growing sophistication from preconceptions to concepts, derived in the first place from symbols and dream-thoughts, and arriving at a higher—more abstract—level, which, he speculated, could be defined through mathematical or scientific formulae. In this scheme it is important to underline that every idea that arrives at the level of conception comes to be utilized for successive experience in the form of preconceptions. The horizontal axis comes to be used initially to record a system of notation, observation, attention, inquiry, and action.

Bion proposed Column 2 in the Grid to indicate the same process, but instead of being used to search for the truth, it is used, rather, to describe those things that are not true, to hide true ignorance of the self and others. However, he came to recognize the formulations of Column 2 as an error; therefore he eliminated them and has thought of elaborating instead a parallel with the Grid, a Negative Grid. At the end of his work in 3 volumes, *A Memoir of the Future*[2], written in the last years of his life, Bion thought to correct another error, realizing that the conclusion of the process of thinking is not action but communication, because in reality action is a method of reducing and impeding communication.

Bion held that the evolution of a thought in the thinker must follow a definite sequence: first of all, translation into a constant configuration (a pattern), then the focusing of attention on it, which stimulates the inquiry or search that finally leads to communication. This method of considering thought is useful also in the psychoanalytic process where there are constant conjunctions, constant configurations produced by the patient in a particular form, which come to the attention of the patient and the analyst, provoking inquiry and then communication. This is the transformation of the initial thought as it becomes progressively more sophisticated.

Although this system seems to underline—as with Freud—verbalization and language as the means of expression of thought, in reality it does not, because it is clearly stated that the initiation of thought is dream-thought. When thought is considered to have its origin in dreams, the emphasis turns to the importance of envisioning it so that it can then be transformed into other symbolic forms. Symbol formation can, in fact, manifest itself in musical, graphic, and also linguistic forms. In child analysis we deal largely with pictures and games with objects and Plasticine; later, also with language. And language can be the ultimate instrument of communication when it succeeds in uniting visual and musical arts and becomes poetry.

Following this, we see that the possibility of thought depends first on the external object relationship and then on that with the internal object, thus implying a vision of the internal object as parental figures that precede the self in their capacity for thought. This view of development does not envisage a smooth process, but proceeds through a succession of quantum jumps, in which each jump implies the acquisition of a new idea and a period of catastrophic change. Bion then considered the passage from the paranoid-schizoid position to the depressive position, the change of values and organization inherent in every part of catastrophic change during growth and development. Thus in every moment of development there is always an oscillation between paranoid-schizoid and depressive positions.

In analysis we are able to see this process with great clarity. We can verify how between one resting-place and another a new idea appears from which the patient retreats, then struggles with anxiety; and this applies not only to the patient but also to the analyst. This formulation allows us to tailor more precisely and rationally the ongoings of the analytic process, limiting it only to communication and avoiding action and counteraction, acting out or acting in the transference. We in psychoanalysis study the evolution of the individual and the evolution of the individual in the family or in relation to his family. These processes of catastrophic change through which the individual develops are paralleled by similar processes of change in the family while it itself evolves. We can verify that our usual method of defining critical points of development in the evolution of the individual corresponds in effect to the acquisition of new ideas—birth, weaning, and so on— and in the analytic situation one can see very well how these processes entail an interior struggle, a retreat, then an acceptance, and that during this period of turbulence nothing is clear.

The nature of transference, whether of a child, an adult, or a patient, leads the patient to be convinced that the analyst knows the truth. Naturally the analyst does not know the truth and must attempt to stabilize the transference situation without feeling too overwhelmed. The great danger the analyst may encounter during his work is to begin to think he knows the truth. In analysis, for example, when the patient makes a step forward towards digesting a new idea, the analyst can see through his behaviour that a new idea is present but cannot know what it is until it is described in his dreams. We find ourselves always in a situation of uncertainty.

Bion designated as K (Knowledge) the emotional element that governs the analyst's acceptance of the ultimate mystery of things. The new theory of affects that accompanies his theory of thinking is indicated by three compartments of the Grid that speak of love, hate, and knowledge as constituting the desire for knowledge. This permits us to formulate better the nature of the passionate contact that is propelled by K (the K-link)—the wish to understand that allows us to hold together the turbulence of love and hate. It permits us also to formulate more precisely a method for modulating the anxiety produced by catastrophic change, the destructive impact of which would otherwise pull the mind towards the negative grid—that is, towards lies and negativity. One mode of retreating from this turbulence is to avoid the emotional conflict and pursue modes of adaptation and opportunistic calculation, thus avoiding thinking. The inquiry or need that is put forward by the patient in analysis, or by the individual in life, is to have a transference object, a person who can represent the good qualities necessary to his development, though not necessarily embody them. Thus the patient asks the analyst to be driven by K, by the desire to understand him; this involves attention, inquiry, arriving at communication. Even if you don't always succeed in understanding the internal state of the patient, the analyst should nonetheless be under the dominance of K—that is, of the desire to understand.

The problem of the thought that is trying to become communication is a complex one owing to the fact that the personality is not uniform but has many parts, each its their own view of the world, and these parts need to be integrated (Bion's vertices). The request that the self makes of its objects, internal or external, is that of aiding it to proceed in development, making itself a focus of integration of its various parts. In the last volume of his trilogy, *The Dawn of Oblivion*, Bion describes the type of internal organization of the personality that makes internal communication possible in relation to thinking, and possible the thought and the confrontation with the catastrophic experience of the new idea. This gives a new significance to the term integration, affirming that the diverse parts of the self can enter into communication.

This vision of development in stages through moments of catastrophic change in the search for new ideas leads therefore to new levels of thought and of organization of the personality, going from conceptions to creativity. It is important to understand that the self experiences creativity as something coming from the object, focusing all the various aspects of the self through the passage from attention to comprehension.

In the third volume of the *Memoir*, the various characters from the first two volumes are found together in a kind of committee—they talk, talk, talk, always the same noisy discourse. Thus one understands that they wish to succeed in something. The new idea in the end becomes the idea of the combined object, and this for Mrs Klein signified the advent of the depressive position.

It follows from this model of the process of individual development as seen in relation to dependence on the external object that the transference object can then be internalized as part of a process autonomous to the individual. This is a crucial step towards creativity and towards enabling the individual to accept new ideas in the service of cultural ends—for the benefit of "the world".

It is clear that the things necessary for creativity are not exactly the same as those necessary for mental health. Creativity is a term which has special reference to artists. While development involves some give-

and-take with objects, creativity comes with a strong feeling of being used by internal objects as a medium to relay knowledge to the world—communication, mission, preaching to siblings. Creativity does not require that there should be an integration of the self, but that there should be an integrated combined object well internalized. Studies and psychoanalytic experience indicate to us nevertheless that internalization of the combined object is a very rare phenomenon. The problem of having inside oneself a capacity for creativity is different from that which Bion defines as "the publication of creativity", because to render public his own creativity, the individual must have the capacity to *represent* the new ideas as they have taken form in the structure of his personality. We see the difficulties that people have in forming a "combined object" relationship with another person, to represent for example to the children. It is obvious that the artist in his studio and the scientist in his laboratory, the analyst in his consulting room, function at a higher level than they function in their own family.

Viewed in this light, then, the evolution of creativity demands the dominance of K—that is, the wish to understand. The predominance of K is that which makes possible what Keats termed "negative capability"—the capacity to suspend action, the possibility of having doubts, the wish to plumb the depths of a problem, to search for truth instead of rushing for solutions or experimental actions. While love and hate alone may urgently push towards action, K is the factor that permits the individual to become a thinking being.

Mrs Klein's adventure of discovery with Richard

When Melanie Klein settled down with her secretary to dictate her notes on Richard, she had a clear summer holiday in prospect, with a schedule free of other work and the delight of the Scottish landscape before her. However, she did not realize what a task she was setting herself: day by day and week by week with a spirited and neurotic boy of twelve in an unfamiliar setting (the girl-guides' cabin near a waterfall), far from home for both of them. But she set out using her usual methods and quickly found the boy responsive and lively. He was talkative, lonely, and inquisitive and soon responded to the drawing materials she provided.

Richard was much concerned with the war, with the Jews, and, naturally, for his father on active duty. Naturally his initial drawings were seascapes with air fights and surface attacks; gradually, his imagination slipped beneath the surface to the world of fish, starfish, and octopi, giving way gradually to a territorial investigation rich with countertransference references. Mrs Klein was, in spirit, investigating the transference objects and part-objects pictured by the war situation. Gradually a list of characters arose: star-fish babies with their greed and competitiveness, fighting the octopi—territorial and colonial. This picture of Mrs Klein's interior world became the "territorial map of the world" with lines and boundaries marking complications of combat, very dependent on the interpretive work.

In many ways the transference was shaping up into a love story, bursting out of the confines of the hut where Richard was dazzled by beauty of the night sky and of Mrs Klein's clothing, but—invaded by Mr Bluebottle flies. Thus Oedipus declared itself, and the breast was discovered, with its strawberry nipples and combined objects. Richard's claustrophobia was about to be conquered.

In all, during a whirlwind process of three months, Richard helped Mrs Klein to clarify major issues of the Kleinian psychology—differentiating internal from external, whole objects from part-objects, and clarifying the oedipal situation by discovering the combined object— discovery at its best, emerging right there from the clinical material, as distinguished from the invention of terminology.

On countertransference[3]

This term, which has achieved a status of its own, is not merely a clever linguistic inversion. We can set it out for investigation, pinned out to dry like a skin. What is it? It is meant to be the analyst's contribution, as in a duet with the patient—meant to harmonize and impose its own rhythm and cadence, in the nature of the chanter or the bagpipe. It need not be lexical or intelligible; one is reminded of Bion's foibles. I remember his saying, in his puckish way, which he knows I hate, that what he is saying is circular, but he is depending on the diameter to give it meaning.

So the first point is that the countertransference is an utterance by the attentive analyst. Second, it represents his focus of attention. Third, it is alleged to contain primitive fragments of thought called "alphaelements" which, when scrutinized attentively, will seem to form a pattern: incipient symbols of emotional meaning. When Bion is depending on the diameter of his excursion, he is hoping it is not nonsense. The circle itself is a primal symbol verging on language, a primitive script, like linear B. Anyone who has listened to Bion knows that he has been chained to negative capability—to the suspension of judgement and action, to waiting, and to tolerating his irritation: "Why can't he be clear, like Phil Pullman?" Because Bion is no charmer, because he is not inventing, he is hard at work in the task of discovery as the circle turns into "O"—or is it Zero? More Dodgsonian Mathematics. The reader is getting tired and developing a headache. Negative capability is not easy. Small wonder that the computer is so popular. And statistics so seductive.

It is difficult to explain the technique of counter-dreaming. It is not enough to fall asleep while the patient is talking. It requires a process of working over the material, focusing and selecting interpretive configurations awaiting a state of satisfaction (rest). The state of observation is essentially a resting state. It is also a state of heightened vigilance. I compare it with waiting in the dark for the deer, grazing at night, seen by their flashing white tails. This nocturnal vigilance is on the alert for movement of the quarry, part-object minimal movements that with patience can be seen to form a pattern of incipient meaning "cast before". This catching of the incipient meaning cast before is a function of receptive imagination—open to the possible, unconcerned with probability. Being rich with suspense, it is necessarily fatiguing, and fraught with anxiety. It is a trial of strength—and faith—that gives substance to terms such as resistance or retreat. However, it is a poetry generator.

In short, the countertransference is an emotional experience that must be caught in your dreams. Now the patient must attend to the analyst to interpret. How does he know what he is talking about? He doesn't—he is "counter-dreaming"; he has, in fact, abandoned "thinking" (science) for intuition (art, poetry): the verbal tradition of Homer.

Notes

1. W. R. Bion, *Two Papers: The Grid and Caesura* (Rio de Janeiro: Imago Editora, 1977.
2. W. R. Bion, *A Memoir of the Future*, single-volume edition (London: Karnac, 1991.)
3. D.M. added the following paragraphs for purposes of the present volume in 2002.

CHAPTER NINE

Post-Kleinian poetics

the Privilege of seeing great things in loneliness

John Keats[1]

yet not alone, while thou
Visit'st my slumbers nightly

John Milton[2]

W hat are the implications for both psychoanalysis itself and for psychoanalytic writing (and reading), of the post-Kleinian view of psychoanalysis as an art form? Bion, says Meltzer, treats psychoanalysis as "a thing-in-itself that existed in the world prior to its discovery by the mystic genius of Freud who gave it form".[3] Bion sees the process of coming to knowledge in terms of transcendence, breaking through the barriers of lies and basic assumptions. "What sort of artists can we be?" he asks.[4] Meltzer also sees psychoanalysis as an art-form, in which the psychoanalyst's quest for meaning is driven by awe of the beauty of the method that can make contact with the mysterious creativity of internal objects. But both have an essentially Platonic view in which the psychoanalytic activity takes place under the aegis of a source of knowledge beyond that already known by the self. The analyst is an observer of the shadows on the wall of the Cave. Whatever the interpretive terminology used during the course of the analysis or in the written formulations of hindsight, the practice of the psychoanalytic method is governed by this underlying Idea of psychoanalysis. Indeed, it is not the analyst who is conducting the analysis; he is being conducted, led, by his objects in communion with those of the patient.

Both Bion and Meltzer regard psychoanalytic theory an inadequate vehicle for expressing or conducting the emotional realities of the transference relationship. At one point Bion recounts wryly, that

> One of the painful, alarming features of continued experience was the fact that I had certain patients with whom I employed interpretations based on my previous experience with Melanie Klein, and, though I felt that I employed them correctly and could not fault myself, none of the good results that I anticipated occurred.[5]

The "good results" did not occur because he was mechanically reproducing the achieved understanding of his selfhood. What he said was "correct", but it was not "true". He was using theory in a prescriptive mode, rather than in the exploratory, quicksilver way of Melanie Klein with Richard, as described by Donald Meltzer in chapter 8. Bion was, during this phase, in an academic, imitative—projective—mode of identification with Klein rather than communing with Klein-as-Muse and her function as container for the Idea of psychoanalysis.

Given the inadequacies of theory, how, then, can anyone, outside the intimacy of the psychoanalytic consulting-room, glean any vestige of the "truth" of the psychoanalytic process—how comprehend anything of the psychoanalytic Idea? How can participants in the psychoanalytic process themselves link up with the Idea that allows new discoveries to be made, making psychoanalysis an aesthetic experience of the present time, not merely a mechanical feat of memory or organizational hindsight? If such knowledge cannot be academically transmitted, does that mean it is impossible for anyone not actually analysed by Melanie Klein to be a true Kleinian—and, indeed, would this external fact be of itself sufficient? Even Bion, after all, suggested that, though he had benefited from his "previous experience" with Klein, he found that it was possible to lose contact with its goodness (as in the case of trying to transmit it to his patient). He learned this from experience, in the same way that Milton recognized through "The Passion" that he had, for a period, lost contact with his Muse. Clearly psychoanalysis would soon die out if it were so exclusive that it became unteachable and therefore untransmittable. The problem lies in the manner of teaching. What, precisely, is being conveyed by an inspired teacher?

The psychoanalytic answer is, *the truth of an emotional experience.* Not the correctness, but the truth. Klein, Meltzer has said, was quite unabashedly prepared to change her mind about something from one day to the next, if her feelings and therefore her judgement changed as a result of new evidence—however emphatic she may have been in stating her original opinion.[6] The truth of an emotional experience is not a simple thing to convey. Meltzer has shown, in his account of the "love affair" between Klein and Richard, how it is not just possible but essential to read the deep grammar of this narrative of a psychoanalysis, if one wants to observe the process of discovery that was taking place at the time.[7] It is not sufficient to understand it only in terms of the theoretical conditions of its era, or even of hindsight. Milton said, "the meaning not the name I call". It is necessary to read beyond the "naming" to the "meaning" and to locate the discovery-process, if we wish to internalize the substance of the ineffable events that took place during that analysis and incorporate them into our own idea of mental development—to make that knowledge food for the mind. It is not sufficient to know what Mrs Klein *said* about Richard: it is necessary to know what she *did*—to find a way of observing what happened in the sessions that was beyond words. Shelley's definition of poetry as "legislative" is equally true of the poetry of psychoanalysis. The poetry of its practice, which enables the having of ideas, predates the philosophical formulation of those ideas. We may rest in the formulation; but what we need to know is the meaning. Coleridge said, the "highest problem of Philosophy" was

> Whether Ideas are regulative only, according to Aristotle and Kant; or likewise CONSTITUTIVE, and one with the power and Life of Nature, according to Plato, and Plotinus.[8]

His view was that ideas, by their very nature, could not be merely regulative and therefore paraphraseable; they had to be understood as part of an organic process. In attributing this to Plato, he was reading the poet-in-Plato, as the poets have always done, rather than the doctrinaire Plato (who banished the poets, etc.). Indeed, according to Cassirer, Kant in fact reinterpreted his concept of "reason" to become "pure reason"—a "constitutive" principle that guided from within, rather than a "regulative" principle of external reference.[9] Formulations and theories are limited as well as temporary; ideas are inexhaustible, since they embody the process of coming-to-knowledge, the "power and life of nature".

This kind of "knowing" is, inevitably, dependent on the quality of the subjective involvement of the inquirer; it is an artistic operation. (Also, of course, it requires sufficient access to the material.) An analogous process to that of reading Richard takes place when we read the poets—and, indeed, when the poets read the poets. We need to enter the state of mind that Meltzer describes as the "countertransference dream". Keats calls it "burning through"—a continually repeated process, until you are "grey-gone in passion".[10] The usual objection to subjective readings is that it is impossible to distinguish validity from "wildness" or craziness. In fact, it is quite easy to judge whether the writer is telling the truth—provided that is the question we ask ourselves—as distinct from merely "endeavouring at effect" (to borrow Keats's phrase), which generally results not so much in wildness as in the dullness of self-promotion. A subjective reading, which is in itself a learning experience, is closer to the scientific reality of the way in which the mind develops than any purportedly objective statement of Kleinian theory or Miltonic doctrine. It partakes of the psychoanalytic, or the poetic, idea that underlies all its inelegant, incomplete "steppings of the imagination towards a truth". When Keats stood at the opening of Fingal's Cave and imagined he saw Milton's Lycidas, Genius of the Shore, guarding the portal to the mysteries of inspired poetry, he posed the question: is this a teacher who encourages the hopeful initiates of poetry, or one who bars it against erring eyes? Keats in a sense chose both answers and investigated experientially the consequences of each mode of learning: that of obedient imitation, based on reading stylistic devices as referential "signs", and the adventurous one of "straining at particles of light in a great darkness"—searching for the symbol of the emotional experience.

To be *merely* a sign-reader is to be a liar, in the Bionic sense of covering-over with self-ish accretions. Ignoring the temporariness of theoretical formulations and applying them mechanically or moralistically results in an impoverishment of internal objects and quashing of the intelligence. It is the precise opposite of Keats's "vale of Soulmaking". Bion repeatedly makes a distinction between "knowing" and "knowing about". We can see how some types of knowing-about may be helpful, while others entail a substitution of the self for the object and so become lies. There is much that can be usefully known about the poets, in terms of culture, technique, biography—and we would be foolish to ignore or neglect anything that may contribute to giving our imagination a foothold. Such knowledge is only useful as long as we remember that history is not accurate in the scientific sense either and can in no way explain the creativity of the poets, which is what we really need to know. Many varieties of lie can shelter under the umbrella of "knowing about": they include scavenging, patronizing, plagiarizing, as well as authoritarianism, exclusivity, grandiosity. As is well known, there will be in any humanistic discipline self-appointed academic guardians of its "laws". But those who are not in touch with their inspiring objects, continuously or at least continually, are all liars. They do not contribute to poetry's legislative function in the Shelleyan sense; they obey the letter, not the spirit of the law. These false guardians legislate against the multitudinous seas of humanity lapping at the shore—the "hungry generations". They know nothing of "the gigantic shadows which futurity casts upon the present" that, Shelley said, characterizes the voices of the poets—echoed by Bion in "the shadow of the Future cast before".[11] In the terms of Bion and Meltzer, they are "two-dimensional".

The "addicts" of psychoanalysis, says Bion, have a "curiously two-dimensional quality".[12] This two-dimensionality is owing to the substitution of signs for symbols. It derives from regarding the psychoanalytic process, or the reading process, as one of deciphering signs rather than discovering symbols. In *The Kleinian Development*, Meltzer noted psychoanalysis' debt to philosophers such as Cassirer, Whitehead, Wittgenstein, who "focussed on problems of symbol formation, notational systems, modes of thought, uses of ambiguity, the meaning of silences, the role of the musical versus the lexical level in communication etc."[13] They were continuing an investigation that had begun in the eighteenth century in the context of the debate about the origins of language, and had been taken up by the German Romantic philosophers and the English Romantic poets, as an inquiry into the nature of a "symbol" (a term adopted into its modern usage by Goethe).[14] Susanne Langer, in the same philosophical tradition, developed her analysis of symbolic qualities and situations in the context of attempting to formulate the nature of aesthetic experience. She shows how art forms ("presentational forms") have a "genuine semantic" of their own "beyond the limits of discursive language".[15] This semantic relates to the articulation of the "forms of feeling". Art forms help us to "conceive" our feelings and our life of feeling, through their tensions, rhythms, resolutions, and spatial interplay. It is in these formal qualities that their meaning resides—rather than in their discursive content or paraphraseable meaning. This is the case even—or especially—

when the medium is verbal, as in drama or poetry (or psychoanalysis). Symbolic forms are conducive to conception, whereas sign-systems stimulate action. A symbol, she writes, "makes things conceivable", whereas a sign "stores up propositions"; a symbol "lets us conceive its object"; whereas a sign "causes us to deal with what it means".[16] By "object", she refers to the "unspoken idea" whose comprehension is the goal of a symbolic or artistic activity.[17] Such a symbol stimulates not action but contemplation.

Langer used music as her starting-point for inquiry, since it demonstrates so clearly the marriage-of-minds that must take place between performer and composer in relation to "the musical Idea" that is beyond them both yet governs the sensuous realization of the symbolic form. The "idea", she says, is listened to or seen feelingly by all participants in the process, whether artist or art-appreciator. It follows from this, moreover, that the "cognitive value of symbols" lies in their being able to "transcend the past experience" of the interpreter.[18] This process of conceiving or apprehending an unknown idea within the mind's "dark abyss" to "make it pregnant" was described by Milton in *Paradise Lost*. It is a voyage of discovery—not alone, but with the Muse, that mediator with the world of ideas beyond the already known. As Shelley said, poets can present the "before unapprehended relations of things"[19]—this accounts for the "legislative" function of poetry in the world of ideas:

> [The poets] measure the circumference and sound the depths of human nature with a comprehensive and all-penetrating spirit, and they are themselves perhaps the most sincerely astonished at its manifestations, for it is less their spirit than the spirit of the age. Poets are the hierophants of an unapprehended inspiration, the mirrors of the gigantic shadows which futurity casts upon the present, the words which express what they understand not . . . Poets are the unacknowledged legislators of the world.[20]

However scarlet may be the "sins" of a poet's selfhood, he says, they are all "washed white as snow" by the eternal value to humanity of their service *as poets*, as vehicles for a knowledge beyond themselves.

In the view of Bion and Meltzer, likewise, understanding psychoanalysis as a symbol-making or artistic activity that makes room for the apprehension of the unknown relieves it from the claustrophobia of two-dimensionality. Meltzer writes that it was his experience with autistic patients, and their withdrawal from aesthetic conflict, that enabled him to fit the "key of alpha-function" (symbol-formation) to "the lock of two-dimensionality". Bion characteristically defines the field of true mental activity—as distinct from "protomental"—in terms of three co-ordinates: the emotions of Love and Hate and their relation to Knowledge, or the vertices of Science, Art, and Religion.[21] The three-ness is significant since it corresponds to the three-dimensionality of a field in which the "links" or "tension between" vertices are what capture the meaning of the experience:

> These fundamental characteristics, love, hate, dread, are sharpened to a point where the participating pair may feel them to be almost unbearable: it is the price that has to be paid for the transformation of an activity that is about psychoanalysis into an activity that is psychoanalysis.[22]

In order for psychoanalysis to be psychoanalysis, not just a veneer or lookalike, it must somehow become a three-dimensional space, containing not enclosing, governed not by ideas in the "regulative" sense but by "the relations of things"—ideas in the "constitutive" sense. Such a container for experience "lets us conceive its object"—the idea of that particular experience, a function of the experience that is psychoanalysis itself. The "field" view of recurring emotional struggle supersedes, in post-Kleinian theory, the Kleinian "phase" theory of a developmental hurdle between the paranoid-schizoid and depressive positions. In Meltzer's account, the replacement of "phase" by "field" is what allowed it to become evident that it was the "aesthetic response" that activated the symbolic realm. Time and again the mind trembles on the brink of symbol-formation, in depressive/paranoid-schizoid oscillation. The tremendous field of force set up by the confrontation between Love and Hate results in dramatic rescue by the K-link, the dormant but innate desire for knowledge that changes the catastrophe-disaster into "catastrophic change", a structural development within the mind owing to its incorporation of a new idea.[23] The K-link, one could Bionically extrapolate, is the knight on horseback who in literature archetypally figures the questing aspect of the personality. The three vertices of the emotional field are established; they are condensed by means of the tension between them, and ultimately the pain bites—with a single stroke of the axe. If the modern aim of psychoanalysis is to "introduce the patient to himself" (as Bion often puts it) and to activate those emotional conflicts that will set the growth of his mind in motion, then it must provide the opportunity for aesthetic encounters such as these. The essence of the psychoanalytic process, in the post-Kleinian view, lies not in reviewing past experiences but in having present experiences. Thinking does not consist in organizing feelings through hind-sight, but in gaining access to feelings, which are then "transformed" through alpha-function into symbols.

By the time of the *Memoir*, "dread" in the field of LHK has become "awe", in its original etymological sense of awesome—the origins of aesthetic and religious experience in the face of the Unknown (Wordsworth's Cliff). Meltzer says that while the manufacture of lies is an active process, done by the self (invention), the discovery of truth is "more passive, requiring submission to the operation of container and contained".[24]

> But perhaps to state [this] as if the analyst were the container misses the point that it is the fitting together of the analyst's atten-tion and attitudes to the cooperativeness of the patient that forms and seals the container, lending it the degree of flexibility and resilience required from moment to moment.[25]

Bion's "container–contained" model is founded on the mother-in-rev-erie, digesting and transforming the infant's anxieties, returning them to the infant in the form of symbols so the anxieties can be thought about. In Meltzer's thinking, the analyst and analysand—Bion's "par-ticipating pair"—work together to make a container, a joint field, which will put their *internal objects* in a position of communication with one another, where they can hold "conversations". Meltzer's descrip-tion of "fitting attention to cooperation" has similarities with Bion's image of the diamond-cutter who intensifies the diamond's brilliance by virtue of reflecting the light back along the same route.[26] The path-way to knowledge is a function of reciprocity. The cutter, like the analyst, merely opens the pathway; the insight is a function of the light itself, Milton's "light shine inwards". We do not "make up" our own minds, Bion said; on the contrary, "our minds are made up for us by forces about which we know nothing".[27] What we do make is the container, the pathway, the irregularity in which an idea might lodge, the "wreathed trellis" for the visitations of Psyche. Analytic "success" depends on the patient's having sufficiently introjected a capacity for learning from experience to be able to carry on his self-analysis. This type of success is to be distinguished from social adaptability, normal-ity, or relief from symptoms. It is useful if the patient can understand the analyst's thoughts about him, on the discursive level of sign-sys-tems. But it is essential that the patient introject the analyst's *capacity to think* about him, on the level of symbol-formation, if he is to be able to continue the process of self-analysis that is the ultimate goal of the "participating pair". This, like all inspiring processes, is not something that is achieved once and for all, any more than the "depressive position" is a badge or qualification. It is something that has to be continually renewed when each new idea sends its premonitions over the horizon of consciousness—the "shadow of the future". Keats, in his great Odes, demonstrated the impossibility of fusion—of being mystically swallowed up, as it were without pain; yet this did not mean death in the sense of abandonment by the symbol-making gods; the nightingale may sing in the next valley-glade.

The word "aesthetic", Meltzer notes, appears for the first time in Bion's work in 1965, in *Transformations*. In Bion's early work there is no distinction between the discursive and the representational— "thought" still means "verbal thought". Initially, Bion seems to have accepted with a certain ironic surprise and reluctance that he was no longer in the domain of the "scientific":

> I cannot support this conviction by evidence regarded as scientific. It may be that the formulation belongs to the domain of *aesthetic.*[28]

Attention and Interpretation, with its formulations of "faith" and of "love, hate, dread", was written in 1970 after Bion had escaped from the "aqueous medium" of London to the "gaseous one" of California, "where he would have to fight for his professional life" (as Meltzer puts it in his "personal mythology").[29] It was there, fighting for his life and throwing respectability to the winds, that Bion wrote his extraordinary fictional trilogy, *A Memoir of the Future*, under the aegis of a voice telling him that it may be possible to tell the truth in fiction even when it seemed impossible in scientific "jargon".[30] In this work the aesthetic perspective finally becomes predominant, fusing and clarifying what had previously been tentative, implicit, obscure, or obscured. Meltzer writes:

> In terms of Bion's concept of "catastrophic change" and the impact of the "new idea" there is no difficulty in establishing what this idea was and the revolution it has wrought in my ways of thinking and working ... The "new idea" was clearly something like: "in the beginning was the aesthetic object, and the aesthetic object was the breast and the breast was the world". Of course I am using the word "breast" as a technical term with only an implication of description, rather than the other way round. On the one hand it seems surprising to me that this idea did not reach me through

Adrian Stokes to whom it was ever vivid; on the other hand it is difficult to say whence in Bion's work it derives. It is not in the Grid; it is only hinted at in *Transformations*; it tags along in a secondary position in *Attention and Interpretation*. Only in *A Memoir of the Future* does it find its place unambiguously. But it had reached me through Bion before that publication had crept into my thought and certainly into my consulting room. Not only had I become aware that the psycho-analytical method had taken on an aesthetic quality in my eyes but I had begun to see, mainly through dreams, that it had done so for some of my patients as well.[31]

The aesthetic quality of the psychoanalytic idea, with all its implications of the turbulent "siege of contraries" in the internal baby's eternal relation to the world-breast, crept gradually into focus until, when fully recognized, it was seen to have been there all along—that is, ever since Melanie Klein during the psychoanalysis of children naturally assumed a maternal role and discovered its combined-object implications.[32]

In Bion's philosophy, the "new idea" that is always on the horizon in any analytic session is feared. It takes on the overwhelming quality that Klein noted could accompany the combined object, and causes premonitions of catastrophic anxiety. In Meltzer's extension of this philosophy, the idea is feared for *the impact of its beauty*:

> If we follow Bion's thought closely we see that the new idea presents itself as an "emotional experience" of the beauty of the world and its wondrous organization, descriptively closer to Hamlet's "heart of mystery".[33]

The emotional experience is a poetic marriage of contrary emotions—love and hate—that may be (Bion says) "almost unbearable". It can result either in "pain" or in "suffering".[34] Pain causes symptoms, whereas suffering, if it can be undergone, is accompanied or followed by a revelation of its meaning. The choice is again one of action or contemplation. Possibly Bion prefers the term "suffering" because of its etymological connection (via the Latin) with "passion" and "passive", with their poetic and religious associations. Meltzer retains the traditional use of "pain", which includes the idea of mental pain, as in Keats's "All is cold beauty; pain is never done".[35] To resolve the painful tension of this conflict into a moment of knowledge requires an act of faith in which the support of the selfhood (what Bion calls "memory and desire") is abandoned in favour of total dependence on the internal object, as with Keats and Psyche, or Milton and his Muse:

The "act of faith" (F) depends on disciplined denial of memory and desire. A bad memory is not enough: what is ordinarily called forgetting is as bad as remembering. It is necessary to inhibit dwelling on memories and desires. They are two facets of the same thing . . .[36]

What is the nature of the "act of faith" in post-Kleinian ethics? To understand the concept of faith requires a return to the nature of pain. Meltzer says that Bion located the origin of mental pain in "that point in growth of a thought where it becomes fixed in dream-myth".[37] But the nature of pain, its qualities, were not defined until Meltzer's formulation of the "aesthetic conflict". This phase in the evolution of the post-Kleinian Idea of psychoanalysis found elucidation in Kierkegaard's "ravings about the absurd" (as he is jokingly introduced by Meltzer).[38] In *Fear and Trembling*, Kierkegaard considers the story of Abraham's intention to sacrifice Isaac in terms of a weaning myth. It is possible to interpret the myth, he says, in terms of the Abraham-baby's faith that the God-mother will provide an alternative form of food (the ram). It is an "absurd" solution, "beyond human calculation". It is not a matter of "resignation" to the inevitable sacrifice. On the contrary, Abraham has faith that God will return Isaac to him (his developing child-self), not in the next world but in this—though he cannot imagine how this may happen. Kierkegaard sees "resignation" as the culminating limit of the self-satisfied Hegelian system of dialectics. He diagnosed himself as being without faith; yet this sharpened his perception of its mysteriousness and of the grandiosity of those who cannot see the problem. The "knights of resignation" have a "bold" look, confident in their moral and social superiority. The "knight of faith", on the other hand, who makes a far more difficult mental "movement", is hard to discern, for he looks quite ordinary on the outside. To all appearances he may be a "bourgeois philistine", or the "cheesemonger vegetating in the dusk".[39] He may be a peasant in the courtyard. He may be a baby on the point of weaning, not resigned to deprivation, but hoping that beyond his own conceptual capabilities, a new form of spiritual nourishment may materialize. The knights of resignation believe in poetry as consolation for the woes of the vale of tears, or in psychoanalysis as the indulgence and promulgation of guilt. It is not their bodies, but their minds, that are two-dimensional. The advantage of this complacent stance is that it holds no pain, no "suffering". But neither is there a pathway for ideas to penetrate and lodge themselves. The nature of the pain lies in the unknown qualities of the object—with its capacity to give, and also to take away.

Bion seems to have come to his concept of faith, as something necessary to alpha-function (symbol-formation), via the Kierke-gaardian route, recognizing that his initial attempts at being a Kleinian analyst were, at times, two-dimensional. What was lacking was the unknown dimension that would transform it from "talk about" psychoanalysis to actually *being* psychoanalysis. In Meltzer's interpretation of this new sign—which Bion calls an "element"—"F" includes within it the fear of the "frightful fiend" of "hallucinosis, megalomania, delusions, catastrophic anxiety". Bion empathized with Coleridge's description of the fiend following at his heels—a fiend of madness that possibly lurks in the corners of everybody's mentality, and whose existence is acknowledged somewhere by all the poets.[40] So Bion's "act of faith", says Meltzer, would correspond not to the child swimming for the first time without his water-wings, confident in Daddy's presence but, rather, to "floating free in shark-infested wa-ters".[41] In *The Apprehension of Beauty*, Meltzer cites the image of the shark from Melville:

> And that same day, too, gazing far down from the boat's side into the same golden sea, Starbuck lonely murmured:
> "Loveliness unfathomable, as ever lover saw in his young bride's eyes! Tell me not of thy teeth-tiered sharks, and thy kidnap-ping cannibal ways. Let faith oust fact; let fancy oust memory; I love deep down and do believe."[42]

Meltzer takes Bion's shark of incipient madness and places it within the aesthetic constellation of emotions, where it becomes the enigmatic quality of the object in the concept of the aesthetic conflict—the oppor-tunity of faith, to "love deep down" in the shark-infested waters of the golden sea. Faith is the moment when Cleopatra applies the asp, or when Gawain offers his neck without flinching for the third stroke of the axe. It is Penelope when she suggests to Odysseus that his bed can be moved. It is when Milton forsakes Christian Doctrine for the dic-tates of the Muse, or Oedipus treads beyond the touch of his daughters, or Keats opens the window—not knowing whether to warm love or to fairy-lands forlorn. Faith is what relieves the mind from the endless circlings of invention and makes discovery possible. This does not mean that all knowledge attained so far by the mind in its soulmaking pilgrimage must be cast aside. On the contrary, each step forward is founded on the utmost potentialities of the previous state-of-mind, in its orientation to the Platonic idea of mental development. What must be "abandoned" in memory and desire is not the real knowledge that has become part of the mind's structure, but the sentimental and tyrannical orientations of wish-fulfilment and nostalgic blame—the invention of causality. Memory and desire are really, as Bion says, the same thing: the self's preconceived idea of how things happen. If indulged too obsessionally, this orientation becomes a "lie", an attitude that preempts concepts from penetrating the crust of complacency. Ideas cannot happen.

The other way in which ideas cannot happen is "misconception". Misconception is the failure to form the "right" symbol—the symbol that truly expresses the emotional significance of the moment. Essentially this is when the infant-self's leap of faith is unreciprocated by the Muse-mother. The model for this type of failure is, for Meltzer, when the baby's presentation of his first well-formed stool is not recognized by the mother as his first creative "thought". The baby has allowed his internal objects to organize his digestion and thereby demonstrates the "binding effect of thought" as opposed to the "evacuatory significance of action". It is a real achievement, a gift, like that given by Milton to the Muse on Christ's birthday:

> O run, prevent them with thy humble ode,
> And lay it lowly at his blessed feet.

If the mother does not appreciate this "humble ode" or make her appreciation felt, the ground is laid for a misconception.[43] Bion begins the story of the significance of the baby's stool in the *Memoir*, in the conversation between P.A. and Roland; they can find no "simple explanation" for the mother and baby's mutual determination and delight.[44] Bion thus makes it clear that there is no "simple" explanation for this simple act, or for the reciprocal joy it produces; though he does not, at that point, explicitly connect it with his predominant concern with the nature of conception *versus* misconception. Meltzer's preferred analysis of misconception is in fact that of Roger Money-Kyrle, who gives it a particular humanistic slant that supports his own wish to free Kleinian theory from its harshly moralistic framework. Meltzer feels that this harshness exists also in Bion's worldview, suggesting it has lost sight of "the Hellenic view of tragedy, of the human condition overwhelmed by forces of which it is not only ignorant, but essentially innocent."[45] Through the possibility of misconception, the weight of guilt and blame is lifted from the essentially well-intentioned analyst or mother-in-reverie, allowing attention to be refocused on the reparative potential of the conversation between internal objects. This is not a softening or compromise position regarding human evil, nor is it (says

Meltzer) merely the expression of a "sanguine disposition". On the contrary, it clarifies the area in which compromise may be a temptation. This area is the other field of failure of symbol-formation—namely, the world of non-emotions, minus LHK. In this field there can be no compromise: it is the Claustrum, the lie-in-the-soul.[46] As Milton's devils so pathetically express their alienation from God:

> As he our darkness, cannot we his light
> Imitate as we please?[47]

In psychoanalytic thinking, as in Milton's, it is only the self—not the objects—who imprison the soul (Satan's "Myself am hell"); as Meltzer says, "the door is always open". Indeed, the formulation made implicitly by Bion of the possibility of a Negative Grid is presented in Meltzer's writings as one of his greatest achievements, owing to the power it gives the analyst not to be blackmailed by the frightful fiend of hypocrisy. Not just the emotional strength, but the intellectual spotlight necessary to artistically show how thought is being undermined.

In *The Kleinian Development*, Meltzer says that psychoanalysis has its "historic roots more in philosophy and theology than in nineteenth-century science".[48] His view is that "the practice of psychoanalysis is an art"; but he elaborates on what this entails:

> It is not possible to make observations and find a language for transformation without there being a Model of the World in the back of the mind. The process of discovery of new phenomena is completely dependent on the explicit and conscious use of a model in order to recognize the emergence into one's awareness of phenomena which cannot be described by the existing model. The evolution of the science is of this inductive-deductive spiral nature, that novel phenomena require an extension of the model, and this extension opens to view other phenomena which not only could not be described before, but could not even be recognized.[49]

The "model of the world" derives from the genuine achieved knowledge of the personality, however incomplete. It is the stage that it has reached in its attempt to "acquire identity" in the vale of soulmaking, where "circumstances" are not only pain-causing events, but opportunities to "school an intelligence" and make it, through successive leaps of faith, into a soul. So long as it is not ossified into a sign-system by memory and desire, it can retain its organic connection with its spiritual mediators in the world of ideas. Clearly the mind, unlike other phenomenological fields, is not susceptible to the methods of physical science; as Bion keeps stressing, the subject of investigation is the same as the tool of investigation, the observer-observed. Yet, insofar as the artistic process is one of discovery, it is ultimately dedicated to contributing to the scientific body of knowledge about the mind. By a process of incremental building-up, we may imagine how with patience (Keatsian "negative capability") eventually "a pattern will emerge", as it does when thinking through individual emotional experiences.[50] Like the participants who—through different activities—are all essentially "listening to the musical Idea", the Idea of psychoanalysis may become embedded in the world of knowledge. The scientific knowledge gained by psychoanalysis and the artistic mode of attaining it are interdependent. Together they result in a "spiral progression". This is owing to the peculiar nature of the mind as an ever-growing, suprasensuous, but still natural domain. Bion writes:

> However prolonged a psychoanalysis may be, it represents only the start of an investigation. It stimulates growth of the domain it investigates.[51]

Meltzer writes:

> The analysts of today may be laying the foundations for a science of great grandeur in the future, in the way that the alchemists laid the groundwork for modern chemistry and its astonishing accomplishments.[52]

And the poets, those eternal alchemists who voice the developmental dreams of humanity, are the unacknowledged legislators of the world of the mind.

NOTES

1. Keats, letter to Haydon, 22 December 1818, in: *Selected Letters*, ed. R. Gittings (Oxford: Oxford University Press, 1975).
2. Milton, *Paradise Lost*, VII.28–29.
3. D. Meltzer, *The Kleinian Development* (Strath Tay: Clunie Press, 1978), III, p. 104.
4. Wilfred Bion, *Bion in New York and Sao Paulo*, ed. F. Bion (Strath Tay: Clunie Press, 1980), p. 73.
5. Wilfred Bion, *A Memoir of the Future* (3 vols., 1975–79), single-volume edition (London: Karnac, 1991), p. 559.
6. See D. Meltzer, "Concerning Signs and Symbols", *British Journal of Psychotherapy*, 14, No. 2 (1997).

7. See D. Meltzer's analysis in *Richard Week-by-Week*, Part 2 of *The Kleinian Development* (Strath Tay: Clunie Press, 1978).

8. Coleridge, *The Statesman's Manual* (1817), *Lay Sermons*, ed. R. J. White (London: Routledge, 1972), p. 114.

9. E. Cassirer, *Rousseau, Kant and Goethe* (Hamden, CT: Archon Books, 1961).

10. See "On Sitting Down to Read *King Lear* Once Again", and "On Seeing a Lock of Milton's Hair", written on consecutive days in January 1818.

11. Bion, *Memoir*, pp. 469, 486. For Shelley, see note 20 below.

12. W. Bion, *Brazilian Lectures, Vol. II* (Rio de Janeiro: Imago Editora, 1974) p. 56.

13. Meltzer, *Kleinian Development*, Vol. 3, p. 21.

14. On the "origins of language debate" and Dr Johnson's idea of "inspiration", see Nalini Jain, *The Mind's Extensive View: Samuel Johnson as a Critic of Poetic Language:* (Strath Tay: Clunie Press, 1991). According to Cassirer, Goethe, reviewing Kant, coined the term "symbol" in the context of establishing the Kantian "ideal" as something which could give a unity to the process of experience, rather than something elevated above it (Cassirer, *Language and Myth*, transl. S. Langer, New York: Dover Publications, 1953). The Greek word *symbolon* originally referred to a small object, broken and divided between two friends or family members as proof of their good faith (belonging to one another). The term occurs in *Oedipus Tyrannos* as the starting-point for Oedipus' quest to find himself (l. 221).

15. Susanne Langer, *Philosophy in a New Key* (Cambridge, MA: Harvard University Press, 1942), pp. 86, 97.

16. Langer, *Philosophy*, pp. 223, 244.

17. Langer, *Philosophy*, p. 259.

18. Susanne Langer, *Feeling and Form* (London: Routledge & Kegan Paul, 1953), p. 390.

19. Percy Bysshe Shelley, A *Defence of Poetry* (written in 1821), in: *Shelley's Poetry and Prose*, ed. D. H. Reiman and S. B. Powers, New York: Norton (1977), p. 482.

20. Shelley, *A Defence of Poetry*, p. 508.

21. Bion, *Brazilian Lectures, II*, p. 96.

22. W. Bion, *Attention and Interpretation* (London: Tavistock, 1970), p. 66.

23. D. Meltzer, *Studies in Extended Metapsychology* (Strath Tay: Clunie Press, 1986), p. 17.

24. Meltzer, *Kleinian Development*, Vol. 3, p. 107.

25. Meltzer, *Extended Metapsychology*, p. 208.

26. Bion, *Bion in N.Y. and Sao Paulo*, p. 15; see also Meltzer, *Extended Metapsychology*, p. 121.

27. Lecture in New York, Bion, *Bion in N.Y. and Sao Paulo*, p. 69.

28. Meltzer, *Kleinian Development*, Vol. 3, p. 75.

29. Meltzer, in A. Hahn (Ed.), *Sincerity and Other Works* (London: Karnac, 1994), p. 471.

30. Bion: see Bion's "Satanic Jargonieur", *Memoir*, p. 302.
31. Meltzer, *Extended Metapsychology*, p. 204.
32. On Melanie Klein's discovery of the "combined object" as the foundation for emotional strength, but also as sometimes overwhelming in quality, see Meltzer, *Kleinian Development*, Vol. 2, pp. 113–23.
33. D. Meltzer & M. Harris Williams, *The Apprehension of Beauty* (Strath Tay: Clunie Press, 1988), p. 20.
34. Bion, *Attention and Interpretation*, p. 18.
35. Keats, sonnet "On Visiting the Tomb of Burns".
36. Bion, *Attention and Interpretation*, p. 41.
37. See Meltzer, *Kleinian Development*, Vol. 3, p. 64.
38. Meltzer, *Kleinian Development*, Vol. 3, p. 97.
39. Soren Kierkegaard, *Fear and Trembling* (1843) (Harmondsworth, Middlesex: Penguin, 1985), pp. 65–69.
40. Coleridge, *The Ancient Mariner*, cited (without reference) by Bion, *Attention and Interpretation*, p. 46.
41. Meltzer, *Kleinian Development*, Vol. 3, p. 99.
42. Hermann Melville, "The Gilder", in: *Moby Dick*, in Meltzer & Harris Williams, *Apprehension of Beauty*, p. viii.
43. In a lecture given at the London Centre for Psychotherapy as part of a series on "Spirituality"; to be published in 2004 by London: Karnac. The "evacuatory significance of action" is described in Meltzer & Harris Williams, *Apprehension of Beauty*, p. 69.
44. Bion, *Memoir*, p. 558.
45. Donald Meltzer, "Money Kyrle's concept of misconception", in: Hahn, *Sincerity*, p. 511.
46. See Bion, *Attention and Interpretation*, pp. 19–20.
47. Milton, *Paradise Lost*, II.269–70.
48. *Meltzer Kleinian Development*, Vol. 3, p. 94.
49. Meltzer & Harris Williams, *Apprehension of Beauty*, p. 204.
50. Bion, *Memoir*, p. 472.
51. Bion, *Attention and Interpretation*, p. 69.
52. Meltzer & Harris Williams, *Apprehension of Beauty*, p. 23.

Rosemary's roots

The Muse in Bion's autobiographies

> Who alive can say,
> "Thou art no poet; may'st not tell thy dreams?"
>
> Keats[1]

> *Paul:*   But he attributed his escape to the Offices of the
> Heavenly Muse— . . .
>
> *Roland:*   You mean to say you think we ought to take his
> description seriously? Of course it's wonderful poetry—
>
> *P.A.:*   "Of course", but Virgil and Homer and Milton were not
> writing "poetry"; they were writing "seriously". They wrote
> poetry because it was the most serious way of writing.
>
> Wilfred Bion[2]

In his quest to discover the truth about himself, Bion uses the freedom of the autobiographical books to remember, or rather to relive in the present, the teaching-by-example of those who contributed to the qualities of his internal objects. Here he endeavours to shed the obscuring veil of respectability that, he felt had always hampered him, and to follow the example of the poets—to "write seriously", despite his intense frustration at feeling unable to achieve poetic expression. In the *Memoir* he invites a gamut of internal voices, ranging from pre-natal somites to "Eighty years old", to engage in a conversation under the aegis of "O", the realm of the Unknown and ineffable. They try to align their conflicting vertices into a receptive pattern in which the truth can lodge. Meltzer writes:

> The new idea in the end becomes the idea of the combined object, and this for Mrs Klein signified the advent of the depressive position.[3]

Certainly Melanie Klein was Bion's Muse, and the *Memoir*, which begins with his archetypal *Dream*, is his self-analysis under her guidance, in the same way that Keats wrote *The Fall of Hyperion* under the guidance of Moneta, or Milton wrote *Paradise Lost* under Urania, or Homer wrote *The Odyssey* under Athene. But, it will be said, Klein is barely mentioned—except to say how unsatisfactory he found the mechanical application of her theories: the magic wand of Kleinian interpretation didn't work after all. He does not even quote Klein in the way that he quotes Freud. No, but aspects or qualities of Mrs Klein-as-object are disseminated everywhere, and the dialogue with aspects of the infant-self is continuous, with its Ps↔D oscillation between the voices of "self-satisfaction" and of receptivity ("awe"). The *Memoir* is in a sense Bion's rediscovery of the personal meaning to him of her concept of the combined object (reformulated by him as container–contained), reviewing his history through the "past presented" and the "shadow of the Future cast before".[4]

This dialogue—or "Bedlam", when all the voices speak together—may be more accessible when approached initially through Bion's more literal autobiography *The Long Week-End*, which helps us to build a picture of the origins of the Muse-elements in relation to a real childhood. Here he describes the mother whose love was deep enough for her to "tolerate the fact" of her children's nastiness, but whose acquiescence to social pressures weakened her inspirational capacity and led to the kind of internal separation that he wryly and bitterly termed "home leave".[5] He describes the father who was both "sensitive" and "a fine shot" but whose brittle anxiety about his son's masculinity made him a vehicle for tyrannical "Arf Arfer" regimentation, substituting the goal of success for the goal of development. Of course, it is not his actual parents that he writes about but his internal dream-parents, as happens in the very process of "remembering", and as—anticipating confusion—he firmly reminds us when he says:

Anyone can "know" which school, regiment, colleagues, friends I write about. In all but the most superficial sense they would be wrong. I write about "me".[6]

It is significant that the first words of *The Long Week-End* refer to his Indian ayah:

> Our ayah was a wizened little woman who, in so far as I connected age with her at all, was assumed by my sister and me to be very old, much older than our father and mother ... [My mother] was not so old as our ayah; my sister and I agreed that *she* was not less than, say, two or maybe three hundred years old, and though this was a ripe age she did not seem likely to die.

Yet we know more about Bion's impossible and indescribable concept "O"—the inscrutable, immutable, ineffable—than we do about his ayah. There is virtually nothing about her in *The Long Week-End*, apart from the passage where she allows his father's wrath to sweep over her like a storm and emerges unscathed and unperturbed.[7] She was presumably an illiterate peasant from the realms of the "untouchable" (which Bion contrasts with the "unspeakable"—the chauvinism of the Raj). Yet we have the deepening impression—as we read his "dreams"—that she, together with aspects of his part-Indian mother, was the original source of the internal Muse whose qualities find reincarnation in Rosemary, the heroine of the *Memoir*, the "whore's child" whose love is not melancholy but fiery and tigerish, capable of transcending the brutish violence of social conformity. This ayah/Muse who, like Mrs Klein, occupies a pregnant dream-silence in the books, is capable of containing his "thoughts" in a way that he evokes as poignantly lacking in the narrative of his childhood. Unlike his mother, who "might die because she was so old", the ayah is of indestructible ageless age, verging on the concept of infinity to the child-mind. Bion becomes acutely sensitive to the space where she is not, and later denotes it "O". Her lack of characterization makes her available for a transferential role—in the *Memoir* she can metamorphose into Helen of Troy as easily as the old Indian Beggar Woman, each of them—like Rosemary's mother the Victorian prostitute—hatched from the compost of civilization:

> My profession is the oldest in the world ... Thais, Eve, Lillith ... there is a lineage which you cannot begin to match ... You did not think, did you, that the poor little guttersnipe from the ghetto, the

virgin's womb, might be more than rewarded by not being abhorred?[8]

When Roland condescendingly attempts to sympathize with the "disadvantages" of Rosemary's upbringing, she contemptuously contradicts his ignorance: informing him that she had "the best of mothers" who religiously protected her daughter from exploitation by society's "young gentlemen".[9] Escape from the confines of social respectability is for Bion a necessary criterion for heroism: the tissue of "lies" must be discarded before the realms of true emotionality can be entered. This idea of the mother/Muse is formulated in the books in apposition to its "negative" antithesis that appears in various guises (the false containers of the tank or trap), most succinctly defined as "Mother England that old whore" who crucifies her sons in the war.[10]

The inspired and original foundation-stone of Bion's post-Kleinian philosophy, his classification of positive as opposed to negative emotions (LHK and anti-LHK) is, Meltzer writes, "deeply foreign to the western tradition in philosophy and theology, but not to the eastern one in which Bion's Indian childhood had dipped him, like Achilles, at the hands of his ayah."[11] After Bion's death, when I was doing research for the Indian film and wallowing in a confused welter of First World War fiascos and mystical philosophies,[12] Mrs Francesca Bion kindly allowed me to look through the books in Bion's large library. I was looking for personal annotations and found very few, but now, looking again at the passages Bion had marked, it is of some interest to note how they confirm the impression his writings convey of the dominance of Eastern, and also classical, influences on his thought, despite his nonconformist upbringing. To judge from his own books, Bion would appear to have had little personal interest in the Judaeo–Christian tradition, other than that idiosyncratically presented by Milton; it is as though the Bible spoke for his culture but not for himself. His Bible is virtually unmarked, though through owing to his missionary background he must have been steeped in it. In the Koran he underlines the idolatry episode where the children of Israel, overhearing Moses talking with God (the parental conversation), themselves "demand to see God", whereupon "they were all struck dead by lightning"—a failed catastrophic change of intrusive identification, dogmatically quashed. Rather, his imagination was fed by "highswelling Soma", flowing from the thunder- and sun-cleft mountain and conveying its ambrosial drink to the gods, the archetypal food of the mind-body. This imagery, as much as the embryological, gave birth to the "somites" of the *Memoir*, those elementary particles of prenatal mind. In the Indian scriptures he found statements of pure mysticism—transcendental fusion with the Godhead—and its many modifications, such as how the "unendurable and unattainable experience must be translated . . . into symbols". Also how intuition is the only means of knowing "the ultimate" and how the *soma*-spirit is "that which makes the mind think, but needs no mind to think", the precursor—along with Plato's *Meno*—of the realm of thought that lies outside the self, waiting for a link with the thinker, in opposition to the world of *maya* (appearance) and its assumptions. This interdigitates with passages marked by Bion in Plato: how "change is always highly perilous" and how there is a distinction between "fearlessness" and "thoughtful courage"—a distinction debated time and again in the autobiographical works, in which Bion seems almost at a loss to find any examples of true courage to endorse until he discovers it in his heroine Rosemary. His fallen companions of the war were not so much courageous as tragic, betrayed by the higher command, through either its ineptitude or its imperial ideology. In Plato, also, Bion marked the distinction between being and becoming:

> All the things we are pleased to say "are", really are in process of becoming, as a result of movement and change and of blending with one another. We are wrong to speak of them as "being", for none of them ever is: they are always becoming. [*Theatetus*]

His variety of mysticism indeed never claimed to "become O" but to be engaged in transformations of "becoming" under the influence of emanations from O.[13] His fondness for metaphors of the circle and of reversal—reversed perspective, binocular vision, looking at a problem from both sides of the "caesura" or "diaphragm"—is part of this solar system. And he anchors the dizziness of cosmic speculation to the earth by means of another internal voice reminding us of the solid reality of a toothache.[14]

It is no wonder Bion felt dissatisfied with seeing Ps↔D as a straight line with no place for transformations and metempsychoses, if in his worldview the process of becoming wise—becoming oneself—entailed a continual confrontation with the dangers of psychic change: "wisdom, or oblivion?"[15] His natural view of development was cyclical, empathizing with the orientation of Eastern and classical religions (the "diameter of the circle") rather than with the linear Hebraic vision. He was drawn to the religion and philosophy of the East—but to the poetry of the West.

Of all the Western poets whom Bion intensely admired—Homer, Virgil, Shakespeare ("the greatest man who ever lived"), Keats (for his concept of "negative capability"), Hopkins (for his "double dark"), the one with whom he probably identified most closely and to whom he refers to most frequently is Milton. After once having a long discussion with Bion about Milton, two points impressed themselves on me as featuring significant aspects of his own struggle. One was his interest in Milton's "letter to a friend", the unpublished manuscript in which Milton poured out his fears, frustrations, and anger that he should have been cursed with a talent for writing poetry, a manner of living much "disregarded and discountenanced" by society. The other was the way Milton comes to terms with his blindness, in the third invocation to *Paradise Lost*. The significant thing was not the didactic argument (which is a poetical commonplace), but the way in which the poetic language shows the necessity for everyday—basic-assumption—modes of seeing to be erased, in order to make room for the type of "blind" vision that is insight. Bion was interested in the minutiae of this adjustment, taking place at the time of writing and going beyond the poet's preconception: requiring also to be artistically read through focusing on the poetic diction. In his own copy of the poem, Bion underlined individual words—"won" "feel" "eyes" "orbs" "nightly" "blind", "knowledge" and "wisdom"—as if to feel his way through the stages. He admired Milton's courage in allowing himself to become a vehicle for his Muse despite the antipathy of his selfhood to the implications of the ideas that arrived in his poem by these "unpremeditated" means.

Bion's marginal markings are of recent date, but they indicate a rediscovery or more formal study of ways of thinking deeply rooted in his own becoming. In his autobiographical books we sense the unbridgeable split between his Indian internal parentage and his European one—that is, the internal objects derived from these cultures, rather than the literal inheritance. In *The Long Week-End* there is the poignant episode in which he overhears his mother ask his father whether he has ever had the experience of religious inspiration—when "a light surprises a Christian as he sings".[16] The honesty with which his father confesses he has not, and his parents' sadness about it, somehow suggests that it was they themselves who directed him to the spiritual world of his ayah, even while they had to obey the social pressures that would entail his going to school in England and then enlisting in the army at the time of the First World War, under the aegis of the puritanical "Arf Arfer" God and the "frightful fiend" who would torment him with post-war persecution, making him run not for his life but for his professional status. The split in internal parentage destroyed him but also saved him, as its resurgence in the autobiographies shows—its qualities distinguished from one another but in a crucial way re-integrated.

The description of the ayah that opens *The Long Week-End* is followed by a vivid picture of the child Wilfred singing with his sister while his mother played the harmonium:

> There is a green hill far away
> Without a city wall . . .

The Green Hill of his mother draws within it the qualities of the Indian landscape that he says he "loved": the "intense light, intense black", the "blazing intolerable sun—how wonderful it was!"[17]

> The parched Indian landscape must have drained all its green into that hill which retained its city wall like a crown within which were tiny spires and towers huddled together against the foes "without".[18]

He says it took him " a long time to realize that the wretched poet meant it had *no* city wall"—"poor little green hill". Even worse, "incredible though it seemed—it was *outside* the city wall", vulnerable to the "foes". Unlike the ayah, who is all-in-all sufficient, the mother is complicated by her allegiances—the things that make her "likely to die". When the child sits on her lap, he feels "warm and safe" at first, then, suddenly, inexplicably, "cold and frightening". The sudden "cold" that sweeps over the mother's warm containing lap derives from the shadow of the primitive paternal god "Arf Arfer" that periodically descends with its "great black wings obscuring the sun" to blot out any evidence of idiosyncrasy in Wilfred. It merges with the cold air of the school chapel at the end of the service:

> Arf Arfer Oo Arf in Mphm, please make me a good boy. I would slip off her lap quickly and hunt for my sister.

(The fusion of the two periods indicates the present "dreaming" nature of even the apparently literal autobiography.) Arf Arfer, with its blackness, derives from the stark contrasts of India, the child's-eye mother-country, with its wonderful "intolerable sun" and its dubious penetration by the Raj-father, who also takes the form of the "goggle-eyed parrot" belonging to his sister, an idol of superstition. This conjunction—of lap and arfer—could induce mystical revelation (as with the ayah's folk-stories) or alternatively, "nameless dread", as when his father sat him on his lap and then treacherously gave him a beating, after having extracted a confession as to why he had hit his sister.[19] (His enraged sister, pointing at him the finger of guilt, reverberates with the famous Kitchener poster; this induction of guilt led to a sort of paralysis in their relationship—he says he learned to stay clear of her.) Later at school this basic-assumption obfuscation becomes the "web of undirected menace" associated with sexual hypocrisy (in adolescence expressed as "boredom") and, during the war, the communal delusion of the safety of the tanks. It led to repeated encounters with the emotional black hole for which "even now I can find no words".[20] Nameless dread is the anti-container for no-thoughts, derived from the combined object in untruthful conjunction—the Negative Grid.

The role of the "father"—or dream-father—is clarified in the twin episodes of the Tiger Hunt and Electric Train, both of which occurred on Wilfred's sixth birthday. After a toy train ordered from England as a special birthday treat failed to work, young Wilfred, together with an Indian servant, attempt a superstitious mode of reparation, smearing the train with ghee and leaving it out in the sun—the power of that "intolerable sun", invoking a deity so much more comprehensible than electricity. The resultant "greasy mess" compounds his engineer father's humiliation over the technological failure, as if undermining his male credibility. "'Full top?' said my sister, who was learning to read." Wilfred asks if this mysterious "Electric City" is "green like the other one"—if it has to do with the mother–father conjunction of the Green Hill.[21] He mutters the children's prayer "Pity my simplicity" ("Simply City") with his eyes fixed on his father's glittering watch-chain, his magic sexuality/city. The Green-Electric City is a rich stronghold of wisdom compared to his own Simply City and yet strangely insecure, "huddled against" its foes as in the stories of the Indian Mutiny that used to frighten him. (One of Arf Arfer's manifestations was "Nickel Sehn"—Nicholson of the Mutiny.) The vulnerability had to do with the rigidity of his father's endeavour to bring up his son in the image of both God and the Raj, smoothly efficient in its mode of colonization. "In a just cause we must fight with clean hands", as he would say later on the outbreak of war.[22] In this his mother was equally complicit—driven, like his father, by anxiety over Wilfred's moral and social adaptability, evinced by the oddity of his questions. Wilfred, indeed, believed that his mother was genuinely "puzzled", but that there was something sinister in his father's attitude of concealment or denial; this seems to become associated with the "Devil entering into him" in the masturbatory excitement of "playing trains" in the midday sun (leading later to his desire to "penetrate the secrecy" of the false Tank/ mother—the concept of intrusive curiosity).[23] The concept of mystery is substituted by secrecy, with its connotations of social hierarchy and privilege. The family with its missionary nonconformism had the air of the anxious or zealous convert to faith in the pure British educational ideal (his father, indeed, was not British, but Swiss). They worried that his Anglo–Indian identity would lead to his "getting ideas"[24] and tried to safeguard him, through discipline, against this possibility.

Thus the child's attempts at symbol-formation are repeatedly thwarted by adult morality (with the best of intentions). This happens on the night of the Tiger Hunt, when the tigress "roars her requiem" over her mate—killed by the hunters, who include Wilfred's father:

> That night, Arf Arfer came in terror "like the King of Kings". The hunt had killed a tiger and the body had been brought to our camp. His mate came to claim him and for the next two nights the camp was circled by great fires and torches burning bright to keep her out. With her great head and mouth directed to the ground so as to disguise her whereabouts she roared her requiem. Even my fear was swallowed up in awe as almost from inside our tent there seemed to come a great cough and then the full-throated roar of the tigress's mourning.[25]

The boy, instead of identifying with the imperial triumph, feels "swallowed up in awe": "She won't eat us Daddy? You are sure she won't?" The tigress is in effect inside his mind ("inside our tent"), a manifestation of the godhead. At the same time he is inside the mouth and mind of the awe/tigress, "swallowed up". In this primal experience founded on aesthetic fear (like Wordsworth's Cliff) Bion depicts the "dread" that demands to be resolved into Knowledge: the "awe-ful experience" described in the *Memoir*.[26] It is the origin of his innate scientific curiosity, which takes a different form from that of his father and finds no answers. Rather, the answer it finds time and again is that this Elephant's Child arouses anxiety in his parents. He wants to know where the tigers, both male and female, have gone and is vaguely fobbed off with "Oh, I don't know, child—far, far away I expect". But he insists:

> "What is he doing now?"
>
> "Who?"
>
> "Jesus—I mean the tiger."[27]

The child is not convinced by the tiger's "death", which in no way separates him from his mate as a combined-object of awesome power.

The phallic symbols of train and gun frighten him not in themselves, but owing to the fear of retribution they evoke from the tiger-goddess (the Mutiny). He wonders continually why he is so "soft", a "moonfaced boy", a "cry-baby". The realism of his fear is denied by the adult world ("felt but not suffered" in his later distinction). However, despite the lack of reciprocity from the adults, the Tiger has fused with the mother/India in his mind and thereby become a symbol, a container for the idea of the god within. It fuses again with Blake's Tyger in the *Memoir* to become the "Great Cat Ra" of the Boy's dream (a dream that recurs during the war):

> *Boy:* Gd-ni . . . [sleeps] Tibs, you are a spoiled cat. No, it's not good saying you are a *Tiger*. If you are a tiger you are really a spoiled tiger—a cat that has been spoiled and has turned into a pussy cat. Cyril laughs when he says "pussy". He says it's a gross word. Now don't you turn into a gross cat Tibs. That's German. I hope I'm not getting afraid of an unspoiled great Kat. Tiger . . . Tiger . . . we learnt in school . . . burning bright. Please sir! Its eyes sir—what dread hands question mark and what dread feet? A stop sir? Yes sir, a proper pause. If the wine don't get you the women must. It rhymes with dust.[28]

The Egyptian Cat, who has existed like the ayah or the Tiger from "the childhood of the race", bears the accumulated ancient wisdom that stretches infinitely beyond the individual's lifetime. As a container for knowledge it springs to life when poetically punctuated—a "question mark", a "proper pause"—a combined-object formulation. Recalling the Electric Train, it comes to a "full stop", but this time imaging the potency, rather than the impotence, of the male component. As a symbol it is degraded or sexually "spoiled" by omnipotence in the form of the children's game (the "otter hunt" when they imprison the house cat in a flower-pot, associated with a "pregnant pot"). In the Boy's view it then takes revenge, by assuming the enemy colours of the "gross" German Kat in the war. The Tiger continues to recur throughout his life, contaminated by projections of Arf Arfer:

> My God! Here they come again. Those howls! It's eerie . . . That is a tiger. No: Tigers are only cats. That is no cat. Arf, arfer's little history of England. You damned hyena? If the wine don't get you then the women . . . [29]

So although by the time of the war, Bion says he has learned to "lie" about the tiger-god internally: to play the game of conformity and forestall the impact of knowledge, this leaves him prey to the anti-symbolic nightmares of nameless dread ("Who'll buy my night-mares?").[30] In these non-developmental phases he is governed by his identification with the failures of his childhood parent-figures to recip-rocate his need for symbol-formation.

The ultimate treachery experienced during his childhood was the feeling that his mother had "abandoned" him by depositing him, aged eight, at boarding-school in England. His last sight of her was her hat bobbing away on the other side of the school hedge. He remembered when she had been called an "abandoned woman" in India, owing to one day wearing a hat to church that was covered in clusters of artificial fruit, its crowning glory a bunch of black grapes.[31] Her luscious hats represented her fertility and emotionality (her beauty) that in hidden ways did not entirely conform with the Raj's propriety—at least, within his parents' circle. Her treachery, however, involved denying her own feelings of sadness as his departure for England loomed:

> "Moth-er! You aren't sad are you?"
>
> "Sad?" She would laugh. "Of course not! Why should I be sad?"
> Well, why should she be sad? I couldn't think.[32]

Her "improper" Indian identity—the one whose love, though gentle, was stronger than narcissism—had betrayed him to society. The em-bargo on expressing her own feelings meant that she could not help him experience his own. He never forgave her and went on perpetual "home leave" during the years of his adolescence, long before the war reinforced this state of mind—a state in which he "couldn't think". The very idea of her became intolerable to him. The type of "abandonment" of which he felt his mother was guilty was reflected internally in what he describes as total ineducability in any real sense, replacing his childish "questioning" attitude by competitiveness and sporting achievement. In self-defence he adopted the "nameless-dread" object that ruled the mentality of his prep-school—the "web of undirected menace" filling the air of an environment where "wig-gling" was rumoured to lead to insanity. ("You *were* making a noise last night! . . .")[33] Even in the "clear air" of the upper school, where—as Bion later realized—the conditions for genuine learning did exist, in the shape of certain dedicated teachers and an enlightened atmos-phere, he felt he was unable to utilize them. He was over-impressed by the competitive aspects and by the cosy-paternal attempts to keep the "simmering sexual pressure cooker" from steaming over, and he neglected the opportunities for humanistic education. Nonetheless these lay dormant in his mind and gradually penetrated his subsequent dreams and thought-processes when his emotional need brought them to the "attention" of consciousness (in the definition of Freud, to which he frequently referred).[34]

Even though social conditions required that school be a "preparation for war", Bion diagnoses his own difficulty in terms of the internalization of an anti-learning pseudo-object. Nobody *had* to submit internally to society's pressures: he discovered some who did not. His distance from educational and emotional reality could be gauged by the sudden fear aroused whenever he came into contact with the occasional student who did appear to be "learning" and who showed him up—in his eyes, and theirs—as a fraud who was concerned with only the superficial veneer of achievement—the badges of honour. One such was the classics scholar whom Bion felt he had to beat—not intellectually, where he had no chance, but by means of a long-distance run in the athletics championship.[35] His formulation of the mentality of "minus LHK" has its roots in what he later terms the "exoskeleton" of worldly success. It is imaged in the "tank mentality" of his War. He was attracted to the Tanks in order to "penetrate the secrecy surrounding them", because of their pseudo-tigerishness as a false container for knowledge; and his first sight of a tank reminds him of a primitive tiger trap in Gwalior that had terrified him as a child.[36] Arf Arfer frightens but at the same time pulls him into line. The tanks "purr" their way into battle like tiger-caricatures but are really dinosaurs, death-traps. As Stegosaurus points out in *The Dream*:

> *Myself:*   God's Englishmen looked so funny going into battle in tanks.
>
> *Stegosaurus:*   Like us. Couldn't move. Sitting target.[37]

The tanks represent the most primitive level of basic-assumption mentality, adopted by "God's Englishmen" of the Raj and public school— as ancient as the primeval goddesses (the ayah, Helen, Rosemary's mother, etc.) but antithetical in significance:

> The whole four had flowered. Hard, bright flames, as if cut out of tinfoil, flickered and died, extinguished by the bright sun. One tank, crewless, went on to claw at the back of one in front as if preparatory to love-making, then stopped as if exhausted.[38]

In their pseudo-creative "flowering" when hit, they spill their vulnerable human brains—"the black guts pouring out of the prehistoric monster".[39] The destructive penetration of the false container represents the state of "minus K", a pretence or substitute for the combined object. In such a state, the soul "dies", as Bion elucidated via his dream-memory of the tank action of 8 August 1818: "It is '–K'. The date in –K is August 7 and August 8."[40] "I died there. For though the Soul should die, the Body lives forever."[41]

The same thing happened when he met his mother again after he finished school and knew he was only a "chitinous semblance" (a "ghost") of himself—"imprisoned in the shell which adhered to me".[42] During the war, he was gratified by her "pride" in his D.S.O. while at the same time despising himself for colluding in what he felt inwardly to be a lie about his "courage". There was not, in his experience, any such thing as courage, only fear in "different directions". Indeed, his mixture of self-satisfaction and contempt blocked his view of his genuine heroism, which, he felt, he could only attribute to mental disorientation caused by fog, flu, and alcohol. It is as though he felt his identity had been restricted forever by the "reversed perspective" of a "poor little ignorant Indian self"—a passionate nature—and its unreciprocating mask, the "trappings of the Empire of Hypocrisy".[43] In such a dualism, there was no room for growth, for real emotionality—there was no Muse. The alternation between sentimentality and harshness (embedded in his mother's warm-cold lap) becomes a feature of his portrayal of his own character in the dialogues of the *Memoir*. When he writes, in the context of the death of his runner, Sweeting, by his side in the War, that the words "I didn't mean it to happen" are "the saddest in the language",[44] the idea of the innocence that lies beyond the guilt has a piteous quality, very different from the rugged, mind-building rage of Sophocles' Oedipus. The thing that he didn't mean to happen was not the physical death—of which he was not guilty, except in the survivor-guilt sense of having escaped Ra-Arfer once again—but the spiritual treachery of his internal response to Sweeting's appeal: "You will write to my mother Sir won't you?" This made Bion intolerably cognisant of his own distance from his "mother", and he found himself silently thinking, "No, blast you, I won't!" The result is: "And then he died. Or perhaps it was only me."[45]

The roots of spiritual "death", however, existed long before the war. Bion reconstructs them in memory when reviewing, for example, the episode when, staying at a friend's home (one of the substitutes for a home of his own), the boys constructed a bamboo aeroplane and prepared to launch themselves in it from the roof of the house, but were prevented in time. The aeroplane is a precursor to the tank, inviting delusions of the false security of omnipotence. What Wilfred learnt from the episode was that Mrs Hamilton genuinely loved her own children, but not him—though he had been considered her "favourite"; it brought him closer to feeling "homesick" than for a long time.[46] It was one of the sparks of contact with his dormant mind, indicating that it was still smouldering. For even during his years of "home leave", his unhappiness was alleviated by certain other parental relationships, at least during his schooldays. One was with Colman, a master who introduced him to an Englishness antithetical to that of "Nickel Sehn" and who comforted him "not by anything he said, but by what he was". At the same time this brought him closer again to the kind of knowledge he could not stand—the richness of past civilization:

> I was dismayed, resentful, of a past so filled with renown that it both stimulated and imposed a dead hand on my inchoate ambitions.[47]

He could not stand it because the sense of richness reminded him of the inheritance of mother/India, which he had "abandoned" because it had abandoned him. Indeed part of his empathy with Colman derived from some sense that Colman could not "stand it" either: he was subject to crippling headaches, which sent him, "dazed and reeling", out of the room. Where Colman suffered headaches—"shellshock" as it became in the war—Bion "ran", to try to escape the intolerable stirrings of envy and jealousy that might disrupt his "home leave". Again he sensed the shadow of Arf Arfer blocking out the sun; his confused desire to respond and symbolize ("inchoate ambitions") was "stimulated" and at the same time flattened by the "dead hand", the hand of negativity. The internal object with which Colman's integrity put him in touch was rich in potential, but weak.

The other England that came to his attention in his school years—though the spiritual use of its qualities likewise lay dormant in his mind—was the world of farming, which he came to know through staying for long periods in the school holidays at the house of another school-friend, Heaton Rhodes. This had a vitality complementary to the inheritance of Milton and Shakespeare and left him similarly awestruck. It derived from closeness to the processes of nature—the realities of "summer and winter", not just on the land, but in the soul: "Heaton and his father had that winter in their characters". They bowed to the nature-god, a force superior to "toolmaking man", and in that sense religious, object-forming. There was no space for the sentimentality of which Wilfred always felt he was guilty. Although entirely different in character, it provided in a sense for the same type of spiritual qualities he had imagined in his ayah and her "intolerable sun"—endurance, timelessness, an acceptance of harshness and the storms of life. "Breeding is ruthless"; and the Rhodes farm bred Kathleen, the spirited girl who, together with his ayah, evolved under the influence of Mrs Klein into his heroine. His mother had defied the Church, in her quiet way, by wearing her "abandoned" hat; Kathleen, one day, simply refused to go, claiming that the parson "gabbled like an 'old cockatoo'". For Wilfred this episode planted (though dormant) the seeds of the eventual demise of Arf Arfer the "goggle-eyed parrot" god:

> Kathleen did not flinch—let me be the sacred poet who only can erect an imperishable monument to her courage—

Her example, he says, made him cognisant of his own "cowardice". He did not quite dare to be "in love" with her. Instead, she joined the ranks of the tiger deities of his inner world:

> She spoke straight; she was fiery tempered. I remember her contrasting sharply with her mother who sat by the firelight, with her calm Mona Lisa expression, watching Kathy confronting her father with eyes ablaze . . . Slaughter, bloodshed, cold, and Kathy's flashing eyes alive with love or hate—those were things I could see or know. But I did not know the meaning of what I saw. The Hamiltons and the Rhodes were providing an education that was not in the timetable. I saw: and was conquered. I did not understand.[48]

The "meaning" Wilfred "did not understand" resided not in Kathleen alone, but in the family context—which also encompassed the lessons in love he learned at the Hamiltons'. What is particularly significant here is the "Mona Lisa" mother who watched these dangerous exchanges between her husband and daughter unperturbed, accepting them as a valid feature of human nature, without feeling the need to cover them over with denial or hypocritical extenuation, as in his own family. Her "timeless capacity for maternal love" frightened Wilfred—recalling the ayah, but without her indulgence. Through his fear he learned that love and hate were part of nature, like summer and winter—that Kathleen's fire and her mother's "coldness" are bred of the same stock, a resilient complement to the wintry "ruthlessness" of the men. He "saw" the Rhodes family pageant, and it "conquered" his

Caesar-like narcissism. At last he has learned something—learned that he "did not understand". What was revealed to him was the emotional tension between Love, Hate, and Knowledge—and the developmental imperative of following the K-link.

In the *Memoir*'s "battle of English Farm",[49] Kathleen and the Mona Lisa reappear as Rosemary, with the hierarchical status of their mother–daughter, mistress–slave relationship revised in the switched roles of Rosemary the "skivvy" and her mistress Alice—who includes aspects of his sister, of whose tiger-like roarings he had become so wary as a child ("I was deafened . . ."). The male–female roles are also reversed, insofar as these had also served the social hierarchy, not internal necessity. Rosemary points out the confusion about who is hunting whom in the realms of container–contained: "you should see what goes on in the psychoanalytical dovecote when feminine intuition obtrudes".[50] She asserts her own dominance, establishing the Bionic pattern of courage as something belonging not to men—who are all boys playing tanks and aeroplanes—but to the masculine-within-woman, epitomized in the bravery of childbirth. Indeed, the pairing of Rosemary and the ambiguous "Man" is one of the unresolved features of the *Memoir*—is it possible for Rosemary to be "danced off her feet", the feet that keep the upper classes and the dominant sex in subjugation to her? "I feel awful", she says at the Party of Time Past: "I can't even faint."[51] This "upturning of the vertices", resulting from his own *Dream*, enabled Bion to put all his Muse-elements into the melting pot, together with his "inchoate" and formless ambitions—real ones, this time: the ambition to know himself by means of the idea of the combined object. It is a mode of knowing that he calls "real common sense"—when the emotional state of opposing vertices penetrates the boundary between them.[52] For what his dream-analysis makes clear again and again is that his torment derived from "not understanding"—from the lack of symbolic reciprocity of internal objects. The function of the *Memoir* is to re-live the points of not-understanding, revivifying their emotional content in the present so that they can be pursued further. These opportunities of ignorance become available to him only in the context of their antithesis—the "lies" of the Negative Grid, which substitute the dinosaur/tank for the tiger/god, an exoskeleton for an endoskeleton, a badge of success for a mind. The way to knowledge opens as the blockage is removed.

Psychoanalysis itself, says Bion, is just "a stripe on the coat of the Tiger"—the Tiger of Truth. "Ultimately it may meet the Tiger—the Thing Itself—O."[53] Nonetheless, the "great hunters of psychoanalytic intuition" give it an honourable place in the real Hunt for the "idea" of the combined object, the idea that is "generative" and that peers over the horizon at the conclusion of the *Memoir*:

> Fancy? Or fact? Just fancy, if there was something about ideas which might make them "generative"! . . . Alice may fear the movement of a "phenomene" in her mind. When an "idea" is created there is, in addition to the actual creation, a series of reactions to the created idea.[54]

The generative idea is heralded by a "blush on the walls of the uterus", which itself requires that Rosemary allow her feet to be "danced with", not merely to "kick out". Alice/Rosemary has become the container for transmission of ideas, the Muse/Tiger that mediates between the infant-self and that "ferocious animal Absolute Truth", the "light brighter than a thousand suns", the "star-shell" in the cold vast of the Infinite. Bion returns to the Tiger Hunt of 1903 and discovers its present meaning. Whatever the "circlings" of his mode of expression, in the autobiographical books Bion is "writing seriously". For the first time he truly discovers and appreciates those other stripes on the Tiger whose presence in his life had previously been camouflaged by his intolerance of "inchoate ambitions". He pays homage to the unsung heroes of his war and childhood—the "men who ought to have been famous", those *ante Biona multi*.[55] They came before him, and their qualities found a place in his pantheon. Above all, he invokes through his "roll-call" those manifestations of the poetic spirit in its many guises—from Odysseus and Palinurus through Bach and Mozart to his previously unrecorded schoolteachers—"E. A. Knight, F. S. Sutton, Charles Mellows."[56]

> What part of England or Shakespeare was it that forged the England that is eternal and will be for ever England? What is foreign soil? Which part is Rupert Brooke, Shakespeare, Milton? Which part will be for ever foreign? Pope was a nasty little man. Who, then, wrote the Epistle to Doctor Arbuthnot? Who knew Doctor Arbuthnot's address so many years ago? Who told Kipling—the worshipper of very ordinary trash—that he ought to write Recessional, and that somewhere amidst the ruck and reel which he not only observed but worshipped there were sinners who might have ears to hear—if he could write? Who told him he could? Who told Bunyan to stop his ears and run; Belloc, that the stupidity of his Church was such that it must have been divine to have survived; Hopkins, that "double dark"

would help him find the "uncreated light"; Freud, that he needed "artificially to blind himself" to explore the dark places of the mind?[57]

Who told "Wilfred R. Bion—Me, Myself"—he could write the *Memoir of the Future*? Did the roll-call of poetic ghosts from the realms of the ineffable enter into him at last in his "run round the bend", in preparation for his "date to meet Fate", jettisoning with relief the garments of imperial and institutional respectability?[58] For, as he insisted, "This is my attempt to express my rebellion, to say 'Good-bye' to all that." Reaching the age of the Biblical "goodbye"—threescore years and ten—he took courage from Keats's statement that no man can interfere with another's telling his dreams.

NOTES

1. Keats, *The Fall of Hyperion*, ll. 11–12.
2. W. R. Bion, *A Memoir of the Future* (1975, 1977, 1979), single-volume edition (London: Karnac, 1991), pp. 244–45.
3. See this volume, Chapter 8.
4. The title of the second volume of the *Memoir* is *The Past Presented* (taken from Milton's *Samson Agonistes:* "present / Times past, what once I was, and what am now").
5. See W. R. Bion, *The Long Week-End* (Abingdon: Fleetwood Press, 1982), pp. 28, 115.
6. *Long Week-End*, p. 8.
7. See *Long Weekend*, p. 17.
8. *Memoir*, p. 79.
9. *Memoir*, p. 297.
10. *Long Week-End*, pp. 265–66.
11. D. Meltzer, *Studies in Extended Metapsychology* (Strath Tay: Clunie Press, 1986), p. 26.
12. This film, directed by Kumar Shahani, was intended to cover Bion's childhood memories and their influence on his dream-life in his autobiographies *The Long Week-End* and *A Memoir of the Future*. It had the support of a loyal and wonderful cast of distinguished actors, including Nigel Hawthorne, Alaknanda Samarth, and Angela Pleasence, but was never finished owing to financial and organizational problems.
13. Bion was suspicious of any claims to "know God" directly: see, for example, *Memoir*, pp. 359, 522).
14. *Memoir*, p. 574.
15. *Memoir*, p. 576.

16. *Long Week-End*, p. 23.
17. *Long Week-End*, pp. 18, 29.
18. *Long Week-End*, p. 9.
19. *Long Week-End*, p. 11.
20. *Long Week-End*, p. 237.
21. *Long Week-End*, p. 14.
22. *Long Week-End*, p. 109.
23. See *Long Week-End*, pp. 9, 29 ("Before I had time to think . . ."), p. 115.
24. *Long Week-End*, p. 15.
25. *Long Week-End*, p. 17.
26. See, for example, *Memoir*, p. 382.
27. *Long Week-End*, p. 18.
28. *Memoir*, p. 441.
29. *Memoir*, p. 97.
30. *Memoir*, p. 282.
31. *Long Week-End*, p. 15.
32. *Long Week-End*, p. 21.
33. *Long Week-End*, p. 90.
34. Freud defined consciousness as an "organ for the perception of psychic qualities"—frequently cited by Bion, e.g. *Memoir*, p. 98.
35. The Run is described in *Long Week-End*, pp. 74–77.
36. *Long Week-End*, p. 115.
37. *Memoir*, p. 122.
38. *Long Week-end*, p. 254.
39. *Memoir*, p. 156.
40. *Memoir*, p. 155; 8 August 1818 . . .
41. *Memoir*, p. 257.
42. *Long Week-End*, p. 104.
43. *Long Week-End*, p. 92; *Memoir*, p. 302 ("reversed perspective", in Bion, does not refer to contraries or opposites but to the same quality flowing in different directions).
44. *Memoir*, p. 256.
45. *Long Week-End*, pp. 249, 264.
46. *Long Week-End*, pp. 72–73.
47. *Long Week-End*, p. 97.
48. *Long Week-End*, p. 75.
49. "English Farm" was also a village near Ypres—see *Long Week-End*, p. 128.
50. *Memoir*, p. 390.
51. *Memoir*, p. 414.
52. *Memoir*, p. 526.
53. *Memoir*, p. 112.
54. *Memoir*, p. 572.
55. In the *Memoir*, Bion is haunted by the phrase "ante Agamemnona multi", which recurs repeatedly, referring to the unknown, unsung heroes who

came before one by chance became famous. See, for example: "No one ever heard of him, but *I* knew what we had lost . . ." (*Memoir*, p. 424). Listing some of his past schoolteachers, whom he felt he did not appreciate at the time, he begins: "Let me now praise men who ought to have been famous . . ." (*Memoir*, p. 560; also p. 396).

56. *Memoir*, p. 560.
57. *Memoir*, p. 42 (citing Freud's letter to Lou Andreas Salome).
58. See *Memoir*, pp. 398, 577–78.

Confessions of an emmature superego
or,
the Ayah's lament

A verse narrative fictionalizing the genesis of Bion's ideas, in the voice of the "ayah" of his Indian childhood. I wrote this originally to be performed by Alaknanda Samarth, who played the child Bion's ayah in the unfinished film of *A Memoir of the Future*. The narrative is spoken by the voice of the ayah-as-goddess, the oriental aspect of Bion's internal mother/object. In the autobiographical books she is a shadowy figure, realized most graphically perhaps in the character of Rosemary: so, like one of Bion's "empty concepts", she can be filled with meaning. She appears in various guises, from the Great Cat Ra (the Tiger) to the knowledge-containing Skull. Her story follows as in a dream-sequence the autobiographical history of the *Memoir* and *The Long Week-End*, from pre-natal life and its passionate origins, through childhood in India and in exile in England, to the war and its re-living through psychoanalysis. The narrative dramatizes the implications of Bion's concept of "home leave" (the enforced distancing from his emotional roots), which may be said to constitute the origins of his differentiation between positive and negative states of emotionality—a clarification that, when successful, leads ultimately towards the birth of thought. For Bion repeatedly describes his actual life-experiences as taking place in the realms of "minus K". It was their re-living in the form of dreams that constituted, for him, learning from experience.

What is to be sought is an activity that is both the restoration of god (the Mother) and the evolution of god (the formless, infinite, ineffable, non-existent), which can be found only in the state in which there is NO memory, desire, understanding.

Wilfred Bion, concluding paragraph of
Attention and Interpretation, p. 129

EM-MATURE: This book is a psycho-embryonic attempt to write an embryo-scientific account of a journey from birth to death overwhelmed by pre-mature knowledge, experience, glory and self-intoxicating self-satisfaction. I was spared any knowledge of the courtship of my sperm with my ovum, but many years later was given to understand that my ancestors had a long and disreputable history extending to the day when an ancestral sperm, swimming characteristically against the current, lodged in a fallopian tube to lie in wait for an unknown ovum.

Wilfred Bion, opening paragraph of
The Dawn of Oblivion, Book 3 of *A Memoir of the Future*, p. 429

Our ayah was a wizened little woman who, in so far as I connected age with her at all, was assumed by my sister and me to be very old, much older than our father and mother. We were very fond of her, perhaps more fond than of our parents. On second thoughts, perhaps not. My mother was a little frightening. For one thing she might die because she was so old. She was not so old as our ayah; my sister and I agreed that she was not less than, say, two or maybe three hundred years old, and though this was a ripe age she did not seem likely to die.

Wilfred Bion, opening paragraph of
The Long Weekend, p. 9

As for that one, the subject of my Song,
He was neither first nor last, but one
Of many seeded in my dark abyss.
In the beginning was the Mother, and I
From the beginning of time was *his* mother.
Before I was called Helen, Hecuba,
Andromache, Penelope, Lady
Macbeth, Medea or Clytemnestra
I was nameless,
10   The unrecognised vegetation, the goddess
Of fertility from whose rotting remains
The mammalian parasites sprang and on whom
They still depend. He was the outcome of a
Passionate conjunction between sperm
And ovum, a blush on the walls of my uterus.
Familiar sickness, in the eternal pattern,
Arose in me, abhorrent as before.
I wondered, has the hour come round again?
What rough beast now, so clumsy and obscure,
20   Slouches towards my sacred river banks
To be born? All my knowledge I gave last time,
Stretching the limits of my philosophy;
How many more times must this container my body
Distend in roughening involutions
To provide a lodgement for an idea
Beyond the reach of thought? Once again
Pulsations cross some coarse irregularity
In me, and without thinking my agents begin
To weave their pearly web over its hideous
30   Grit, and the thing is not concealed but grows
Hugely, though tiny, and seizes my attention.

Once again the fierce dispute between
Damnation and impassioned clay is set
In motion, and I am disturbed alternately
By the dogma of its prematurity,
And by needy questionings, which penetrate
Despite myself (unanswerable as they are),
And which I find myself enveloping
40   In the cathedral of my many arms,
Whose tendrils at alarming speed increase
In volume and complexity. Though from

Experience I know it cannot be done
I try to relax desire and memory, and
Respond to the moment's urgent minutiae—
The creature's thin amoeboid tongue-lappings.
O the selfishness of the unborn! To them
I am an undiscovered country, in which
The mystery of their being is ensphered.
50   Yet these figments of imagination pass
Through me like volcanic upheavals,
Leaving me permanently changed, and even
On the seventh day there is no rest.
To calm the murderous feelings they arouse
I have to quickly wrap the foetal idea
In a fiction, since I know that so disguised,
The truth may yet slip through. Crudely the humans
Try to verbalise it in their scriptures:
"Drinking deepest draughts of soma, the belly
60   Like an ocean swells, like wide smooth
Streams from the cope of heaven. Making light
Where there was neither light nor form, they issued
Forth like babes unborn, together with
The dawns." In hope, I sent the humans artists
But they would not see; I sent them prophets
But they would not listen. And yet I sense
How from the beauty of my ugliness
May one day spring forth mind, a light
Brighter than a thousand sons.
70

                              In heaven
Meanwhile, as Psyche-Soma fought their war
Of contraries, I arranged for us
A barrier of communication,
A diaphragm of common-sense, to remind
The new gaseous medium of its once
Watery existence: remembering how
Disguised, the truth can slip past even my
Archangelic vigilance. Just so, many
80   Incarnations ago, Satan slipped into
The Garden of Eden wrapped in rising mist, and
Inspired the serpent's head, possessing him
With act intelligential, abhorring not
My virgin's womb—no rib from Adam's frame

But an invisible blush on the white
Radiance of my eternity,
A noise inaudible, pain impalpable,
Not hell but held with integrating force.
The engineer his father saw it not,
90 The woman's invisible tool, heard not
The still small voice the serpent used
To Eve, enshrouded as I was by the
Imperial drapery of the Empire
Of Hypocrisy, obsessed as he was
By man as a tool-making animal. He gave
His son the electric train, the key to electric
City, yet turned away from the Indian sun
Whose rays in fierce and rhythmic circulation
Enriched the air with sounds and sweet
100 Noises that gave delight and hurt not.
His parents, over anxious for the light
That may surprise a Christian while he prays,
Could not pity his simply city
As he played. He played as little Krishna,
And I was the Great Cat Ra.
And when I smothered with ghee the childish
Engine, weathering with ease the father's
Storm, for I was used to turbulence,
They said, the devil has got into him.
110 *Don't run about in the sun!* What sun?
The cold flowed over his mother's lap, the frightening
Cold, the voice from the hole in the Marabar cave.
Whoever was that screaming? Later, it was
The apparition of the old beggar
Woman, and worse, the grey shapeless dream
Which made him wake up sweating, to wish that
It was only a war.

That night Arf Arfer came
120 In terror like the king of kings, the sun
Obscured by the beating of his great black
Wings. The hunt had killed a tiger,
And to her mate the tigress roared
Her requiem. Intense the light, and blackness
Intense; as suddenly darkness fell and noise—
Real noise—burst forth: the yelling, hammering,

Shrieking, roaring, croaking, coughing, bawling,
Mocking of innumerable beasts.
The Great Cat Ra was armed to the teeth, no longer
130   Content to passively absorb their sins
With enigmatic smile. And he was the rat
Being systematically clubbed to death.
O tiger tiger burning bright,
In the forests of the night! Beware
False Beauty's painted face, a mousetrap,
Eyes like teeth. The secret weapon
Of male and cunning she-devil was closed
To him, he felt, and hostile to his wormlike
Wiggling, a waste of spirit in expense of shame.
140

The time had come, they thought, to implant
An endoskeleton in this moonfaced
Elephant's child, a chick with pieces of shell
Adherent, sadly lacking spine and
British stoicism. And though I later
Regretted it, I did not resist,
For alien voices spoiled our intimacy,
Curdling our common sense, so that we had
No language. Discordant voices shrieking
150   All together made the place a perfect
Bedlam. Hell hounds! inordinately
Proud of daring to defy the arms
Of the Omnipotent. Then that cub—
The Ignorant—tried to set a trap
For me, the Great Cat Ra, to catch my ancient
Wisdom in a common pot! He thought he'd shut
My teeming womb of royal kings, from whence
No more would issue forth. I do admit
That momentarily I was truly stunned
160   By such a narrowing of our perspective.
How long, I wondered, till perception's doors
Are cleansed, and vision infinite released
From one-eyed Error's tyranny? An otter
Hunt, he called it—revenging on me
His father's imperial tiger hunt.

Mother you're not sad are you? Sad?
Not sad! she lied, and I was silent. We're not

Omniscient, we immortal becomings,
170 Though lazy minds believe we are, and no
Freedom or fulfilment can be ours
Unless our embryonic thoughts progress
To their terrestrial fruition.
And this one at an early hopeful stage
Of evolution had shown undoubted
Native intelligence, when his mouth firmly
Grasped the nipple as though he'd actually
Expected it to be there waiting for him.
With preconceptions as accurate as that
180 I naturally believed in his eventual
Tolerance of wisdom. I acquiesced
Therefore when he was sent away to school
In Norfolk—an enlightened institution
Open to light surprises yet with academic
Reputation unassailable,
Its lid of unimpeachable morality
Pressed gently, firmly down upon
The simmering sexual pressure cooker.
It was the beginning of a long home leave.
190

He realised now his mother was abandoned,
An abandoned woman whose churchgoing hat,
Undulating above the strictly clipped
Hedgeline, bore lascivious clusters
Of black grapes. Did she abandon him
Or he her? *I didn't mean it to happen*—
The saddest words in the language. I gave him
Extra-curricular education in the form
Of Mrs Hamilton, sad in her apprehension
200 Of responsibility for an outsider
Who engendered lethal folly in her gang
Of boys, omnipotent aeroplane-makers,
Precursors to the tank and offspring of
The electric train. I gave him Mrs Rhodes,
Whose capacity for maternal love
Smiled timelessly behind her
Mona Lisa gaze and transfixed him
With the fascination of its necessary
Cruelty, the tiny vestigial spore
210 Of ruthlessness in the farmer's task

Of breeding, showing him how horny handed
Tons of soil soiled the white radients
Of eternity and turned them into
Many-coloured life. Later in awe
He observed the lonely cathedral of Ely
Below the great expanse of the fenland sky
Riding the landscape like a huge ship,
A shadow matched by the procession
Of clouds above, Ely of the other
220 England—Cromwell, Milton and Hereward
The Wake—the other Mother whose pregnant
Expectations laid a dead hand
On his inchoate ambitions, impressed
By his resentment of a past renown,
Unfathomable in its blue water, blue sky,
Reed-concealed snipe and white reflective sails.

Distant khaki moving rhythmically
Replaced those inchoate ambitions
230 With another marching song—not genuine
Battle orders even, such as Cromwell
Would have given, but playful bible stories.
But that also was part of the game, he felt,
For he had learned at school that games
Were a fitting prelude to war. That training
Nearly complete, there came at school the day
Of his final run, and he felt he had to win
At any cost—and the cost was final indeed.
He ran like one that on a lonesome road
240 Doth walk in fear and dread, because he knows
A frightful fiend doth close behind him tread.
The fiend his Rival was a classicist,
A scholar with a passion strangely
Genuine, inspired by Homer and by Virgil
In an endoskeletonal way. For they,
Like Milton, could plant eyes. Instead,
He numbly exchanged the white feather,
Given by the disdainful girl to a great
Big boy like him, for a medal bright,
250 A Hero Dress. *Couvre-toi*, he thought,
With a hat, *flannelle*, or glory, any feathers
For the chick to make his mother proud

And hide his hatred, knowing in his heart
He carried openly on his chest a sentence
Of almost certain death. An exoskeleton
Was his at last, and none could see
That nothing propped him up within
But fear, not even fear of death
(A not ignoble sentiment), but the fear
260 Of being branded as a fraud, the medal
Whipped away and replaced by the feather,
Fight-flight's imperial insigniae.

I couldn't blame his mother, for she was left
With only a chitinous semblance of himself.
Where was his father's fight-with-clean-hands?
Nothing is clean nowadays, she sadly said.
But when after the battle he and I came
Face to face again, and manifest
270 Madness reigned in his eyes, I noted
In my own soul certain black and grained
Spots of conscience, a correspondent
Sickness to his own, for now I understood
There was no anaesthetic for those who suffered
Home leave; they break down at a chance
Of hatching out, and I found myself
Impelled to internalise his story.
Canst thou not minister to a mind diseas'd—
Who'll buy my nightmares? I will—
280 If you have tears to shed, shed them now.

By age nineteen, he said, his ways were set.
He joined the Tanks to penetrate the secret
Of their strength, and fired by intrusive
Curiosity, he watched on their home ground
The training manoeuvres as the tanks, slow
As saurians in some mating ritual,
Clawed each other heavily up the hill.
Playfully on sports day the small tanks
290 Tyrannosaurus and young Stegosaurus
Tossed between each other their communal
Rudimentary brain; but a permanent
Lodging for this anomaly within
Their armour plate was never found. How far

Removed, I thought, from the early education
I gave him in the jungle! Privileged
To worship tigers, of whom he had a healthy
Awe, he chose instead to be obsessed
With armoured tanks: drawn irresistibly
300 To climb inside their heads and even—with
Ambition high and dizzy in th'extreme!—
To get himself appointed Tank Commander.
And anyway, he said, once you got inside
It wasn't really as bad as it had seemed.
For in the tank they got together to hold
Scientific meetings, taking compass
Bearings on the follies of the world,
Men like trees walking in the fog,
Detectable ingeniously through holes
310 In the armour plate. O words, words, words!
Many civilizations have been mine,
And if this one should come to a violent end
It is only of minimal significance
To me, since there are plenty of other suns
In the universe. But it angers me that words,
Of all things, should become a tank-like trap,
Definitory caskets that prevent
The birth of foetal ideas which may be crawling
Curiously between earth and heaven.
320 Not words, I told him—*woods*! It's there in the jungle
That you've got to live—yes Purgatory,
That dismal hole.

When the Intelligence Officer
Loomed before him, questioning if he'd seen
The dry cretaceous ground superseding
The alluvial, the forehead of a soldier
Rose before his eyes; and he watched
Curiously, as when the sniper fired,
330 The alluvial brains bulged out at the back.
I fixed his eyes upon my brow so he
Might guess what time behind its hollow
Crown enwombed, might know the nameless dread
That dogged his run against the classicist,
That foetal other self that negativity
Had thwarted him from trying to become.

Was he then responsible for that death?
His chest swelled with the D.S.O., his death
Warrant—but no, death struck the other one,
340 His runner Sweeting, chest-blasted at his side.
Sir, you will write to my mother won't you? No,
Blast you, I know no Mother! The pregnant child
With feral eyes slipped silently down
The cellar steps, observing unobserved.
Beyond in the soft mud lay wounded men
In pieces, crying softly like marsh birds.
It was August 8th, on the Amiens–Roye road, the day
He died, a-theist, a-chronous, a-moral, a-sthetic.

350 Again the tanks purred on, then burst
Into flower and came to a stop, the black guts
Pouring out of the prehistoric monster,
And this made it more real-like, we burnt a treat!
Was that, he wondered, the transformation
Signalled to him lately by the Intelligent
Fool? For though the soul shall die the body
Lives for ever. At this point, wrapped in mist,
The ancient goddess Soma repossessed
His fragile psyche, having consulted
360 His embryonic mind's constituent units
Of primal germplasm, and enveloped him
In raging fever, which explosively
Ejected him and his crew before his tank
Got shelled. Her primitive preservation
Quashed the treachery of the ego-shell.

So now we had another chance—both he
And I, for I was learning too. One life
Is not enough, and we internal beings
370 Have evolved through centuries our negative
Capabilities. Punishment we discarded
Long ago, and now I am beginning
To believe that even worship isn't
Very efficacious. Our procedure
Is cyclical not linear, for we re-present
Times Past, what once he was and what is now.
Don't go down the unconscious, Daddy!
The timid voices cried—but the old mole,

My new Intelligence Officer,
380 Delved into his vale of sorrows
Driven by the Resurrection Blues
To archaeologically reconstruct
The features of its vale of soulmaking,
Excavating the intense shadows thrown by
The intense brightness of the eastern sun,
The shadows that like the poets' phrases
Throw forwards into the future of the past.
He knew now not to seek for light surprises:
Be shellèd eyes, and listen to the double
390 Dark, the intimate impulses of the sudden
Onset of the tropical night—real noise.

I gave him the licence
Of a Fool in the Court of Beauty,
The privilege of one who wished to become
A psychoanalyst, and in the burial ground
Of the court at Ur, he began to meet
His ghosts. In the psychoanalytical
Dovecote, where feminine intuition
400 Obtruded like sniper-fire, he discovered
The laws of mental cannibalism, sucking
Out the mother's brain like an eggshell,
Degrading the Tiger to Alice's own pussy,
A smile with teeth. He unearthed the battle
Of English Farm, the meeting of the internal
Invading forces that destroyed and built
His mind, and there he suffered other
Episodes of sanity—the shell-shock
Which in the other war he'd been
410 Insufficiently robust to endure,
Nor could he seep away. In Sweeting's
Shattered chest, pitifully covered
With its vain field-dressing of lies,
He found the gaping wound of his own mind
And opening his imagination
Guessed how to unwind its superficial
Sanitisation, the obscuring fog
That masquerades as the Holy Boast
Of civilisation. Yes, here comes Priest
420 And he's running round the bend, and what's that

Small atomic bomb in his hand, its sparks
Flying upwards from its mind-less origins
Into the postsaurian desolation
Of the brilliant Absolute? So black
And bright, so astronomical a hole
They might regret the price they have to pay.
What a marvellous day it is! And I
Only am escaped alone to tell thee.

430   *Sir, you will write!* Yes, now he could write
Of his mother. Now he could give names to those
Ante Agamemnona multi, the unsung
Heroes and heroines of his inner life:
Kathleen who had the courage to become
The pregnant child with feral stare; Colman
Who showed him Ely riding in the clouds,
The pregnant *idée mère* that heralded
The loss of memory and desire. He sung
Of Auser and Roland the ones he loved, who braved
440   The hunter's shot of invading Man—the Man
Who believed in God's goodness, himself
An avatar of God, armed not with a toy
Electric train but with an automatic
Chocolate bar fuelled with lightning fire.
Yes, that's his howl! calling his mate,
Calling his partner for the becoming dance.

As for introducing him to myself,
I knew that he could not survive if I
450   Allowed him to see me as I really am.
So I became Rosemary, the whore's
Daughter—not Mother England the top-drawer
Whore—the other one, the best of mothers,
Poor little guttersnipe from the ghetto
Sacrificed to the spirochaete,
Returned to vegetable eternity,
The fossil stone from whose deep veins
Michelangelo will call them out
At last. Luckily I was reconciled
460   To having an ugly soul, serviceable
And tough, being the sole of a servant's boot.
It's true that with the increased leisure

I had to follow my interests after
The reversals of English Farm, I had become
Interested in P.A., despite
His shell of puns and platitudes. Come in
Equivocator! Kiss my foot. Stroke
The stripe on the coat of the Tiger. Yet even I
May fear to give an interpretation;
470   I prefer to demonstrate by example
The underlying pattern of the facts
Of feeling, knowing that only the Love-Hate
Spectrum will ever have any lasting effect.
And there was no-one I hated more than Man;
My eyes pulled with threads of invisible steel;
My feet emitted microwaves when they
Twinkle twinkled on the hard slum pavements
Of my street. I was in two minds whether
To keep him dangling or dispense with him.
480   *When are you going to make up your mind?*
Chorus the voices of the civilised
Committee of post-natal souls. Makeup?
All their expensive education
As futile as eyeshadow! No, I told them, not so—
I let my mind make me up. Dancing with Man
I experienced all the strangeness
Of reversed perspective: in one
Direction helplessness, and in the other,
God. It flows both ways, from intuition
490   To abstraction. Could this be Love,
The Thing-in-Itself? I confess it had not
Occurred to me, when I was Rosemary,
That in dancing I might also be *danced with.*

And does the thing have independent existence?
Too late, says the mocking bird, too late—
She's gone, remembering all your sins.
He was only a small stain on the red
Radiance of my eternity, the merest
500   Instant in the never-ending realms
Of our becoming. But since our dances, like
The poets' phrases, cast their shadows forward
Beyond the knowledge of their generation,
We could view his story as a trap

For light, fusing with integrating force
Its web of contraries to generate
An underlying pattern, a container
For that ugly monster, the kicking
Foetus of thought, product of his birth
510 And death—which are only, after all,
Directions of the same activity,
So next time it endeavours to take form
The ending may be a happy one.

REFERENCES

References to the poem are by line number.

Abbreviations

> *Memoir:*   W. R. Bion, *A Memoir of the Future* (1975, 1977, 1979), single-volume edition (London: Karnac, 1991).

> *Long Week-End:*   W. R. Bion, *The Long Week-End* (Abingdon: Fleetwood Press, 1982).

6   "Before I was called Helen . . ." (*Memoir*, 358); "Out of the rotting syphilitic remains of human flesh . . ." (*Memoir*, 486); Rosemary as Beauty (*Memoir*, 340).
15   "An idea has as much right to blush unseen as any blush" (*Memoir*, 276).
19   Yeats, "The Second Coming".
20   Bion was born in a tent on the banks of the River Jamuna in 1897.
24   The "roughness in which an idea might lodge" (*Memoir*, 265, 268, 429).
26   *Hamlet*, "thoughts beyond the reaches of our souls".
32   Keats, "On Sitting Down to read King Lear Once Again".
48   *Hamlet*, the "undiscovered country" of thought. The intrauterine landscape (*Memoir*, 430ff).
50   "Figments of imagination" (*Memoir*, 306, 378, 395, 418–20, 571).
51   The "imminence of an emotional upheaval" (*Memoir*, 538).
55   The "fetal idea" and its "metaphor" (*Memoir*, 417–18).
56   "Disguised as fiction the truth occasionally slipped through" (*Memoir*, 302).
60   Leonardo's "swirling masses of water" and turbulence (*Memoir*, 156).
64   *Memoir*, 35–36.
67   Rosemary on beauty and ugliness (*Memoir*, 128); the Old Woman—"like the beautiful girl I have built-in ugliness" (*Memoir*, 145).
68   ". . . a light brighter than a thousand suns" (*Memoir*, 358); "the autistic

wisdom begins to hatch out of its shell" (*Memoir*, 412); "a mind will be generated ... Like maggots in the warmth of a rotting dung heap" (*Memoir*, 474); the "empire of the mind" finding a home in Shakespeare (I, 133).

72 Psyche and Soma—"the meaning does not get through" (*Memoir*, 433–35); "the coming together of the pre-natal and post-natal personalities" (*Memoir*, 551).

74 "... make communication possible through the barrier" (*Memoir*, 539).

75 "Real common sense" (*Memoir*, 526); the "screen, caesura" (465); "our forgotten fishy selves" (501); gas and "spirit or soul" (527).

80 Milton, *Paradise Lost*, Books IV and IX, 180–91.

83 "... the virgin's womb might be rewarded by more than not being ab-horred" (*Memoir*, 45, 79).

85 Shelley, *Adonais*, "life stains the white radiance of Eternity" (*Memoir*, 51, 465).

87 "blushing so invisible, noise so inaudible ..." (*Memoir*, 51).

88 "It wasn't hell—held perhaps" (*Memoir*, 275); "the ideas hold me" (*Memoir*, 257).

90 "the still small voice, the one the serpent used ..." (*Memoir*, 46).

93 The "Empire of Hypocrisy" (*Memoir*, 302); hiding the "empire of mind" (133).

95 "Man as a tool-making animal" (*Memoir*, 42, 85; *Long Week-End*, 246, 287).

97 The toy electric train sequence is in *Long Week-End*, 12–16.

99 "Sounds and sweet noises" (*The Tempest*, III.ii.134).

102 The "light surprises" (*Long Week-End*, 13, 24; *Memoir*, 287).

103 "My Simply City" (*Long Week-End*, 13); "poor little ignorant Indian self" (*Long Week-End*, 92).

108 His ayah "trembled as the storm beat about her ..." (*Long Week-End*, 17); "turbulence" (*Memoir*, 229).

109 "The Devil entered into me" (*Long Week-End*, 29–30); also Rosemary's mother, "the devil has come over you" (*Memoir*, 65).

112 The Voice (*Memoir*, 67, 71, 135); "nameless dread" (M, 77); the old woman (M, 145); the shapeless dream (*Long Week-End*, 237).

119 Arf Arfer (*Long Week-End*, 17; *Memoir*, 97).

124 Jungle noise (*Long Week-End*, 18; *Memoir*, 65).

131 "I was having an unusual view of sport" (*Long Week-End*, 198, 209, 362).

135 "The painted visage" of Arf Arfer (*Long Week-End*, 29); the Cheshire cat (*Memoir*, 59). *Hamlet*, III.i & iv.

139 *Long Week-End*, 23, 32, 46. Shakespeare, sonnet.

142 WB a "sissy" (*Long Week-End*, 22), "moon-faced" (*Long Week-End*, 105); "bits of shell" (*Long Week-End*, 81); "eggshell of belief" (*Long Week-End*, 224); worship of the Curzon-style exoskeleton (*Long Week-End*, 48); the exoskeleton and the "heaven of middle-class England" (*Long Week-End*, 194); pre-natal exo- and endoskeletons (*Memoir*, 431); "preservative function" of the shell (*Memoir*, 478).

151 Bedlam (*Memoir*, 443); "hell hounds" and the "otter hunt" (*Memoir*, 440–41; *Long Week-End*, 68).

153 "Who durst defy th'Omnipotent to arms", Milton, *Paradise Lost*, I.i.49.

161 Blake, "perception's doors", *The Marriage of Heaven and Hell*, pl. 14.

167 Mother "not sad" (*Long Week-End*, 21).

169 Being and becoming (*Memoir*, 183).

183 School "enlightened" (*Long Week-End*, 49, 80, 85).

188 The "sexual pressure cooker" (*Long Week-End*, 78).

191 Mother an "abandoned woman" (*Long Week-End*, 15, 33).

196 The "saddest words . . ." (*Long Week-End*, 256).

198 "an education not in the timetable" (*Long Week-End*, 75).

199 Mrs Hamilton (*Long Week-End*, 72–73).

203 Toy train a precursor to the tank (*Long Week-End*, 16).

207 Mrs Rhodes' "Mona Lisa" smile (*Long Week-End*, 75); Rosemary a "cruel snake" (*Memoir*, 273).

211 "Cromwell, a farmer" and his discipline (*Memoir*, 200).

212 "white radients" adapted from Shelley (*Memoir*, 51).

215 Ely Cathedral (*Long Week-End*, 97); the eternal England (*Memoir*, 42).

223 "inchoate ambitions" (*Long Week-End*, 99).

225 Waters of the "formless infinite" (*Memoir*, 156); "blue skies and blue water" (*Memoir*, 280); "blue language" (*Memoir*, 386, 574) snipe diving from blue sky to blue water on the Broads "shot with green" (M, 279).

218 *Long Week-End*, 108.

231 "Battle orders I wanted—not Bible stories" (*Long Week-End*, 134); "in my soft feminine way I preferred success" (*Long Week-End*, 101).

235 A prelude to war (*Long Week-End*, 93).

237 The Run (*Long Week-End*, 94–96).

239 Coleridge, cited in *Attention and Interpretation*, p. 46.

246 *Memoir*, 225, 283.

249 The white feather and "couvre-toi" (*Long Week-End*, 102, *Memoir*, 442); the "great big boy" and the D.S.O. (*Long Week-End*, 277); the "state of mind . . . more impenetrable than 'gloire' or 'flannelle'" (*Memoir*, 396); the "Hero Dress" (*Memoir*, 423).

252 "mother proud" (*Long Week-End*, 111, 187, 190); WB proud (*Long Week-End*, 187); worship of the D.S.O. (*Memoir*, 156).

252 His hatred (*Long Week-End*, 266).

255 The death-sentence, and "love had died" (*Memoir*, 149–50).

257 The uselessness of an exoskeleton "for an endo-skeletonous animal" (*Long Week-End*, 194).

262 The shell, the "insignia of distinction" (*Memoir*, 282).

265 The "chitinous semblance" (*Long Week-End*, 104).

266 "We should fight with clean hands" (*Long Week-End*, 109).

267 *Long Week-End*, 266.

270 *Hamlet*, III.iv.89.

274 "no anaesthetic . . ." (*Long Week-End*, 115).

275 "They break down . . ." (*Memoir*, 411).

277 *Macbeth*, V.iii.40 (*Memoir*, 98, 375).

278 *Memoir*, 282.

282 *Long Week-End*, 193.

283 *Long Week-End,* 115.

288 *Long Week-End,* 254.

290 Albert Stegosaurus and Albert Tyrannosaurus (*Memoir,* 84); their reversed perspective (*Memoir,* 93); Sade v. Masoch (*Memoir,* 104).

301 Milton, *Paradise Lost.*

306 Compass bearings (*Long Week-End,* 233–34, 243); "ingenious manipulation of symbols" (*Memoir,* 92).

308 *Memoir,* 38, 53, 67.

310 "Words, words, words!" (*Hamlet,* II.ii.192; *Memoir,* 276).

316 The tiger-trap at Gwalior (*Long Week-End,* 32).

317 "I'm only an idea of yours . . . definitory caskets prevent my birth" (*Memoir,* 276).

319 *Hamlet,* III.i.128.

320 *Long Week-End,* 114; Milton, *Lycidas,* line 193.

321 The "dismal hole" and the Party of Time Past (*Memoir,* 406).

324 The "Intelligence Officer" and the cretaceous skull (*Long Week-End,* 138, 154, 165; *Memoir,* 453–54).

330 "The mud had seeped into the place where our minds were supposed to be" (*Long Week-End,* 126).

331 Keats's Moneta, *The Fall of Hyperion,* I.277.

332 The "hollow crown"—Shakespeare, *Richard II,* III.ii.160.

338 *Memoir,* 156; "You wear the Past as if it were a decoration" (*Memoir,* 393).

339 "And then he died—or perhaps it was only me" (*Long Week-End,* 249); "No, blast you" (*Long Week-End,* 264); *Memoir,* 256; barring him from his mother (*Long Week-End,* 266).

343 *Long Week-End,* 281; *Memoir,* 256; association with his own "animal eyes" (*Long Week-End,* 126).

344 the "observer observed" (*Memoir,* 216).

345 *Long Week-End,* 142.

346 8 August 1918, "minus K" (*Long Week-End,* 249, 265; *Memoir,* 155, 159, 256).

350 *Long Week-End,* 254.

352 "like dinosaurs in a prehistoric catastrophe" (*Long Week-End,* 240); "blackened bodies" (*Long Week-End,* 251).

353 *Memoir,* 156.

356 "For though the Soul should die . . ." (*Memoir,* 257).

360 "lowly glandular origin of thought" (*Memoir,* 79); "primitive elements of thought" (*Memoir,* 229); susceptibility of "germplasm" to catastrophic implications, and "germ of phantasy" first step to perspicuity (*Memoir,* 539).

362 "not fear this time—fever" (*Long Week-End,* 260); "pyrexia of unknown origin" (*Memoir,* 476).

363 "'Get out!' I shouted'" (*Long Week-End,* 262); "I shot out" (*Memoir,* 476).

369 Keats's "uncertainty principle" (*Memoir,* 207).

373 "unearth the forgotten god from his mound of worthless adoration" (*Memoir,* 412).

375 "The proper approach to confusion . . . continue cyclically" (*Memoir,* 197).

376 *The Past Presented* from Milton's "present / Times past" (*Samson Agonistes*).

377 *Long Week-End*, 143.
378 the "old mole"—Hamlet's father/ghost (*Hamlet*, I.v.170).
379 "sleepwalking" troops (*Long Week-End*, 254) "impressed my hidden re-
      serves of intelligence" (*Long Week-End*, 256).
381 The Party of Time Past (*Memoir*, 406).
386 The thought "generators" (*Memoir*, 234), "throwing forward into the fu-
      ture" (*Memoir*, 383), after Shelley's *Defence of Poetry*.
389 Gerald Manley Hopkins (*Memoir*, 271).
390 "intimate impulse" (*Samson Agonistes*, 224).
391 the "sudden onset of tropical night" as contrasted with "light surprises"
      (*Memoir*, 342).
393 "the licence of a fool . . ." (*Memoir*, 340).
397 The burial ground at Ur (*Memoir*, 36, 59, 133, 162, 306).
398 "afraid to meet my Ghost" (*Memoir*, 256); the dovecote (*Long Week-End*, 60;
      Memoir, 29); the "psychoanalytical dovecote . . ." (*Memoir*, 390).
401 "mental cannibalism" (*Memoir*, 159, 164).
403 (*Memoir*, 441).
405 English Farm—part of the battlefield at Ypres (*Long Week-End*, 128); set-
      ting of the *Dream Memoir*, Book I).
410 "not robust enough . . ." (*Long Week-End*, 236); shellshock (*Long Week-End*,
      256; *Memoir*, 516); "Break up, down, in, out, or through?" (*Memoir*, 539).
413 "I pretended to fix it across the gap" (*Long Week-End*, 248).
414 "And then he died. Or perhaps it was only me." (*Long Week-End*, 249).
417 Opacity of memory and desire (*Memoir*, 190).
418 "Homo sapiens' new toy" (*Memoir*, 135); Priest's commentary on the Run
      (*Memoir*, 398).
423 "dead bones gave birth to a mind" (*Memoir*, 60); dinosaur-thoughts with-
      out a thinker (*Memoir*, 84); "whether the human animal will survive a
      mind" (*Memoir*, 160).
425 "Holy light" and the "star-shell" (*Memoir*, 204); "Absolute Truth" (*Memoir*,
      239, 499); the price (*Memoir*, 508); being "too imaginative" (*Memoir*, 284).
428 Melville, *Moby Dick*; Priest (*Memoir*, 398).
430 "this book" (*Memoir*, 86); "if somites could write" (*Memoir*, 470).
432 "ante Agamemnona . . ." (*Memoir*, 67, 120, 264, 396); "the shame of having
      survived" (*Memoir*, 450).
434 Kathleen (*Long Week-End*, 62; *Memoir*, 72); Rosemary, "what a woman"
      (*Memoir*, 300).
435 Colman's patriotism (*Long Week-End*, 97).
437 "idées mères, thought generators" (*Memoir*, 196).
439 Auser (*Memoir*, 423–24); Asser (*Long Week-End*, 271–72); Roland, shot by
      Man (*Memoir*, 352, 394).
441 Man has "evidence of God's goodness" (*Memoir*, 351); "does Man remind
      you of God" (*Memoir*, 421); who "owns the owner of the idea" (*Memoir*,
      561).
444 Man's chocolate bar (*Memoir*, 378).
445 *Memoir*, 397.
449 *Memoir*, 296.

452 Mother England (*Long Week-End*, 265).

453 Rosemary's mother (*Memoir*, 79, 297, 324).

457 The "stone" within art's splendour (*Memoir*, 333); the "wisdom" hatches out of its "shell however stony" (*Memoir*, 412); cyclical process.

460 Rosemary's soul (*Memoir*, 424); "tough" (*Memoir*, 399); "they knew I could fight" (*Memoir*, 538).

464 Rosemary's interests (*Memoir*, 335).

466 *Memoir*, 278, 387; puns "first step in a new language" (*Memoir*, 465).

467 P.A.'s speech—"from that warfare there is no release" (*Memoir*, 396).

468 Psychoanalysis a "stripe on the coat of the tiger" (*Memoir*, 112).

469 The fear of giving an interpretation (*Memoir*, 362, 517).

471 "underlying pattern" (*Memoir*, 200, 472, 512, 533); "facts of feeling" (*Memoir*, 434, 536).

472 The love-hate spectrum (*Memoir*, 362).

474 Rosemary on Man (*Memoir*, 400).

483 Make up (*Memoir*, 407); Man—"My prize is more than I can wear" (*Memoir*, 404).

487 Reversed perspective (*Memoir*, 164, 209).

489 "the awe-ful experience" (*Memoir*, 382); "I feel awful, faint" (*Memoir*, 414).

490 Love "the ultimate" (*Memoir*, 183); the noumenon (*Memoir*, 180); Rosemary the "real thing" (*Memoir*, 354); conversation the "real thing" (*Memoir*, 477).

493 The shock of being "danced with" (*Memoir*, 414).

495 "thought without a thinker" (*Memoir*, 168); "independent existence" (*Memoir*, 353).

496 The "brain fever" bird (*Memoir*, 453).

498 the "rosy stain", *Memoir*, 85.

502 The "Future casting its shadow before" (*Memoir*, 469, 486); the poets (*Memoir*, 383).

504 "trap for light" (*Memoir*, 190).

505 "integrating force" (*Memoir*, 200); Rosemary as "generator force" (*Memoir*, 390).

507 *Hamlet*, III.i.90.

508 "What saurian engendered thought?" (M, 352); foetal kicking as an "idée mere" (*Memoir*, 271); foetal ideas (*Memoir*, 417).

511 Birth and death the "same activity" (*Memoir*, 352).

BIBLIOGRAPHY

Works cited frequently in the text

Literary works

Available in many editions; the following are cited in the text:

Blake, William. "The Tyger". In: *Songs of Experience*, and in: *The Marriage of Heaven and Hell*. In: *Complete Writings*, ed. G. Keynes. Oxford: Oxford University Press, 1966.

Coleridge, Samuel Taylor. The Ancient Mariner. In: *Poetical Works*, ed. E. H. Coleridge. Oxford: Oxford University Press, 1969.

Coleridge, Samuel Taylor. *Biographia Literaria*, ed. N. Leask. London: Dent, 1997.

Gawain-poet (author anon.). *Sir Gawain and the Green Knight*, ed. J. R. R. Tolkien & E. V. Gordon (revised N. Davis). Oxford: Oxford University Press, 1967.

Gawain-poet (author anon.). *Sir Gawain and the Green Knight*, ed. B. Stone. Harmondsworth, Middlesex: Penguin, 1964.

Homer. *The Odyssey*, transl. R. Fitzgerald. London: Collins Harvill, 1988.

Keats, John. *The Eve of St Agnes, Hyperion*, "La Belle Dame Sans Merci", and "Ode to Psyche", in *Complete Poems*, ed. J. Barnard. Harmondsworth, Middlesex: Penguin, 1973.

Keats, John. *Selected Letters*, ed. R. Gittings. Oxford: Oxford University Press, 1975.

Milton, John. "Ode on the Morning of Christ's Nativity", *Lycidas*, and *Paradise Lost*, in *Poetical Works*, ed. D. Bush. Oxford: Oxford University Press, 1966.

Shakespeare, William. *Antony and Cleopatra*, ed. M. R. Ridley, Arden edition. London: Methuen, 1971.

Shakespeare, William. *Othello*, ed. M. R. Ridley, Arden edition. London: Methuen, 1971.

Shelley, Percy Bysshe. *A Defence of Poetry*, in *Shelley's Poetry and Prose*, ed. D. H. Reiman & S. B. Powers. New York: Norton, 1977.

Sophocles. *The Three Theban Plays,* transl. R. Fagles. Harmondsworth, Middlesex: Penguin, 1982.

Wordsworth, William. *The Prelude,* ed. J. Wordsworth, M. H. Abrams, & S. Gill. New York: Norton, 1979.

Psychoanalytic and theoretical works

Abraham, Karl (1924). A short study of the development of the libido, viewed in the light of mental disorders. In: *Selected Papers on Psychoanalysis.* London: Hogarth, 1973. [Reprinted London: Karnac, 1979.]

Bion, Wilfred Ruprecht (1970). *Attention and Interpretation.* London: Tavistock.

Bion, Wilfred Ruprecht (1975). *The dream.* Rio de Janeiro: Imago Editora. (Reprinted in a single-volume edition: *A Memoir of the Future.* London: Karnac, 1991.)

Bion, Wilfred Ruprecht (1977). *The Past Presented.* Rio de Janeiro: Imago Editora. (Reprinted in a single-volume edition: *A Memoir of the Future.* London: Karnac, 1991.)

Bion, Wilfred Ruprecht (1979). *The Dawn of Oblivion.* Rio de Janeiro: Imago Editora. (Reprinted in a single-volume edition: *A Memoir of the Future.* London: Karnac, 1991.)

Bion, Wilfred Ruprecht (1980). *Bion in New York and Sao Paulo,* ed. F. Bion. Strath Tay: Clunie Press.

Bion, Wilfred Ruprecht (1982). *The Long Week-End.* Abingdon: Fleetwood Press.

Bion, Wilfred Ruprecht (1973). *Brazilian Lectures, Vol. I.* Rio de Janeiro, Imago Editora. (Reprinted in a single edition: *Brazilian Lectures.* London: Karnac, 1990.)

Bion, Wilfred Ruprecht (1974). *Brazilian Lectures, Vol. II.* Rio de Janeiro, Imago Editora. (Reprinted in a single edition: *Brazilian Lectures.* London: Karnac, 1990.)

Bion, Wilfred Ruprecht (1977). *Two Papers: The Grid and Caesura.* Rio de Janeiro: Imago Editora, 1977. (Reprinted London: Karnac, 1989.)

Bion, Wilfred Ruprecht (1991). *A Memoir of the Future,* single-volume edition. London: Karnac.

Freud, Sigmund (1910c). *Leonardo da Vinci and a Memory of His Childhood. S.E., 11.*

Freud, Sigmund (1918b [1914]). From the history of an infantile neurosis. *S.E., 17.*

Freud, Sigmund (1921c). *Group Psychology and the Analysis of the Ego. S.E., 18.*

Freud, Sigmund (1923b). *The Ego and the Id. S.E., 19.*

Freud, Sigmund (1927c). *The Future of an Illusion. S.E., 21.*

Freud, Sigmund (1930a). *Civilization and Its Discontents. S.E., 21.*

Freud, Sigmund (1939a [1937–39]). *Moses and Monotheism. S.E., 23.*

Klein, Melanie (1957). Envy and gratitude. In: *The Writings of Melanie Klein, Vol. III.* London: Hogarth.

Klein, Melanie (1959). Our adult world and its roots in infancy. In: *The Writings of Melanie Klein, Vol. III.* London: Hogarth.

Klein, Melanie (1975). *Narrative of a Child Analysis. The Writings of Melanie Klein, Vol. IV.* London: Hogarth.

Langer, Susanne (1942). *Philosophy in a New Key.* Cambridge, MA: Harvard University Press.

Langer, Susanne (1953). *Feeling and Form: A Theory of Art.* London: Routledge & Kegan Paul.

Meltzer, Donald (1978). *The Kleinian Development.* Strath Tay: Clunie Press.

Meltzer, Donald (1986). *Studies in Extended Metapsychology.* Strath Tay: Clunie Press.

Meltzer, Donald (1992). *The Claustrum.* Strath Tay: Clunie Press.

Meltzer, Donald (1994). *Sincerity and Other Works,* ed. A. Hahn. London: Karnac.

Meltzer, Donald, & Meg Harris Williams (1988). *The Apprehension of Beauty.* Strath Tay: Clunie Press.

Stokes, Adrian (1967). *The Invitation in Art.* London: Tavistock.

Williams, Meg Harris (1983a). Underlying pattern in Bion's *Memoir of the Future. International Review of Psycho-Analysis,* 10.

Williams, Meg Harris (1983b). Bion's *The Long Week-End. Journal of Child Psychotherapy,* 9 (1).

Williams, Meg Harris (1985). The tiger and "O". *Free Associations,* 1.

Williams, Meg Harris (1986). "Knowing" the mystery: Against reductionism. *Encounter,* 67 (1).

Williams, Meg Harris (1997). Inspiration: A psychoanalytic and aesthetic concept. *British Journal of Psychotherapy,* 14 (1).

Williams, Meg Harris (1998). The aesthetic perspective in the work of Donald Meltzer. *Journal of Melanie Klein and Object Relations,* 16 (2).

Williams, Meg Harris (1999). Psychoanalysis: An art or a science? *British Journal of Psychotherapy,* 16 (2).

Williams, Meg Harris (2005). The three vertices: Science, art and religion. *British Journal of Psychotherapy,* 21 (3).

For a full list of papers by Meg Harris Williams, see: www.artlit.info

INDEX

Author index

Main entries are shown in italics.

Subject index

Or in moment of dire need, as Gogarty*
    Recalled their beauty in the perilous river,
Recall those desperate wings against the wind
    Struggling to rise from the long, dark water

As men from knowledge strive to mysteries;
    Then yield; recall the soft returning surge
When water receives them once more, and in dusk they burn
    On the smooth lake in phantom, silver fires.

Roland J. Harris, extract from "Swans"

*friend of James Joyce